German Painting
in the 20th Century

BY FRANZ ROH

with additions by JULIANE ROH

New York Graphic Society Ltd.

GREENWICH, CONNECTICUT

THIS BOOK is an abridgment of the first part of *German Art in the 20th Century*, published by New York Graphic Society in 1968. The original German edition was created and published in 1958 by F. Bruckmann Verlag, Munich, Germany, under the title *Geschichte der Deutschen Kunst von 1900 bis zur Gegenwart.* For the English language editions, Juliane Roh has contributed additional material covering the period from 1955 to 1968.

Translated from the German
by Catherine Hutter

Edited by Julia Phelps

SBN 8212-1106-4
Library of Congress Catalog No. 68-12367

Printed in Germany

CONTENTS

FOREWORD

By "German Painting" we mean here "Painting in Germany," the art that developed on German soil, even if it was created by an Austrian (Kokoschka), a Russian (Kandinsky), or a Hungarian (Moholy). This definition should not be interpreted as nationalistic presumption, for cultural environment is more significant than the birth certificate. Justifiably the French consider the Spaniard Picasso and the Russian Chagall as members of the School of Paris.

Moreover, we will sometimes pursue the further development of artists forced to leave Germany, so that we may present a full picture of their personalities.

We do not share the skeptical view that it is impossible to survey and evaluate one's own time. There is some subjectivity in all philosophical judgments. Even epochs distant in time have undergone extreme fluctuations in assessment–one has only to think of how much opinions have changed in the course of the last century on the late antique Laocoön or on the aesthetic value of Ottonian miniatures. The advantage of a period closer in time lies in our ability to interpret its works more intensively out of the spirit of the era. For our study we have had at our disposal a virtually unbroken documentation. I have known most of these artists personally.

COLOR PLATES

INTRODUCTION

Art Movements

Expressionism, Constructivism, New Realism, Surrealism, Nonobjectivism, Tachism–all these "isms" are cited as characteristic of our century. And there will certainly be further variations, for styles in art sweep over us like the stars in the sky. From 1900 to approximately 1940, however, we experienced such diverse world events and modes of creation that we may assume we face an era in which this variety of form and expression will be fused. Periods of synthesis tend to follow revolutionary phases; they should not be cursorily dismissed as signs of exhaustion.

Impressionism was followed in Germany by a group consciousness that was promoted at first by the artists themselves and subsequently was supported by the critics. In contrast, the next stage was characterized by the proliferation of completely individual modes of expression. Then the emergence of Tachism as the dominant movement of the 50's led back virtually to the point of departure –Impressionism–for Tachism is actually a nonobjective form of Impressionism. Recently, however, there has been a tendency towards quiet, contemplative form (the Monochromists), and constructivist order prevails in at least one group (Program ZERO, etc.).

In our century, the development of expression and of the arts has been quick to change. Still, we must be cautious about attaching too much importance to this unstable tempo, for every era's judgment of itself seems to be distorted by lack of perspective. Conversely, we tend to ascribe too much uniformity to eras long past and to be unaware of their actual tensions. Seen from a greater distance in time, the many "isms" of our century may one day be recognized as various nuances of one and the same antirealism. For all of them have one thing in common: gone is the artist's desire to mirror objects in a prescribed world; instead he wants to depict the forces that may lie behind them. In Impressionism it was the life-stream of light and air, in Expressionism the power of color, in Surrealism the fantasy of the dream. Each time a different style led far beyond objective reality, until the latter disappeared absolutely in abstract painting.

This four-part development could be seen as a unity, as a gradual crescendo impelling the work of art to become increasingly the organization of inner expression. We may understand the finale of this development better if we refer cautiously to the analogy of absolute music; as in absolute music, the means of painting–that is to say line, structure, color, and space–have become an end in themselves; their importance lies in their intrinsic value.

Inner Poverty?

To look upon this consistent devaluation of the objects of the outside world as a dehumanizing force is, I believe, mistaken. If it were so, we would have to see something inhuman in other art forms, such as architecture and music, that shun a relationship to the world around them. Controversies of this nature bring to mind an academic question that played an important role in post-medieval culture: was a representation of landscape or still life of equal value to a composition with human figures? In our day and age, questions about the character of an object–we could go so far as to say questions about the object *per se*–have become irrelevant. Some interpret this as a *Verlust der Mitte*, a departure from the middle way; others see it as a purification process through which the arts have become more specific.

In the development of man, art first served magic, then religion; later it furthered the discovery and reproduction of external nature, however strongly the emotions of the artist may have been mirrored in his work. By casting off the straitjacket of these dominions through titanic processes of transformation, the artist has probably penetrated to the very core of all artistic endeavor.

There are many who believe that the painting of symbols alone must be monotonous, but I believe we can demonstrate that in abstract art the greatest contrasts are again possible. A concentric or eccentric perception of life, a harmonious or demonic world outlook, an optimistic or pessimistic display of color, a surface or spatial arrangement, a linear or painterly form of expression, an open or closed organization of form–all may be realized in abstract art.

In Paris, which may still be considered the decisive art center, it has often been said that Germany's contribution to twentieth-century art was belated, or even that it was a coarse variation of French developments. In the meantime, however, a fairer view has been accepted, and we can now determine accurately in which cases modern art emerged later in Germany than in France, in which it developed simultaneously in the two countries, and which are the occasions when German art should perhaps be given priority.

In architecture and industrial design, with the activity of Van de Velde at the turn of the century and of the Bauhaus in the twenties, we have instances where the decisive stimulus originated in Germany. Similarly, in the plastic arts Hermann Obrist developed abstract sculpture in Munich shortly after 1900, when it had not even been thought of in other countries, France included. As for painting, we have Kandinsky: in Germany around 1910 he created one of the first forms of purely abstract painting; its particular quality was not developed further elsewhere until much later, after his emigration to Paris in 1933. Paul Klee discovered his sublime dream world in Germany and is recognized as a precursor of related styles. In other categories, different countries led the way.

On the whole, temporal discrepancies in the artistic development of nations seem to shrink as the delight in exchange intensifies. The numerous exhibitions circulated throughout the world and the color reproductions distributed to all four corners of the earth gradually produce simultaneity of progress. Such a joint development, which does away with the isolation of former cultures, could be considered regrettable without that prevailing diversity that is guaranteed by outstanding artistic personalities, or if typological schisms of stubbornly conflicting styles did not arise periodically. For many countries the cultural stability that was determined solely by isolation has been lost, but regional characteristics of style undoubtedly remain, thanks to such characteristics as the variety of landscape, local traditions and mores, and special rhythms of the local idiom.

German Impressionism, for instance, was completely different from French. Liebermann's paintings were sandier-gray in tone and more severe in form. Corinth's pictures were more sensually aggressive, rougher in texture than the late works of Manet. Nolde's pictures and those of the Brücke group were coarser, more barbaric, more massive in effect than those of the French Fauves of almost the same period. Nolde may remind us of Rouault, but the color contrasts of the latter seem more harmonious. And when one compares paintings of the German Blaue Reiter group with various works of the French Cubists, one sees that the French works are more systematic and formal in effect, because of the Latin rationale, even when the object is fragmented. In Germany form became less an end in itself. Kandinsky (in his early works) lashed out furiously and improvised; Franz Marc used cubic refractions only as counterpoint for his color harmonics. In France, even with Picasso, the bizarre remains somehow under the control of reason and taste, whereas the German masters often strove for a freer, more primitive expression. In the most recent abstract art, such regional contrasts also play a part.

Artistic Decentralization in Germany

The development of the arts in France in the twentieth century took place mainly in Paris, traditionally the great art center dominating the entire country; in Germany the development occurred in various places as a result of the absence of political centralization and the consequent emergence of cultural centers in Germany's many principalities and small states.

Berlin was the focal point for the late German Impressionists because Liebermann, Corinth, and Slevogt spent the most important years of their lives there, and the metropolis, as is usually the case, also sheltered the leading art dealers and collectors. Berlin remained important for later periods as well, but German Expressionism originated in Dresden where the Brücke group was founded, even though the artists later moved to the German capital. Munich had already gained prominence at the turn of the century with the Jugendstil and became important subsequently through the Blaue Reiter group. Art in Frankfurt was transformed by the personality of Max Beckmann. A bold artistic life burgeoned in Cologne with Dadaism and the originality of Max Ernst and his disciples. Stuttgart received its artistic character from Adolf Hölzel, Oskar Schlemmer, and Willi Baumeister. The little town of Weimar became the center of a new art form through Van de Velde, and after him, through the Bauhaus (which later moved to Dessau).

The art academies scattered across the country only partially served these new movements, but they periodically became centers of attraction for the aspiring young student by appointing to their faculties interesting personalities, as was done in Düsseldorf, Breslau and Hamburg.

Cultural Parallels

Although all special fields within a culture exhibit specific structural characteristics so that they diverge when one tries to compare their development, a certain mutual *Zeitgeist* may be said to prevail. In our epoch it seems that all fields of activity have thrown off some alien element in order to become more specific. Painting seeks independence from earlier representational forms. A new emotional lyricism evocatively shakes off many syntactic limitations. Modern physics, concentrating ever more intensely on mathematics, indulges in obscure abstractions. In art as in science, the end-effect is also supposed to illuminate, perhaps even lay bare, the method used to bring about the result. In both disciplines the formula dominates rather than the object, and instead of being evaluated rationally and technically, everything is conceived as hermetic. Einstein asserted that "the most exciting thing we can experience is acquaintance with the mystical."

The growing interest in inner expression, which in painting and the plastic arts became more and more an end in itself, at first brought with it an increasing alienation from the objects of the outside world, which had been mirrored in earlier art, no matter how subjectively. Painting next proceeded to abandon also the illusionistic space created by perspective, for which art had had no need prior to the Renaissance. With Impressionism perspective began to lose importance once again. The painters of the twentieth century speak constantly of the plane; since they wish to avoid imitation of external nature, they confine the representation of objects to a single visual plane. In the history of art such procedures have been introduced whenever there has been a desire to pass from mere reproduction to symbolic presentation, and nature becomes simply a starting point for the projection of inner expression. At any rate, the result is a complete amalgamation of outer and inner experience, through which life is conceived more and more as a single, gigantic process.

For the same reason, German poetry, from the late Rilke through Trakl to Gottfried Benn, tends more and more to abandon all description in order to give expression to mysterious perceptions through a system of sounds. In the novel many authors refuse to use an objectified plot, chronologically devised. Their efforts are bent toward mirroring reality through the opinions of their characters, through fluctuations of memory, flashbacks and projections, or, as in Joyce, by a flood of simultaneous associations. Drama often abandons the traditional boxlike stage separated from the audience and the old unity of time and place as well, in order to join poet, poem, and listeners in unique fashion. Music rises out of the close confines of fixed tonality and passes from one key to another. Often the conception of key is abandoned completely. Dissonance is accepted as an insoluble end in itself and at the same time as the symbol of a life that remains painful.

Today only the more conservative creators, who continue to do valuable work, cling to perspective in painting, tonality in music, and chronological sequence in narrative. In the visual arts also dissonance is often an end in itself, and extreme liberties are permitted in color and form. But the observer who is not wholly attuned tends to look upon every true union of creativity and life as "barbarism" whenever it becomes discordant.

Modern architecture has also expanded its conceptions of unity. The architect felt constricted by the closed, boxed-in room; now he plans interiors with as many rooms as possible opening out and encroaching on one another; the whole is held together by glass walls in order to make another link with free space, that of the exterior. The dividing supports are drawn inward so as to be hidden from the outside, giving the floors an effect of floating in space.

Science has discovered that a too-facile conception of basic principles has prevailed. Greater caution is observed in the formulation of exact forecasts. Psychologists no longer place as much value as they once did on human consciousness and refer more and more to the power of the subconscious, which drives us all. Freud influenced Surrealism and its *expression automatique;* here the object world seems as two-faced as the soul of man in psychoanalysis. Biology tells us of the capricious mutation of genes; atomic research introduces an irregularity coefficient into the motion of the most minute particles; the theoreticians of physics draw space and time together. In modern politics, whatever trend is followed, ever closer attention is being paid to undercurrents of collectivism (mass psychology, etc.). The relativity of power has been exposed, but so has that of our social structure. Many doctrines, including materialistic interpretations of history, now deal with a destabilizing coefficient which formerly was often overlooked. In today's philosophy we find the ideas of *Grenzsituationen* (limit-situations: Jaspers) and *Angst* (Sartre) playing an ever greater role.

All such attitudes reveal not only uncertainty, but also a productive broadening of our approach to life. And as always, the various fields lie in mysterious connection with one another, producing a universal *Zeitgeist.* That the procedure itself sometimes seems more interesting than the final result could be interpreted as a refinement of our thought processes.

Today we realize that the so-called laws of nature we lay down are always replies to the questions we ask of the universe. In this sense all experience, including scientific experience, is today seen "subjectively." In our exploration of nature we fashion it "thoughtfully." But that is just what the modern artist is constantly stressing. Faced with this attitude it seems senseless to deplore subjectivity of expression in abstract art only. Even in the representational works of our time the artist has been aware of the tension between his model in nature and the pictorial structure he is creating, and he has often had to struggle to resolve this relationship.

At the same time many creative artists see a secret union between themselves and earlier phases of mankind in which a form of calligraphy, equally unrealistic, predominated. Kandinsky and Klee reverted to a cryptography of inner communication, but like all expression of this type, theirs differs from those of earlier cultures in its lack of the compulsory overtones of magic and religion through which every work of art was formerly approachable. Today's calligraphy speaks primarily to kindred spirits.

But we should not reproach the artist of today with this reservation, for it lies in the nature of all modern culture, in which the value judgments of the individual prevail over those of society. The abstract artist will no longer be so lonely when the public, still attuned to the realism of past centuries, has divested itself of the idea that it must find repeated everywhere the objects of our external world. In absolute music, which is met for the most part with appropriate understanding, these cultural, pre-fixed symbols are lacking.

The first major movement we must examine is Impressionism. It had developed in France over the last thirty years of the nineteenth century but was transplanted to Germany only around 1900, and then in a very general way. Liebermann, Slevogt, Corinth, Uhde, Trübner, Zügel, all of whom belonged more or less to the movement, proceeded from the momentary appearance of objects and sought to achieve a sketchlike, unstudied effect by dissolving their plasticity. They achieved only partially that luminous division of color in complementary stages so much stressed by the French.

Max Liebermann (1847–1935) started with a dark-toned, highly objective realism which places him somewhere between Millet, Courbet, and the seventeenth-century Dutch painters. But from the beginning he shunned the anecdotal aspects that had dominated the genre painting of the nineteenth century. "The fascination of the naked truth" was his goal early in life. "If it is already beyond my powers to paint a goat as rich in form, color, and motion as I see in the animal standing before me, how could I possibly paint Wallenstein's Death?" Liebermann's development as a painter falls between the muted, "objective" realism of a Courbet and the "subjective" realism of a Manet. Not until shortly before 1900 did his style become more relaxed and begin to absorb color and light. Objects became the conveyers of atmosphere. Humans, animals, and plants suddenly seemed to be woven of the same substance. "Drawing is omission," he now declared.

Bergson's philosophy of a general *élan vital* had stirred many Germans. Objects were to appear only as the emanations of a general life force. But the impatient strokes which now appear on Liebermann's canvases are united by the same cool discipline that always dominated his paintings, even when the subject was rearing horses or excited polo players.

In his portraits, to which he devoted himself increasingly after 1900, we sense a strong psychological approach. The person portrayed is sharply individualized. Every portrait should include a nuance of caricature, he declared in a statement directed against the "refined," dark, glamorizing style which Lenbach, for one, had cultivated before Liebermann. And with his psychological approach, Liebermann was a step ahead of the French Impressionists.

In his landscapes he favored ash-gray tones. His dry, grainy color seems to contain some of the sand of Brandenburg or the asphalt of Berlin. He deviated from the French Impressionists in color and composition. His later garden landscapes recede in depth and are dominated by a latent geometry, and in his paintings that include several figures, this geometry is again evident in the handling of the foreground. The French Impressionists rejected this order and instead developed a glowing sense of color. But one should not measure Liebermann's austere color against the brilliant scale of Monet or Renoir, both painters he admired.

Liebermann, who played a decisive role in founding the Berlin Secession, spoke up with ready wit against the reactionary influences of the time, as personified by the court painter Anton von Werner, the art historian Henry Thode, and the Emperor Wilhelm II himself. He wrote about Israels, Degas, the woodcuts of Manet. His work, *Die Phantasie in der Malerei*, is a belated German acknowledgment of impressionistic realism. He differentiated between literary and pictorial fantasy, yet he made a statement that should not be forgotten today: every *good* realistic painting always includes a hidden act of transformation. In Impressionism, the seed was already planted that was to lead to the emancipation of the media of painting, which broadened in such extraordinary fashion in our century. Liebermann already declared that it was a matter of indifference whether one was painting a Madonna or a head of cabbage; he went so far as to quote a sentence by Schiller which was later to become very appropriate: "There lies the real artistic secret of the master–he effaces the original material through the form."

Liebermann lived for eighty-eight years, during which he passed through three stages: first, one in which his realism was violently attacked; second, one in which it was viewed with the highest regard; and finally, a stage in which he himself was unable to recognize a style which was in the ascendancy.

Max Slevogt (1868–1932), born a generation after Liebermann, left south Germany at the turn of the century and after a short stay in Frankfurt settled in Berlin. There he was exposed to Impressionism, and he became a disciple. "I admired Manet so much because through him I could sense what made the world so beautiful." Slevogt brought German painting into the great European current. "Such a joyful, thunderous stream of strength, health, and beauty issues forth from the culture of France that we must not fail to honor this enormous bounty, especially since we are so prone to recognize the fact that Germany gave the world an incredible abundance of music in the same century."

If Liebermann's Impressionism is austere, Slevogt's is lighter and above all richer in color. Here bold inspiration won over solid construction. No muted gray hues, but instead autumnal splendor in his landscapes. His palette shows the colors of the western Palatinate, of Rhine wine, of Tiepolo's paintings in Würzburg (where he went to school). Light greens, gleaming yellows, gay blues vibrate. In his portraits, which are uneven in quality, he stresses psychological elements more than the French, who convey everything in terms of the painting itself. His spirited portrait of the Portuguese singer D'Andrade gives one a sense of the musical-dramatic vitality of the painter, who himself wanted to be a singer. Slevogt painted individual portraits and many-figured compositions (sometimes rather jumbled), but above all pure landscapes.

Lovis Corinth (1858–1925) stands between a sensuous, substantial kind of realism (which at first horrified people because of its coarse point of view), and a free-flowing, impressionistic, colorful style. When dealing with sensual women, boldly interpreted Greek or Christian mythology, or landscapes bursting with life, he was more forceful than Liebermann or Slevogt. He attended the Academy of Fine Arts in Munich and the Académie Julian in Paris, and lived nine years in Munich; then in 1900 he moved to Berlin. His powerful naturalism was such a drastic protest against the idealistic German classicism of Anselm Feuerbach and Hans von Marées, and also against the pseudo-vital pictorial rhythms of the Jugendstil, that he was called the butcher of painting. Although he turned his back on the art-gallery tone of the nineteenth century, he favored a scattering of dull grays. Everything is created out of the wet paint in an absolute furor. He threw himself into the force of life and wanted to make the work of art visible *in statu nascendi*. His close friend, the poet Eulenberg, said of him, "The strong smell of hides in his father's tannery evidently overpowered the boy at an early age." He painted in slaughterhouses, "amid stiff cadavers, steaming stomachs, and glistening entrails." He saw even the growth of plants in an animalistic fashion. The forcefulness of the brush was more important to him than impressionistic luminosity. He continued to struggle tenaciously with

1 Lovis Corinth, Walchensee, Landscape with Cow, 1921

old-fashioned mythological compositions, although they did not suit his sensual approach to realism. In his subject matter we find Golgotha, St. Anthony, Samson, Odysseus, Mars, and Zeus. Great projects *(Perseus and Andromeda,* 1900*)* stand beside overwhelming and labored compositions *(The Temptation of St. Anthony,* 1908*)*. The French Impressionists had wisely renounced this dated content, but Corinth was un-French, like his great pupil, Max Beckmann: two demonic masters, the first a product of Realism, the second of Expressionism.

Corinth's goddesses act like bouncing wenches; his hard-drinking heroes speak a cab-driver's German. Today he touches us most when he approaches life without any literary circumlocution, in his landscapes, in his abundant still lifes, in his animal pictures. His friend Max Halbe assures us that "he painted without first drawing, straight onto the canvas, and worked in the wet paint. With a portrait he often began by setting a nose or a pair of eyebrows or a mouth on the canvas, and let the rest emanate from them, executing what followed with a very quick hand."

He began with a massive, dull display of color which clung powerfully to the objects portrayed, until his technique became increasingly free. Gradually Corinth achieved the broad color style that paved the way to his later period. A chronically shaking hand caused by a stroke influenced his style rather movingly. The effect of the involuntary vibrato of his brushstrokes is not that of the feebleness of age, but of a deeper vitality. In his late self-portraits he sometimes captured his robust yet already failing individuality with demonic grandeur. The Walchensee landscapes of his last years (Plate I) are filled with convulsive torrents of color and look as if they had been whipped up by a storm. They abandon completely the realistic pictorial legacy of the nineteenth century and pass to the freest forms of expression. The next generation could use them as a starting point. Kirchner, speaking as an Expressionist, stated, "At first he was mediocre, but in the end he was truly great."

The oeuvre of *Fritz von Uhde* (1848–1911) takes us a short way into the twentieth century. We need touch on him only briefly, but he is interesting as one of the first Germans to accept the wave of French Impressionism. In this he was a step ahead of Liebermann, and therefore for some time many eyes were turned on him and his even brighter palette and lighter style which contradicted academic methods. His early works, with clear colors, remain his best. Later, driven by compassion and social consciousness, he turned to painting the poor.

11 Hans Purrmann, Room with Balcony, Montagnola 1949, Private collection

(In this subject matter following Millet, Courbet, Daumier, Lepage, Israels.) Uhde explored this sentimental vein in a more colorful way, but like Israels, was rarely convincing. After this Uhde turned to religious themes, transferring sacred events to a modern proletarian milieu. Only rarely did Uhde succeed in uniting the lingering sentimentality of the nineteenth century with the vital demands of Impressionism as he saw them. His work is an example of the unfortunate German tradition of trying to encompass too many aspects at once, instead of deciding wholeheartedly for one of the available possibilities.

Uhde's friend *Hugo von Habermann* (1849–1929) brought something very different to the art of southern Germany around 1900. A vigorous, billowing force swept across his canvases. He employed the surging movement of late Baroque art in his portraits and diagonally placed nudes.

The work of *Heinrich Zügel* (1850–1941) lies somewhere between objective realism and the new conceptions of light in plein-air painting. He was more impressed by the realism of Constant Troyon than by the Impressionists, and the bodies of his animals were not meant to merge flatly into the atmosphere but to emerge as heavy, blocklike forms from accentuated depths. Zügel went out into the country with huge canvases that had to be anchored against the wind. When the Munich Secession was founded in 1892, he fought energetically with that group against the twilit hues and weak colors of the studio promoted by the conservatives of Lenbach's circle. "You have to create form with color," Zügel would tell his pupils. But he was not as gifted nor as capable of development as Liebermann or Corinth. This stouthearted son of a shepherd was attuned to cattle and flocks of sheep, themes that he painted repeatedly, gradually using lighter and lighter colors. A chronological parallel throws light on how conservatively Zügel interpreted animals in spite of the wide, free sweep of his brush: when he was at the height of his realistic style, another Munich painter of animals, Franz Marc, was already conjuring up on his canvases dreamlike abstractions of everything animalistic. Along these lines, as we shall see, a totally new era in south German painting was to arise.

In west Germany, *Wilhelm Trübner* (1851–1917) was painting on much the same level as Zügel. We are concerned briefly with his last period. Trübner gradually developed into a landscape painter. He began with a dark tonality, with almost sculptural overtones; then his brushstrokes became more colorful and began to glow as if liberated. Yet his style remained weighty; some of his paintings give an effect of masonry. Gradually, he began to use the chlorophyll-green impasto of the French Impressionists, which gave a colorful strength to his robust, sometimes too-thickly-painted planes. Juicy green fields and meadows, blue seascapes that seem almost lacquered, off-white buildings stand energetically in their frames. If Slevogt sometimes improvised too spiritedly, then Trübner certainly constructed his pictures too statically and heavily.

DIVISIONISM

Impressionism was followed by Divisionism, a kind of Pointillism which was developed more consistently in France. Instead of the swirling, irregular color *commatica* of the Impressionists, the Divisionists sought a more serene approach, constructing a systematic color mosaic. *Chromo-luminarisme,* as this method was called, was initiated in France, not Germany. Seurat died in 1891, and the theories relevant to his work had already developed in the 1880's, but the work of the German Divisionists does not appear until the twentieth century. In France as early as 1880, when Impressionism was still very much alive, David Sutter announced a Neo-Impressionistic program; it was then formulated by Félix Fénéon in 1887, and also by Signac and Cross. It proclaimed the alliance of the artist with science, an alliance which would allow the artist to act autonomously. The breaking down of all colors into the elements in the spectrum was decisive in order to allow their blending in the observer's eye; black and brown were to be eliminated entirely. The "stones of color" were to be arranged with a feeling for the surface plane.

Although the introduction of this style, with its classical effect, into the world of impressionistic color seems especially characteristic of the Latin world, it was also introduced and adopted in Germany. *Curt Herrmann* (1854–1929) painted in this manner. In 1911 he wrote a book, *Der Kampf um den Stil,* in which he advocated "the organization of the three-dimensional on the plane surface instead of stereoscopic illusion." This theoretical aim was to become one of the chief goals of our time, and with good reason.

Herrmann did not find his way to Pointillism until he was about forty years old, at the beginning of the twentieth century. He was the director of a private art school in Berlin which was oriented towards this method, and he fought energetically for the new directions. Signac, Bonnard, Matisse, and in Germany, Van de Velde, were his friends. Later he developed a rather strange rhythm without, however, joining the Expressionists. Yet at that time he wrote, prophetically indeed, "Not only the form but also the color that fills the form is subject to rhythm, and the real obligation of modern painting is to achieve thereby an absolute balance between contrasts, complexes, and complementary appearances and values."

The simplifying luminosity of Neo-Impressionist pictures brought a storm of protest from the conservative devotees of the art-gallery tone, for instance Menzel, who rejected this new, lighter world of color as inartistic and brutal. With pointillist color dots whose size was supposed to be proportional to the picture's format, the essential aim of the artist was to give the new painting a surface stability. *Paul Baum* (1859–1932) became fascinated by Neo-Impressionism at the turn of the century. He allied himself with Herrmann and the contemporary Belgian painter, Rysselberghe, but the group had only a small following. Neo-Impressionism did, however, infect the Italians (Segantini) and the Belgians (Rysselberghe and Van de Velde). It also made its influence felt in the decorative murals of that era, although they were more affected by the Jugendstil. Neo-Impressionism may be considered one of the steps that led away from representational painting. The flow of color–through Impressionism–and the mosaic handling of color–through Neo-Impressionism–became practically ends in themselves.

Ludwig von Hofmann (1861–1945), more than any other painter in Germany, brought a light palette to large-scale decorative painting. In 1889 he was in Paris and saw the work of Puvis de Chavannes and Maurice Denis. He turned away from the somber twilit depths of Marées, yet it was that painter's solemn compositions which he really wanted to develop further. Thus blond Arcadian landscapes, peopled by young, innocent figures, now blossomed under his brush. This direction was called New Idealism; Hölderlin and Marées became its spiritual ideals. Stefan George, central figure of this new aestheticism, wrote sonnets to Hofmann. There was a Utopian, eurythmic feeling for life in the murals Hofmann painted for the Weimar Museum (1905–1906), for the Weimar theatre (1906), for Jena University (1909), and for Van de Velde's theatre at the Cologne *Werkbundschau* (Trade Union Fair) in 1914. Beside these large-scale assignments there are small, gentle, harmonious pastels that give no evidence of Pointillism. Hofmann's later paintings included figures, but adhered too rigidly to a lyric mood. In the effort to replace the diffuseness of the genre painters with a unity of color and line, too much true expression was lost. Only the Swiss Hodler combined the tendencies.

Among the nature-lyricists we must first mention the Worpswede painters. As early as 1889 they formed a group, seeking to express their devotion to a gentle, quiet profundity in contrast to the immediacy of the Impressionists. Red-brick houses, green and blue ironwork, and heavy-hanging thatched roofs stand reverently in their pictures. Trees, human figures, animals, detach themselves from the North German plain, quietly articulating space. The paintings of the peat-digger village of Worpswede, near Bremen, with black-sailed skiffs lying in its canals, with its pines and birches, evoke a dreamy feeling for life.

Fritz Mackensen (1866–1953), *Otto Modersohn* (1865–1943), and *Heinrich Vogler* (1872–1942) treated their paintings like poetic impressions. In 1895 these painters exhibited at the Crystal Palace in Munich, and scored a huge success with their rather artificial interpretations. Colors were rendered with delicacy, all shapes were slightly elongated. The young Rilke expressed his admiration of this craftsmanlike Worpswede approach in an elegiac whisper: "One is so fearfully alone among the blossoming trees and the brooks that flow by"–but this is hardly one of his more enduring insights.

Like these gentle souls, *Hans am Ende* (1864–1918) and *Karl Vinnen* (1863–1922) were ruled by a longing to escape, but it was not that more powerful, creative need which had driven Gauguin from Europe seeking strength in concentration on exotic forms. The Worpswede painters were also in revolt against an earthbound Impressionism, but they never achieved the freedom of pictorial structure that Gauguin had discovered. For this reason they had already lost all importance when the Brücke artists introduced their powerful colors and forms in 1904.

Meanwhile the painter *Walter Leistikow* (1865–1908), living in Berlin, represented a similar muted reaction against the Realists and the Impressionists. In oppressive, twilit colors, Leistikow depicted the melancholy surroundings of Berlin, not the lively suburban areas, which remained a theme of the Impressionists. He painted the pine woods of the Havelsee with a wide, softly stylized shoreline; figures were banished from these tranquil canvases. This cultivated, well-to-do man was a close friend of Liebermann and Corinth, and with them he founded the Berlin Secession in 1898 and subsequently the Deutsche Künstlerbund (German Federation of Artists) in Weimar, both institutions opposed to the conventional ideas of the German middle classes.

The Dachau Group

The Dachau group joined forces in 1893, somewhat later than the Worpswede painters. But they too were unable to escape entirely a certain decorative weakness, and their influence on German painting was also brief. The Worpswede school had devoted itself to the landscape of the north German heath, while the Dachauers were attracted to the south German moors that run along the Amper River. Muted colors amid thin, rolling mists, trees with flecked silver-gray trunks and crowns that seemed to hover in the sky like small clouds were organized into tasteful compositions by painters such as *Ludwig Dill* (1848–1940), or *A. Langhammer* (1854–1901). *Adolf Hölzel* (1853–1934) is the only Dachauer who was important for the further development of German art as it began to turn toward abstract painting; this influence, however, was felt through his teaching in Stuttgart, after his Dachau period. We shall return to him.

The Scholle

The painters of the *Scholle* (Native Soil) school were also devotees of a decorative picture form. The Scholle had flourished in Munich from 1899 and was represented by the art journal *Jugend*, founded in 1896. Japanism, Jugendstil, and the influence of the Nabis were here united in favoring a lighter and more broadly conceived tonality. The contrast between Munich and Berlin at that time was also reflected in their leading art periodicals. The Berlin *Kunst und Künstler* was interested only in the fine arts and reported very factually on Realism and Impressionism; the *Jugend* stood for the merging of the fine arts with literature and humor, all under the heading of the *Jugendstil*, absorbing, notably in its illustrations, the already passé influences of Toulouse-Lautrec and Beardsley. For many of these painters the Paris World's Fair of 1900 was an important event.

In *Fritz Erler* (1868–1940) we find this ornamental style represtented most purely. He decorated books for the publishing house Pan, stylizing the world of German legend, and painted huge festive triptychs, some religious, some mythological, that spread out endlessly like tapestries. The surface was intended to dominate; on it, decoratively simplified figures in subdued blond tones were interwoven in a rather hieratic manner. He decorated the interior of the Kurhaus in Wiesbaden, the town hall in Hannover, and also passenger vessels. His new, esoteric choice of colors was intended to overcome at last the dingy brown art-gallery tone of the masters of the nineteenth century. For a time his immaculate formal structure was valued in Germany as a new world of art.

Qualities of the Jugendstil and the Scholle were carried on by the Silesian *Adolf Münzer* (1870–1952), the Munich painter *Angelo Jank* (1868–1940), the Tirolean *Leo Putz* (1869–1940), and the Saxons *Max Eichler* (b. 1872), *Walther Georgi* (1871–1924), and *Walther Püttner* (1872–1953). Today their only historic value lies in their determined rejection of all genre painting. Most of them were preoccupied with the idea of incorporating the picture in wall space or room, but in doing so all of them succumbed somewhat to a summary poster style, devoid of any profound message–and this at a time when the quality of genuine poster art was at a very high level, especially in Munich. The liveliest of the lot was probably the Palatinate painter *Max Feldbauer* (1869–1948), who depicted massive horses and soldiers in glittering uniforms, undeniably with a certain power.

An artist with a unique position was the problematic *Franz von Stuck* (1863–1928), who chose to treat everything demonically. He painted *Sin* voluptuously, a woman with full breasts and glowing eyes, with glistening snakes wound round her. In an enormous painting he pictures *War:* Death rides, as if in a drama, over decaying bodies that cover the ground cadaver-white as far as the eye can see. The themes of Böcklin are enlarged upon, and the ashen flesh of the figures of Albert von Keller (a painter of interiors) is combined skillfully with decorative horror figures inspired by Munch. If one compares his paintings with the works of Max Klinger, who was just as theatrical and also worked in every kind of medium, then Stuck's work seems less overcast by the aestheticism that was dominant in Munich at the time. In any case, he must have been a stimulating teacher of new forms and expressions, for Marc and Kandinsky were among his pupils and always thought of him with gratitude.

Max Klinger (1857–1920) is of interest here because of his efforts to synthesize all the possibilities of his time, an attempt in which he sometimes succeeded through quite ingenious means. Today he is underrated. A Brahms enthusiast and disciple of Nietzsche, Klinger was a link between the genre painting of the nineteenth century and the freely roving fantasy which followed. Late classicism, a few impressionistic features, veristic psychology and the symbolism of the Jugendstil are united in him, sometimes mysteriously, as in *The Blue Hour* and the *Brahms Fantasy*. In *The Cycle of the Glove* he anticipates some aspects of Objective Surrealism, whose followers later admired his prescience.

Let us turn for a moment to the pure draftsmen, who are beyond the scope of the present study but should be mentioned for their important contributions in these years. The best of them in Germany at the beginning of the twentieth century found common ground in the weekly *Simplizissimus*, which began publishing in Munich in 1896. Among these political satirists were *Th. Th. Heine*, *Olaf Gulbransson*, *Eduard Thöny*, *Bruno Paul*, *Karl Arnold*. There were also important graphic artists active elsewhere: in Berlin *Heinrich Zille* (1858–1929) and the social tragedian *Käthe Kollwitz* (1867–1945), as well as the Austrian-born fantasist *Alfred Kubin* (1877–1959).

Rarely do the various trends in art succeed one another in an orderly fashion. Thus, in the period between 1900 and 1910, we find simultaneous directions: in France, Impressionism, the Nabi movement, and Fauvism; in Germany, Impressionism, Jugendstil and related styles, and early Expressionism. This last ran parallel to French Fauvism and originated in north and east Germany, whereas half a decade later the activity of the Blaue Reiter group is centered in south Germany.

Paula Modersohn-Becker (1876–1907) was a serene forerunner of Expressionism. She painted the peasant women and flaxen-haired children of Worpswede, but differently from the other artists active there. "Mothers, breasts, the human body, children... how strange her heavy hand on flesh, humans, the earth," her friend Hoetger said. From 1899 she was a member of the Worpswede colony and married the painter Modersohn. But she soon outgrew the lyricism practiced there. Heavier colors appear in which the brushstroke is visible, and large, constructed forms within containing outlines. One must keep in mind that the Brücke painters had not yet appeared on the scene, that the German students of Matisse were still far away in France, and the developments that appeared in France in 1880 occurred in Germany only shortly after 1900.

Modersohn-Becker avoided all emotional expression and conceived humanity as blocklike and quiescent. She did not attain in her figures the exotic sensitivity of a Gauguin, and sometimes her peasant children have big potato heads, inexpressive and apathetic. Already in 1900 she wrote from Paris that construction was the order of the day, and in 1902, "I believe that when painting one should not always think of nature." At the same time she longed for the themes of her homeland; she gradually abandoned earth colors and achieved a more expressive and brighter tonality. She died at thirty-one. As in the case of Van Gogh, deeply felt letters and diaries helped bring a quicker understanding of her style, which was new to the Germany of her day.

A painter who worked towards Expressionism but without identifying himself with it was *Christian Rohlfs* (1849–1938). His birth date places him in the generation of Liebermann, Uhde, Trübner. It is therefore all the more astonishing that after painting for a long time in the traditions of the nineteenth century, he should have adopted an entirely new style at the age of fifty. Certainly he is the only member of his generation who did not shut himself off from the revolution of Expressionism after 1900.

Even before 1900 the influence of French Impressionism caused his color to blossom. In 1901 the collector Ernst Osthaus, on the advice of Van de Velde, persuaded Rohlfs to move to Hagen; there, in the Folkwang Collection then being assembled, he could study choice examples of the western painting that would eventually prevail over Impressionism. At this point Rohlfs might have found his way to the cruder style of the emerging Brücke, but he was forestalled by his strong lyrical sensibilities, which sought a more malleable form of expression. A dreamlike quality and a beautiful sense of balance are typical of his color in comparison to that of his friend Nolde, for instance, with whom he worked in Soest from 1905 to 1906.

Gently flowing landscapes, churches, still lifes, and religious themes were his domain. He used veiled, batiklike colors, and discriminating, though somewhat unexciting, harmonies, very occasionally introducing a kind of lyrical-grotesque quality. He favored the color chords of cadmium yellow, rose madder, burnt sienna, and delicate green lake. Working with a binding agent he mixed himself, he brushed his colors on gently, or used a coarsely woven cloth instead of a brush, with the weave itself playing an effective part, as did also the texture of canvas or Japan-paper ground. In the last two decades of his life Rohlfs painted mainly on paper in water-tempera. In 1927 he moved to Ascona, Switzerland, where he saw flowers and landscapes as if through a light veil laid tenderly over simplified forms. But he had no intention of ignoring external reality. "Nature," he said, "should be drunk like fine wine, not like water, and one should be happy that it exists." Although Picasso said of him, "*pas du tout boche*," his lyric style was still too crude for the Nazis. In 1938, neglected and senselessly disgraced, Rohlfs died in his Hagen studio, alone, at eighty-nine.

Emil Nolde (1867–1956) was a chief founder of German Expressionism. He was a hard-living, introverted peasant from the coast, born in Nolde (North Schleswig) of Frisian-Danish descent. While the oxen bellowed for food, the boy was painting or drawing on carts or stable doors, using chalk he found in marl, or he was kneading figures out of clay. "I tried to paint with elderberry and beet juice, I liked red-violet so much." In 1889, a roving artisan, he came to Berlin, "a manure pit out of which grew lilies and roses." Next he proceeded to Munich, where he became acquainted with the nature-lyricism of the descrip-

Emil Nolde,
Prophet, 1912

tive Dachau school. He met Adolf Hölzel, who was already feeling his way toward new color harmonies. But Nolde's color remained muted and indefinite. "I painted landscapes with clouds in clusters or reaching convulsively across the sky like big dark fingers casting shadows far ahead of them." In 1900 in Paris he was impressed at first by the subtle color distinctions of Manet and by the dramatic mobility of Daumier. Then in 1905 stimulating new sources of power were revealed to him by the German collector Osthaus: Van Gogh's dynamics, Gauguin's feeling for forms in space, and the abstract power of the exotic. Yet he was also haunted by Munch and Ensor.

It is not surprising that from 1905 to 1907 he joined forces with the Dresden Brücke, where a passionate give-and-take now developed on German soil. From this the powerful structure of German Expressionism was to arise, primordial amid conventions grown flaccid, and therefore shocking to the general public. Instead of the scattered, fleeting tonality of the Impressionists, we now find powerfully combined thrusts of color planted sturdily in a broad black framework. Instead of small, separate brushstrokes, masses in a "barbaric" color key roar at us; instead of Impressionism's transient image from the outside, we find in Expressionism the urge to attain a powerful statement from within, made by a creator who reforms and opposes the pressures of nature. We find those deformations which were at first so bitterly contested but were later accepted as new expressions in depth from an interior world. But the Expressionists, unlike Kandinsky, never wanted to blot out utterly the beloved objective world, however freely they treated it.

Nolde did not in any way stress the contours that were to become of such paramount importance to his colleagues. The powerful organization of his pictures is based entirely on intense, glowing colors, which pour over the surface like lava, sometimes fiery, sometimes in a dark mass. Nolde's Expressionism flowed like an energizing bloodstream through all German feeling for color. His short affiliation with the Brücke was soon dissolved because he was an unsociable individual. From 1909 religious compositions dominate Nolde's oeuvre, raw as in his earliest days, ecstatic, with a fierce solemnity: in 1909, *Whitsuntide* and *The Last Supper;* in 1911, a nine-panel altarpiece, *The Life of Christ;* in 1912, *Maria Aegyptica;* in 1915, *The Burial of Christ;* in 1929, "*So That Ye Shall Not Become As Little Children.*" He fell upon this ancient sacred territory with such fervor, and interpreted its themes so drastically, that howls of rage went up from his viewers. But Nolde, unperturbed, wrote, "The fact that during the Renaissance the Apostles and Christ were painted to look like Italian scholars may have given the clergy the idea that this traditional treatment had to remain constant."

In his secular paintings he amalgamated exotic masks, primitive sculpture, elfin creatures, and colored material, using them to find his way back to the expressive force of earlier cultures. It is indicative that in 1913 he joined an ethnological expedition that led him via Russia, China, and Japan to Polynesia. He was receptive to primitive art, just as Picasso had been to African sculpture in 1907. "My interest in things foreign, in the primordial and primitively racial, was very strong... W. von Bode [Director of the Berlin Museum] was still vehemently opposed to primitive art... clearly and frankly I expressed my opinion of Liebermann and his all-powerful position" (1910). French Cubism made no impression on Nolde. "I think highly of Franz Marc's efforts toward a grandiose form, and I love his animals, but the prismatic things are foreign to me."

Nolde's unpretentious flowers and landscapes, in which his tendency to deform is less noticeable, gradually became popular. Rampant, glowing plants; damp, reclaimed land with windmills; spring-green meadows with cattle and paddocked horses; the dark blue North Sea under rain-swollen clouds–everything swings wildly in space. Here one feels the natural breath of life, but Nolde had no intention of abandoning his principles. "The farther one can remove oneself from nature, yet remain natural, the greater one's art." One must compare such theorizing with the opposite viewpoints of Liebermann and the nineteenth century to understand the giant step that had been taken. At the same time, impressionistic principles remained valid. "I avoided all blending of cold and warm, which has to result in muddiness and the death of all luminosity." Nolde's late watercolors remained for the most part airy and fluid, and his form consistently immanent.

In today's world of artistic individuality, we rarely come across antipodes greeting each other with respect from afar, but Nolde saw in Paul Klee "a butterfly fluttering in celestial spheres," and Klee wrote farsightedly, "The abstractionist, earth-withdrawn or earth-fleeing, sometimes forgets that Nolde exists... in him the hand of man creates, not without weight, in a calligraphy not without blemish... it is the mysterious, full-blooded hand of the netherworld."

DIE BRÜCKE

In June 1905, four students of architecture at the Dresden Polytechnic Institute formed a group: Ernst Ludwig Kirchner, Fritz Bleyl, Erich Heckel, and Karl Schmidt-Rottluff. Their purpose was to give the visual arts a strong, fresh impetus, to free themselves of Realism, Jugendstil, and Impressionism. They were enthusiastic disciples of Van Gogh and Munch, the Germanic elements of the new style of painting. Simultaneously with the French rebels, the *Fauves*, they found a source of strength in the barbaric figures of primitive art. Their first shows, held in a lamp factory near Dresden, went unnoticed or were reviled. The name, *Die Brücke* (The Bridge), expressed the desire to link all those who, like its members, opposed the individualism of the nineteenth century. The name originated with Schmidt-Rottluff, but it was Kirchner who drew up the program. The alliance was of short duration and unintellectual, being based actually on nothing much more than an exchange of intuitive and practical ideas. In 1906 they were joined by Nolde, and then by the Saxon Max Pechstein, the Finnish Symbolist Axel Gallén, the Swiss Cuno Amiet, and the Hollander Van Dongen, who came from Paris and acted as a connecting link with the Fauves. The last to join, in 1910, was Otto Mueller.

The artistic aims of Die Brücke were: an abstracting, primitive style, the use of unbroken color, the dissolution of impressionistic aerial perspective, and a dynamic blocking-in of form. What Gauguin had achieved by emigrating to the primitive world of the South Seas, these painters arrived at home: an attitude toward life that was again primitive yet at the same time forceful, that rejected the shallow life of big-city civilization. Certain concepts of the medieval guilds were once more crying out for revival. Their aims were similar to the yearnings of Ruskin and William Morris in the nineteenth century–in the latter case, a renaissance of the crafts, combined with a pallid revival of the Gothic. But only the Bauhaus was to succeed in collectively influencing daily life and in a less sectarian way, attaining its goals through a rationalized approach and through its influence on industry.

The Brücke experienced the fate typical of small groups composed of exceptionally strong individuals. In the beginning, just as it was possible for a time to confuse the Cubism of Picasso and Braque, so too the work of the Brücke painters was sometimes difficult to differentiate; soon, however, the masters developed their own individual styles. In 1913, when Kirchner wrote a retrospective chronicle, the group was already breaking up, although a loose association was still effective among its members until 1920.

For a long time the Brücke style was attacked by art academies and the more conservative public, and also by the lyricist Munch, who declared it augured ill for the future. The disciples of French Cubism also disapproved, perhaps because they were more oriented towards form, whereas the Expressionists emphasized expression, of course, and gesture. Cubism had undertaken to develop a plural vision deriving from exotic art, while German Expressionism, drawing a fresh feeling for nature from the same source, remained rooted in a reality which it wanted only to simplify expressively. Kirchner expressed the group's aims in his chronicle of 1913 as follows: "Uninfluenced by today's currents of Cubism, Futurism, etc., the Brücke fights for the humane culture that is the foundation of true art." And in 1917 he wrote, "The great mystery that lies behind all events and things sometimes becomes spectrally visible... we can never express it formally, all we can do is present it symbolically in form or word." A painting "is the circumscribing of a great mystery, and in the last analysis does not depict the individual personality, but a fragment of the spirit or emotion afloat in our world."

What a contrast to Dürer, who years before had confidently proclaimed an objective realism: "Abandon not Nature in thy estimation that it may be found better within thyself, for thou art being misled. In truth, art lies *in* Nature. He who can extract it, possesses it." Nowhere are the opposing epochs more sharply mirrored than in these avowals of two extremely masculine German artists.

The most mercurial and headstrong member of the group was *E. L. Kirchner* (1880–1938, Plate IV). As an architectural student he was influenced by early German graphic art. In Munich, where he attended the art school of Debschütz and Hermann Obrist, he was exposed to various currents: a major Neo-Impressionist exhibition, the drawings of Toulouse-Lautrec in the magazine *Pan*, and color plates by Vuillard and Bonnard in the journal *Insel*. But the northern world

III Max Beckmann, Black Lilies, 1928

IV Ernst Ludwig Kirchner, Family at Table

of Munch and German late-Gothic art excited him more, and modern French art actually remained alien to him. "For the Latins," he said in one of his exaggerations, "beauty lies in appearances, others seek it *behind* things." In 1904 he returned to his architectural studies in Dresden, along with Erich Heckel. Both were strongly influenced by the Ethnological Museum there, and by South Sea island carvings more strongly than by the more delicate Japanese woodcuts. In 1905, their friendship with Schmidt-Rottluff and Nolde led to the formation of the Brücke. They painted in an exotic manner circus subjects, suburban life, or summer scenes on the Moritzburg lakes, in which human figures and nature were pantheistically interwoven.

Kirchner may be distinguished from his friends by his energetic draftsmanship, his more angular, one might almost say Gothic, construction, his curves that converge or radiate. In spite of the passionate color, the graphic scaffolding of his work gives a dense effect until gradually the painting is dominated by a coniferlike arrangement. All perspective seems tilted, as if one were looking up.

In 1911, when the Brücke painters had moved to Berlin to take up life in the more cultured metropolis, the radical magazine *Der Sturm* became interested in Kirchner especially. In this second phase of his work his forms grow even more narrowly angular, his colors cooler and more transparent. Now his tonality is dominated by light blue, purple, black, a special shade of salmon pink, green, and yellow. But his psychological demon seems to grow more exaggerated. Mercilessly, treating his subjects like puppets, he captures the eternal schism between man and woman–even the Berlin prostitute–in all their roused sensuality, jammed between animalism and the machinery of a big city. Yet he does not accuse, as did Dix and Grosz later. While the latter, as social realists, eventually underwent a crisis in their art, Kirchner avoided this because his problems of color and form remained active. In 1913 Kirchner wrote the story of the Brücke; the account was so subjective that it was instrumental in the group's breakup.

At the start of the First World War Kirchner fell ill, and in 1917 he settled in Davos, broken in health. Gradually there appeared in his paintings a sturdy peasant and mountain world; his colors became stronger and healthier, his forms were resolved more rectangularly, his structural organization was firmer. In 1926, probably under the influence of the post-Cubist Picasso, Kirchner's symbolic period began. Bold linear loops and broad contours now form an abstract, highly individual rhythm. Divided objects are pulled together, the unity of others is broken up, figures and heads are shown from several angles in Janus-like double vision. But in the end Kirchner reversed himself: in 1936 he wrote, "My work grows richer in detail... I think. The older man loves details. To shape them from the greater thing is delight and joy." Although he now became interested in Picasso and Klee, he found the former too intellectual, the latter too frivolous. In 1938 chronic pain and the German political and cultural catastrophe plunged him into a despair that ended in suicide.

Erich Heckel (b. 1883), a Saxon like Schmidt-Rottluff and Pechstein, was also one of the great masters of German Expressionism, but he had a much gentler approach to life. His early themes included the twilight world of variety artists and clowns, also primitive foresters, seafarers, peasants, and gypsy-like girls, in strange contrast to the realistic scenes of city life that the public expected. He laid out his canvases with powerful wedges of color, but the forms thus hewn were concerned more with the things of this world and with realistic space than were Kirchner's. Consequently Heckel was able to bring atmosphere and light to his landscapes. Sky, clouds, and distance are more dominant than in the paintings of his friends in the group. At times he preserves the vanishing point and allows the horizon to arch imperceptibly, thereby developing a definite feeling for space between his exotic figures and greenladen treetops. Above all, tension and order were balanced in his paintings.

After this period of demonic expression, intense color, and angular forms, a gentler benevolence toward all creatures becomes evident in Heckel's work. From 1920 his colors grew softer and less stirring. In 1940, decorative elements even began to appear. Such a development may be found quite often in sensitive natures who have at first been carried along by stronger colleagues–in Heckel's case, probably by Kirchner and Schmidt-Rottluff. But other associations also play a role. In 1910 he met Franz Marc in Munich; in 1912 he worked with Macke and with Feininger. That same year, with Kirchner, Heckel painted the chapel at the Cologne Sonderbund Fair. The First World War brought him in contact with Ensor and Beckmann in Belgium. The most important years of his life were spent in Berlin. When his studio was destroyed by bombs in 1944, he moved to Hammenhofen, on Lake Constance, where the gentle landscape may have been dangerous for the strength of his art. In 1949 he was given a professorship at the Karlsruhe Art Academy.

The youngest member of the Brücke was the Saxon *Karl Schmidt-Rottluff* (b. 1884). According to Kirchner he started off with "a monumental Impressionism," working until 1910 with thick, exciting gobs of color flowing freely from the tube. In 1906 he painted with his friend Nolde and in 1907 with Heckel. In 1911 he went to Berlin, which enchanted him. Military service followed, after which he saw Italy, Paris, Rome. Under the Nazi regime he was removed from the Prussian Academy and forbidden to paint, but after the Second World War he was given a professorship at the Berlin Academy.

He was never one of those painters who are swayed by outside influences. The themes are constant: powerfully mobile landscapes, primitive figures, robustly conceived portraits, and still lifes which are heavily weighted in the foreground. His paintings are never experimental in form. His forms fill the space blocklike, as if hewn with an axe. His colors gradually attained a barbaric power through complementary contrasts, surpassing anything undertaken by other members of the Brücke. His painting, unlike Kirchner's, was not articulated by vertical graphic lines within the form. An unbroken architectonic power lies in his pictures, a forceful tonality with an almost symbolic color structure. "I realize that as far as I am concerned, I have no new art program, only the inexplicable longing to grasp what I see and feel, and to find for it the purest expression." Nevertheless, latent struggles underlie his development. His brilliant colors often clash with the weight of his construction. After his thickly flowing early Impressionist style had disappeared, he began to work with larger, flatter pictorial elements, although by 1912 Cubist forms also strive for recognition. Schmidt-Rottluff, however, never analyzed form as did the French Cubists. His pendulum swings back and forth between such possibilities until, in 1920, his "zone painting" appears: color blocks and space areas are separated no longer by the simple, single stroke of a color-laden brush, but by means of complementary color halos which frame the objects and create color zones around them. In his watercolors, largely landscapes, Schmidt-Rottluff's color is subdued, sometimes almost flaccid. But in his late period the pictures glow once more with bold and luminous colors.

In view of his style, it is easy to understand that he was also a sculptor, like Kirchner and Heckel. At that time everyone was collecting African sculpture, with its severely cut, barbaric juxtaposition of positive and negative forms.

Since 1950 Schmidt-Rotluff has been cutting heads and figures from small pieces of limestone which he himself picked up.

The Silesian, *Otto Mueller* (1874–1930), was the least passionate of the Brücke group. Though older than his friends, he was admitted to their circle only in 1910. He painted slim or woodenly angular adolescent girls who daydreamed under dull green trees placed diagonally in his compositions, their crowns bending lyrically over the figures. Mueller's paintings are flat, limited in plasticity, devoid of rounded forms. But under the influence of the Brücke he adopted stronger outlines and a more angular figure composition. The life of the east European gypsy was to him what the South Sea islands had been to Gauguin.

He should have been a muralist, so great was his command of large flat surfaces, as is evident from the cycle of figures he painted covering the walls of his studio. The close correspondence of his colors suggest the last light of day and suit his personal elegiac view of life. Often we find a composition of nothing more than pallid green, ocher or sulphur yellow, brown or gray interwoven with black; occasionally there is a matte red. Because he painted on coarse sackcloth–in the beginning with oil paint, and after 1911 with pigments mixed with lime–his pictures give the impression of Gobelin tapestries.

Mueller was a small man, taciturn, with a sallow complexion, blue-black hair, and melancholy eyes. He always wore an amulet, and he believed in ghosts. In 1907 Mueller moved to Berlin; in 1910 he traveled in Bohemia with Kirchner, and in 1919 he was offered a professorship at the Breslau Art Academy. He was always frail and died in 1930, not living to see his work destroyed by the Nazis.

Max Pechstein (1881–1955) was the least difficult and most carefree of the Brücke painters. His nature was boyish and fresh, but for all that, he was less experimental, less inventive and sensitive to the new visual signs of the times. He differed from Kirchner just as Macke, in the Blaue Reiter group, differed from Franz Marc. Pechstein's themes were similar to those of his fellow painters: dancers and music hall artists, bathers on the beach, the sea with its fishermen–especially the fishermen of the Kurische Nehrung, the spit of land on the Baltic Sea where he spent his summers. In 1906 he joined the Brücke, but disappeared again in 1907 into the relaxed atmosphere of Italy; then in 1908 he settled in Berlin. He was the first German Expressionist to become generally accepted and successful. His forms remained more representational, his figures more tactile, his composition more conventional, thus providing a less antagonizing form of Modernism. Pechstein was not really in step with the radical innovations of this group; with him, the Brücke opened out into the general stream of modern art. In fact, his departure from the group was felt to be a betrayal of its specific quality. Nevertheless it was Pechstein who confronted the "old" Secessionists in Berlin with a "New Secession," and he became its president.

In the wake of Gauguin's flight to Tahiti, Nolde had gone to Polynesia, and Picasso, Kirchner, and Heckel had come under the influence of African sculp-

Max Pechstein, Head of a Worker, 1912

ture; in 1913–1914 Pechstein visited the Palau Islands in the western Pacific Ocean. The exoticism we have mentioned frequently should not be interpreted as a flight from Europe or as a sign of degeneracy, as it was seen by the conservatives. It resulted in recharging European art with fresh blood. Such a development seems always to take place when art forms lose aesthetic distance or have been consumed by the mere reproduction of nature. The First World War surprised Pechstein in Palau. The Japanese took him prisoner, but after a breathtaking escape as a ship's stoker, he managed to get back to Germany. He was at once drafted into the army and shortly after was wounded. A letter written in the summer of 1919 shows how well he survived these ordeals. "I am working and absorbing strength like the moss that swells in the rain and transforms the forest into something miraculous. I am living in a state of ecstasy; I eat the air and could break my brush in the rapture of creation." He was inundated with commissions, including orders for the design of mosaics and stained-glass windows, and in 1926 he designed the stained-glass windows for the Labor Exchange building in Geneva. He was also prolific as a graphic artist.

Pechstein produced his most vital paintings and drawings around 1910, and he never completely abandoned exotically forceful form and color. As in the case of Heckel and Schmidt-Rottluff, his later style was softer, the colors lighter and less exciting, and balance was stressed, but the quality of the work was still high. Today the later work is underrated. After Pechstein's appointment to the Art Academy, the Nazis, insatiable in their desire to destroy all modern art, banned this popular Expressionist as degenerate.

The Saxon *Conrad Felixmüller* (b. 1897) may also be counted among the Expressionists. He became interested in the new art forms in 1914, and his work was published by Herwarth Walden in his magazine *Der Sturm*. Felixmüller painted somewhat in the manner of the Brücke masters, but more wildly, turning to a politically oriented Expressionism. The development of his style was extremely mixed in aim and form. At one time he toyed with both Cubist and Futurist vocabulary; he was drawn also to popular realism. Eventually he adopted an eclectic manner. Basically his art suffered from the influence of the class struggle, sociological realism pulling him–and others–away from aesthetic problems of form, with inevitable dualistic results.

The Silesian *Ludwig Meidner* (1894–1966) brought so much pathos to German Expressionism that the Brücke painters, who were certainly filled with urgency and passion, seem disciplined in comparsion. Meidner's paintings and graphic art were so convulsive that one understands the virtual inevitability of a reaction against this kind of emotionalism (a reaction that would take the form of the New Objectivity). From 1912 Meidner exhibited in the Sturm Gallery. From 1925 to 1932 he devoted himself to literary work, for words moved him no less powerfully than the visual. Of his writings, *Hymnische Prosa* and *Gang in die Stille* are noteworthy. In 1936 he was forced to emigrate, but he eventually returned to Germany and in painting turned gradually toward realism.

Conrad Felixmüller,
The Artist and his Wife,
woodcut, 1915

With *Heinrich Nauen* (1880–1940) Expressionism veered westward to absorb Lower Rhenish influences, becoming almost mournfully elegant. Nauen placed flat, leaflike, elongated figures diagonally across a wide canvas, partly in curvilinear and partly in triangular patterns. His color was light in key and extremely varied. He planned wall decorations whose effect depended on distance, and from 1912 to 1913 he completed such a series at Drove Castle near Düren. Because of the subjectivity of this approach, however, he was incapable of devising a simple, adequate theme for such a major assignment. As a result we find juxtaposed in one room a classical Amazon battle, a modern harvest picture, an almost medieval Pietà, and a scene from the life of a contemporary woman—all done in the same style. The promise in his early work of a spacious style that was sensitively dynamic in composition was never altogether fulfilled.

The life of *Wilhelm Morgner* (1891–1917) underwent many transformations. He painted foresters in their native habitat, herdsmen, strange self-portraits, and above all, religious themes. Strange contradictions murmured within him, yet he sought unity: profound agitation and harmony, the medieval mysticism of his native Soest with its seven church towers, Kandinsky's modern art–all these he wished to unite harmoniously. The Expressionist phase through which he passed (Nolde and Rohlfs also worked in Soest for a while) lent his work a rhythmical order. His languid colors gave the effect of a heavy woven texture, and in these years his originally objective art comes close to absolute painting. In his later pictures we find the green that clings to old garden walls, a beautiful brick red, a burnt yellow; blue, on the other hand, he tended to avoid. In his best pictures color is applied in long, broad stripes, drawing foreground and background together into a single plane. He was in touch with the Blaue Reiter group and influenced by Italian futurism. His *Entry into Jerusalem* is not altogether dissimilar in style to the medieval paintings in the churches of Soest. Making a critical selection from his varied works (235 paintings and almost 2,000 sheets of graphic art), one could assemble an oeuvre that is much too little known. Had Morgner lived longer, he would in all probability have developed a more lavish palette. After all, he wrote, "Now I want to capture in color the God who made the world, the strength that bears the earth... to transform this life into a color-form symphony." But in 1917, when he was only twenty-six, appeared the bleak words, "missing at Langemarck."

THE BLAUE REITER AND RELATED TRENDS

While the Expressionists of the Brücke were still clinging passionately to the forms of the world around them, a second movement was experimenting even more freely with color and form, the Blaue Reiter.

A fruitful impetus for the development of painting came from Munich after the reforms of the Secession and Jugendstil had outlived their day. A decisive influence on the artistic climate was provided by the presence there of the following painters, all of them less interested in an intensification of expression than in giving a many-sided spiritual meaning to form and color: Kandinsky, who had moved to Munich as early as 1896, Jawlensky and Marianne von Werefkin (all three Russians), and Franz Marc and Paul Klee, both of whom also arrived in Munich before 1900. At first they were strictly disciples of Cézanne, Van Gogh, and Gauguin, but soon they became receptive to the simplifications of the Fauves. Kubin and Klee brought their surrealistic graphic imagination to the group. Kandinsky founded the Phalanx, a school of painting which in 1904 was exhibiting Neo-Impressionist work.

In 1909 the *Neue Künstlervereinigung* (New Artists' Federation) was formed, with Kandinsky, Jawlensky, Kanoldt, Kubin, Erbslöh, and the two women, Werefkin and Gabriele Münter. They brought in the Russians Bechtejeff, Kogan, and the dancer Sacharoff; the French painters Girieud and le Fauconnier, and the Germans, above all Marc, Hofer, and the art historian Otto Fischer. Paintings by Picasso, Braque, Derain, Rouault, and Vlaminck were shown, which gives an indication of the European radius of the group. Otto Fischer formulated what they had in common with the Brücke, which had preceded them: "Color is a means of expression that speaks directly to the soul. Color is a means of composition. The true nature of things is not captured by correct drawing but by a powerful and mobile, penetrating and permeating outline." Unfortunately he added, "A picture without an object is senseless." But controversy raged more over the goal of the greatest possible freedom for art than over nonobjectivity.

In this historic hour a schism developed among the artists themselves just as a new exhibition was being planned. The more fainthearted gathered around Erbslöh and Kanoldt; the more aggressive sided with Kandinsky and Marc. The quarrel was mainly about a painting of Kandinsky's, a *Last Judgment*, which was rejected as too big and bold. Kandinsky, Marc, Kubin, and Gabriele Münter left the New Artists' Federation, and in December 1911 they organized the now historic exhibition *Der Blaue Reiter*, which traveled from Munich to Cologne, Berlin, Hagen, and Frankfurt. In Munich, where it was shown at the Thannhauser Gallery, it included, among other works, paintings by Henri Rousseau, Delaunay, Macke, Kandinsky, Marc, Campendonk, and Münter; Arnold Schönberg was represented as an amateur painter. Klee and Feininger did not join until later. In 1913 the more important members of the Blaue Reiter group exhibited at the first German Salon d'Automne, in Berlin. This lively international interplay broke off in 1914. Kandinsky and the other Russians had to leave Germany; Macke was killed in action in 1914, Marc in 1916. Kandinsky, Klee, and Feininger were not to meet again until the Bauhaus years.

The name *Der Blaue Reiter* (The Blue Rider) came from the *Almanac* compiled by Marc and Kandinsky in 1911 and published by Piper the following year. On the title page was Kandinsky's little figure on horseback. "We intend to publish an almanac that shall voice all the new and true ideas of our day. Painting, music, the stage... much will be clarified, above all through comparative material... we shall bring old glass painting, French and Russian folk drawing, side by side with material of our own and of others." Kandinsky argued "the question of form," Marc wrote about the Fauves, Burliuk discussed related tendencies in Russia, Allard reported on Cubism and Busse on Delaunay, Schönberg wrote on modern music. Thus as early as 1911, almost all phases of anti-naturalistic expression were being discussed collectively, and this may be considered the philosophical import of the manifesto. "The great success of the publication," Kandinsky said later, "was proof to us that it was born at the right time. Encouraged, we made plans for the next issue, which was to unite the powers of artist and scientist."

All in all, this group was less fierce, less violent in expression than the Brücke. The latter included far more urban realism in its themes. In the Blaue Reiter group there was a great thirst for beauty and the romantic, although we must differentiate between two separate currents: some members inclined more strongly to Expressionism and French Fauvism, others bowed to the experimental form of analysis that Marc called "the mystic inner construction." He himself went through both phases and brought them to a harmonious conclusion.

In accord with the historic law of inertia, this new form of Expressionism at first provoked intense opposition. The *Münchner Neueste Nachrichten* wrote: "One either comes to the conclusion that the majority of its members... are incurably insane, or that we are dealing here with shameless bluffers who are well versed in the sensationalism of our times and intend to make the most of a favorable opportunity." Marc replied furiously, "Our sensibilities have become so blunted, our eyes so attuned to banality, that the most superficial comparisons with nature are seen as useful criteria of art; our minds have become so lethargic that they can no longer tell the imitative impulse from the driving force of art."

Franz Marc (1880–1916) was a profoundly peaceloving nature mystic; a revolutionary creator of form but one with a Franciscan spirit; a rich colorist yet an abstract thinker. He was blessed with precise knowledge of the shapes of nature (as is proved by the drawings made in a veterinary school in his student days), yet at the same time he developed melodic rhythms, sometimes lyrical, sometimes dramatic (Plate VI). The supple unity binding his forms and their rounded beauty of shape and color have led some critics to call his art decorative.

Marc's rapid development reminds one of Raphael. Both men lived at a turning point in time, acting to reconcile its contradictions; both died in their thirties; both in a few short years passed effortlessly through multiple phases of growth. Marc began with simple, lyrical impressions of nature and moved to an intense expression of the hidden inner spirit of animal life; from here he undertook Cubist-like analyses of form, adding to them Futurist variations, arriving at the very end at an abstract art. For each one of these steps any other painter would have required a decade; Franz Marc explored all these possibilities in eight years.

From representing people he turned to painting animals, for he saw in them a less isolated form of existence. He painted them in embryonic positions, as if resting in the sheltering mother-body of the earth. He drew the limbs of deer or cats so that they look like snail shells, thus joining aspects of nature that actually are widely separate. Marc raised our perception of the animal to completely new heights. In 1912 he went so far as to hope "to create symbols that shall belong on the altar of a future religion of the mind, behind which the technical creator shall disappear.... The art of the future shall be the form of our scientific convictions." As he sought an ever more unified composition, he said, "Our minds already sense that the fabric of natural law hides something behind it, a greater unity." He also grasped intuitively the mutations going on in other art forms. In 1911 he wrote to Macke, after an evening of Schönberg's chamber music, "Can you imagine music in which tonality has been completely abandoned? I was reminded constantly of Kandinsky's large compositions which are written, as it were, in no single key... when listening to this music which lets every tone stand by itself... so that the conceptions consonance and dissonance don't even exist. A dissonance is simply a consonance that is more widely spaced... an idea that today absorbs me constantly in my painting."

Marc was the son of a mediocre Munich painter. His pallid early paintings are interwoven with surging Jugendstil curves combined with impressionistic handling. Until 1908 he painted chiefly single animal figures; then he turned to rhythmic compositions of animal groups. When Macke and Kandinsky became his friends, the former led him to a more luminous palette, the latter to a certain abstraction. During this time he painted large compositions of horses in which he let the colors rise to a crescendo. In 1910 he said, "I am constantly mulling over my system of complementary colors, the only way out of my insipid color scheme." (Macke had commented that the Germans unfortunately had a tendency to use light for color.) In 1911, using a palette based on the three complementary contrasts, red-green, blue-orange, yellow-violet, Marc painted his *Three Red Horses*, "their forms monstrously strong and clear so that they can take the color." From 1912 elements of Cubism enter, chiefly in the prismatic color scale of Delaunay, whom Marc, together with Macke and Klee, visited that year. After he had been dazzled by the Italian Futurists at a Berlin exhibition, his forms began to splinter dynamically across the canvas. In his *Tower of Blue Horses* (1913) the expression of form was no longer dependent on the bulging animal bodies but manifested a demanding life of its own. Marc considered *Animal Destinies*, painted the same year, his masterpiece. He wrote in a letter to Macke, "the trees bared their rings, the animals their veins," and on the back, "and all being is flaming sorrow." He was thirty-six years old when he was killed at Verdun. Marc's death was a great loss to German art because he had succeeded in extracting syntheses from almost all the progressive directions in the European painting of his day. Toward the end he experimented more and more often in purely abstract painting, in which he wanted to reveal only the radiance and motion of the cosmos.

August Macke (1887–1914) brought simple tone, fresh in color, into the melodics of the Blaue Reiter group. Franz Marc's complicated emotionalism and the revolutionary intellect of Kandinsky, who was twenty years older, were foreign to him. Macke said, "For me, work is a joyous encompassing of nature."

After the Düsseldorf Academy, Macke made trips to Italy and the Netherlands, and after 1907, increasingly often to Paris. The Berlin collector Bernhard Köhler made a carefree life possible. In an abbreviated manner Macke experienced the stages of development that were usual in those days: from 1907 to 1909, a form of Impressionism, but even so, in 1907 he wrote that he had tried "to assemble colors on a board without any objects in mind... what makes music so enigmatically beautiful, also has a magical effect in painting." He was still inspired by Cézanne's rejection of apparent form. In 1910 he became friendly with Marc. He saw a comprehensive Matisse exhibition in Munich which enflamed his color, without, however, inducing him to break up forms. From 1912 he worked, like Marc, with a Cubist division of color. In 1913 Delaunay and Apollinaire visited him in Bonn. In Delaunay he admired the way in which the painter worked without chiaroscuro, yet achieved a strong forward and backward motion. "All the Futurists do is *illustrate* motion." While Marc was experiencing Cubism metaphysically, as "inner construction," Macke employed Cubism to attain a transparent, simultaneous, and sensuously strong pictorial architecture. In Macke's prismatic color division there lies something juicy and worldly. While Marc was absorbed by animal symbolism, Macke remained true to the city-dwellers; he painted people in ordinary parks or looking at shop windows, although he used a tropical color scheme.

From 1913 to 1914 he lived on the Thunsee and became friendly with Klee, with whom, early in 1914, he made a successful trip to Kairouan, the old Tunisian Berber capital; there Macke produced radiant, clearly constructed watercolors and hundreds of drawings. Later in 1914 Macke entered the army and was killed in action almost immediately. Marc wrote mournfully from the front, shortly before his own death, "With the elimination of his harmonies, all color in German painting will diminish by many degrees and will be duller, and drier in tone."

Alexei von Jawlensky (1864–1941) emerged from Russian folk art and blended a true fervor for color with the aspirations of German Expressionism and the French Fauves (Plate V). He painted gigantic heads with huge eyes; their firm scaffolding, which is so effective seen from afar, reminds one of icons, but his colors burn. Macke's colors had a noonday glow; Jawlensky painted with the fire of evening. Spread between dark outlines, red, blue, orange, cadmium yellow, and chromium-oxide green press forward, often with ecstatic power. While his younger countryman Chagall was moving gradually toward dreamlike, ephemeral themes, Jawlensky adhered to a static, decidedly monumental form of expression. The square format suited his tendency toward the compact. From 1917 he painted a series of mystic heads and also *The History of the Saviour*. "In my latest works I have rejected the magic of color in order to concentrate on a spiritual profundity." Gradually these faces were filled only with silvery light areas, until, in a short final phase, we find only the muted colors of night.

Before these mystical heads he had painted heavy half-length figures, landscapes, and still lifes. Following family tradition he entered the Moscow military academy at the age of eighteen and was soon made lieutenant of a grenadier regiment–but a lieutenant who burst into uncontrollable tears while listening to Beethoven's *Pastoral* Symphony. During vacations on the estate of the young painter Marianne von Werefkin he painted the Tartar steppes. He served his regiment as captain, but in 1896 emigrated to Munich with Werefkin and entered the art academy of which Kandinsky soon became director. Thus two Russian aristocrats fought through to the creation of a revolutionary art form. They were soon followed by another Russian officer, Bechtejeff. The impresario Diaghilev, whom Jawlensky had known in St. Petersburg, made it possible for him to exhibit in the Paris Salon d'Automne. All in all, the Russian contribution during this opening phase of modern art is noteworthy.

In Munich, Jawlensky's studio and the salon of Marianne von Werefkin became gathering places for the revolutionary artists. Here an international atmosphere prevailed, seething with new ideas. The dominant spokesman was Kandinsky, with whom Jawlensky painted summer-filled landscapes in Murnau. To Kandinsky's friend, Gabriele Münter, Jawlensky said, "A portrait does not have to be a likeness. A hundred years from now, no one will know what the sitter looked like." This is the group that in 1909 formed the Neue Künstlervereinigung, whose shows were received by the public with scorn and ridicule. Jawlensky did not join the Blaue Reiter until 1912.

With the outbreak of the First World War, Jawlensky had to leave Germany. He lived rather wretchedly on the Lake of Geneva, where he painted small landscapes from his modest window. "Variations" were now his chief concern. In 1921 he moved to Wiesbaden and immersed himself again in his abstract heads. In 1924, with Kandinsky, Klee, and Feininger, he formed *Die Blauen Vier* (The Blue Four), a group which enjoyed its greatest success in the United States. But in 1929 he began to exhibit symptoms of paralysis and was able to paint only small heads, called *Meditations*, faces and visions that gave the effect of a double cross which at first glowed magically, only to darken later. In 1938 total paralysis put an end to his last, most serious efforts. The Nazis forbade the showing of his paintings, and he died a broken man in 1941.

Wassily Kandinsky (1866–1944) was soon recognized by his friends as the true leader of the group. Elsbeth Macke wrote, "There was about him a peculiar and fantastic aura, combined with a strange pathos and dogmatism. His art was like a doctrine, a world viewpoint." Paul Klee declared that he had "developed an increasingly deep confidence in him," and Marc, in spite of occasional doubts as to Kandinsky's humaneness, declared, "Kandinsky's art is as prophetic as his word; he is the only seer in our group."

He was born in Moscow in 1866, thus belonging to the generation of the Impressionist Max Slevogt. Kandinsky, however, was a pioneer of the next generation, though late in terms of his own personal development. "Until I was thirty, I longed to be a painter... at the time it seemed to me that art was a forbidden luxury in Russia." In Munich he failed the entrance examination for a drawing class at the academy, but Franz Stuck accepted him in his class. In 1900 he began to create independently and in 1903 was already teaching at the private art school, Phalanx. From 1908 he lived with Gabriele Münter in Murnau or in Munich. In 1910 he wrote his manifesto, *Über das Geistige in der Kunst (On the Spiritual in Art)*, published two years later by Piper, a total program for the nonobjective aims of the new painting.

In his early work, Kandinsky painted figures objectively, in the decorative Jugendstil, sometimes even in a mosaic of color. He was in full control of conventional forms, contrary to the assumptions of some of the naive opponents of his later abstractions. He abandoned Stuck's pallid colors for a restless, forceful tonality that already seemed inclined to go beyond the controls of the object. Moscow under the setting sun had created in him an enthusiasm for the value of color *per se*, but the abstract folk art of Russia had played its part too. "There I saw peasant houses, their interiors covered with paintings, nonobjective ornamentation without theme, furniture, dishes, all painted. I had the impression of stepping into a painting that told no story." Finally he became excited by Monet's *Haystacks*, and by Matisse, who had almost completely transformed the object into pure color. Three currents, therefore, coalesced in producing the great turning point: nature itself, an old folk-art tradition, and the pioneering in color of the moderns (Plate X).

Kandinsky's nonobjective painting may be best understood as a form of dynamic expressionism, a movement of inner feeling that fought to escape the limiting effect of the fixed object. In 1937 he wrote, "I went from Expressionism to abstract painting slowly, through endless trial, despair, hope, and discovery. You can see that I never had anything to do with Cubism." "When in a picture," he goes on to say, "a line is freed from objective description and functions as a thing in itself, its inner tone is not weakened by the obligation to play a secondary role; rather it recaptures its full inner strength" (1912). And with all this he knew, in 1941, that "the object by itself has a pervasive spiritual note that is art for art." Since his experiments were rejected everywhere as too intellectual, a further confession is important in which he says he never used a form "that had developed from logical rather than emotional perception."

The second phase of his development, between 1910 and 1920, he called his dramatic period, for now his colors and unreal forms force their way out and beyond the memory of the object, as if a volcanic power had been released. In this phase the pictorial elements separate, lines thrust beyond the color mass, transparent color is detached from the color of the ground. Yet the paintings preserve an irrational unity. In his theories he constantly introduces analogies to absolute music, but he did not rob painting of its unique nature, for he never rejected the specific properties that do not belong to music–line, color, and space. His first completely nonobjective painting is dated 1910; he was already forty-four. "A frightening abyss, a wealth of significant questions worth an answer came to me. And the most important one: what is to take the place of the

V Alexei von Jawlensky, The Red Shawl, 1909. Otto Stangl Gallery, Munich

VI Franz Marc, Two Monkeys

missing object? The danger of becoming decorative stood clearly before me." The problem of perspective also troubled him. The intrinsic weight of colors varied, and for this reason they produced different spatial effects, resulting in a pictorial depth "that brilliantly replaced the former depth-through-perspective."

It is deeply moving to witness his inner hesitation in constant struggle with instinctive confidence. "In those days I stood alone, because my painting was being passionately rejected. What I had to endure in the way of abuse was fantastic. 'An untalented swindler' was the favorite phrase." In 1914 the declaration of war drove him to Switzerland and from there he returned to his homeland and Moscow. After the Russian revolution he was offered professorships at home, but under Communism the opportunities for modern art were short-lived, and so he returned to Germany in 1921. Gropius called him to the Weimar Bauhaus in 1922 (his work there will be discussed later). At the Bauhaus he joined Klee and Feininger again, and was able to develop a full career as a teacher while consolidating the foundations of his theories. The interaction of Kandinsky and Klee at Weimar reminds one of the friendship that once flourished in this same place between Schiller and Goethe: a dualistic, extremely rational and controlled vital empathy (Kandinsky) opposed to a monistic, irrational sensibility (Klee). Again antipodes joined forces and interacted.

Of the woman painters associated with the Blaue Reiter, *Gabriele Münter* (1877–1962) was the most prominent, through her friendship with Kandinsky. From her landscapes in a bright chromatic key, still lifes in forceful colors, flower pieces and portraits, radiates a tone which is sometimes dark, sometimes luminous, expressive yet always harmonious. She came to Munich to study in 1901, Kandinsky became her teacher, and soon after that she lived with him in Murnau until the First World War. While he was developing his method of nonobjective painting, she remained faithful to an objective world, which she embraced in a friendly fashion, except for brief efforts in other directions. She loved Bavarian folk art and the old *Hinterglasmalerei* (paintings on the reverse side of glass). Her south-German form of Expressionism, very rich in color, therefore developed into something less massive and glowing than Jawlensky's. Her paintings remained serene, even when she used warm and cold reds, ultramarine and Prussian blue, together with black and white, also used as colors. In the course of her long life her colors gradually became somewhat more transparent and lighter.

She spent the First World War in Scandinavia and Lapland. In 1931 she moved back to Murnau, where she pursued her work, never spectacularly, yet never quite forgotten. Pleasant outline drawings in which she captured friends on paper give evidence of her ability as a portraitist. Often she painted in the evening because the effect of such painting was more powerful when seen later in the daylight. Even Münter's art, which no one could have called extreme, excited the fury of the National Socialists, and her paintings were removed from an exhibition in the Munich Art Academy. In her later years, made sedentary by age, she tried her hand again at abstract art, as if she felt that her cycle was about to close and she wanted once more to recall her former mentor.

Heinrich Campendonk,
Interior,
woodcut, 1918

Heinrich Campendonk (1889–1957) was also a member of the Blaue Reiter. The style of his paintings and graphic art lies between Chagall and Marc. Strange animals and human forms are depicted in primeval coexistence amid willful vegetation, with a primordial connection to each other. But his compositions are not as melodically symmetrical nor as resplendently improvised in color as Chagall's. Campendonk's animals are unfamiliar creatures that belong to a rather gloomy amphibian world. His colors are heavy with chthonian moisture. Whereas Marc seemed to be reaching harmoniously and ethereally upward, Campendonk gives an impression of groping downward. Later, however, his leaning towards the fantastic conflicted with his tendency towards decorative space composition. After a trip to Italy in 1920, during which Giotto and the mosaics of Ravenna made a profound impression on him, he developed an affection for static or monumental form. He was able to give it expression in decorative commissions: he designed stained-glass windows, primarily for churches, but also for public buildings in Amsterdam.

As a young man in his hometown, Krefeld, Campendonk was led through the teachings of Johann Thorn-Prikker to work in a rhythmical, decorative style. In 1911, through Marc and Kandinsky, who asked him to join them in Upper Bavaria, he was inspired to create fantasies in which he used cubist forms. In Bavaria the colorful fire of *Hinterglasmalerei* excited him. Although he did not succeed in reviving this folk art, he remained faithful to it. But even here he worked less with outline and more in color areas into which he subsequently scratched the drawing, thus achieving varied graphic effects. Later he turned again to glass painting and in 1937 created a huge painting on glass, several yards square, for the passenger ship Nieuw Amsterdam. In 1926 he was appointed to the Düsseldorf Academy of Arts; in 1933 he was dismissed as "degenerate," the National Socialists removed eighty-seven of his works from German museums–and simultaneously, he received the Grand Prix at the Paris World's Fair. Campendonk emigrated first to Belgium and then to Holland where he taught at the academy in Amsterdam. He became more and more introverted, never again took part in German exhibitions, and disappeared prematurely from the consciousness of his country.

We owe the foundation of the Bauhaus primarily to Walter Gropius, whose innate qualities fitted him exceptionally well for the task. Gropius quickly grasped new possibilities, and at the same time possessed the intellectual capacity to develop a unified program; furthermore, he was a gifted organizer, capable of translating his ideas into reality. Although he gave the impression of absolute determination, he was so broad-minded that he could combine under one roof opposing personalities of such stature as the humanist Schlemmer, the innovator of form Kandinsky, the dreamer Klee, and the geometrist Moholy-Nagy.

The Bauhaus was founded in 1919 in Weimar and in 1925 moved to Dessau. It may be considered the fourth attempt made in this century to form a working community of artists in individualistic Germany. The first was associated with the Jugendstil and led–only transiently–to those "craft workshops" which added refinement to the aesthetic surface. This was followed by the Brücke, which injected new strength into the life stream of modern art through form and color, but lasted only as long as the friendships of the group were maintained. The same applies to the Blaue Reiter. But the Bauhaus was based on architecture on the one hand and on a connection with industry on the other, with the result that much of the romanticism and introverted aspect of earlier attempts at unity were overcome. The idea of the medieval workshop took on a new shape: sculpture, furnishings, lighting, weaving, dance, and other forms were brought under the encompassing aegis of modern architecture. But most important, a new method of teaching was evolved here that enabled the further development of much that had already been achieved. No effort in any other country had ever succeeded in uniting so many highly individualistic masters under one roof. Now, for a few years at least, a constructive union was achieved in Germany that was able to overcome all individual eccentricities.

The concept of the Bauhaus was based on the combination of planning, handwork and the machine, rejecting all projects conceived on paper. Toward this end it was decided to proceed from one general basic course which should include, beside the study of nature, a demonstration of methods of composition with the most varied materials and designs. But the Bauhaus met with vehement opposition. The conservatives suspected too much "machine culture"; the moderns were against the inclusion of crafts. Then came the National Socialists, who considered Bolshevist the entire form world of the Bauhaus–at the same time that the Bolsheviks themselves had proscribed Bauhaus ideals and were propagating an art identical with that of National Socialism.

The Bauhaus sought a connection between its workshops and industry; as many students as possible should be able to earn their living. The experimental was encouraged, partly to shake off all imitative styles, partly to further the development of forms representative of the spirit of the times, but above all to give the student the opportunity to discover his own specific talents, which could evolve only in actual contact with the material required. The dangerous separation of fine and applied art disappeared. The Bauhaus included cabinet-making, pottery, metal shops, weaving, mural painting, work in glass, typography, and architecture, and all were interrelated. At first each department was under the direction of a master-craftsman and an artist; this scheme was abandoned in Dessau, where architecture was more heavily stressed after the construction of Gropius's buildings for the school. Today these buildings count as the most important examples of architecture of the energetic twenties. To the department of architecture were now added teachers of construction, statics, and descriptive geometry.

When the Weimar administration switched from the left to a "nationalistically oriented" policy, the school, which on the whole had been unpolitical, was considered dangerous and was liquidated. Through the farsightedness of the mayor of Dessau, the Bauhaus was able to settle immediately (1925) in that city, and on an enlarged scale. Nearly the entire staff of masters moved there with Gropius: Feininger, Kandinsky, Klee, Schlemmer, Moholy, Muche; former students such as Josef Albers, Herbert Bayer, Marcel Breuer, Hinnerk Scheper, Jost Schmidt, and Gunda Stölzl became teachers. They now had a stage, and Schlemmer was able to broaden his ideas on pantomime and the geometrical human figure–ideas later to be re-expressed in "unliterary speech." Moholy brought freer, more modern possibilities of expression and communication to subjective photography. Dance and pageantry were also drawn into the curriculum.

As closer cooperation developed, an increasing number of outsiders spoke lightly of a "Bauhaus style," but Gropius rejected this formulation. "The aim of the Bauhaus is not a style or system, not a dogma or canon, not a prescription or fashion. It will be alive as long as it does not cling to form but seeks the fluidity of life behind all mutable form." Marcel Breuer wrote at the time that "every good and purposeful object should fit into any room, just like any living object, a flower or a person." Many of the extremely varied courses conducted by Kandinsky and Klee have been published; beginning with the elements of painting, they taught a new way of thinking about plastic form.

Wassily Kandinsky became a decisive influence in the Bauhaus. He had arrived at a differentiation among three aspects of his work: he called *Impressions* works which had evolved from objective motifs; his *Improvisations* were the result of feeling or sensitivity of "inner movement"; the *Compositions* were thoroughly thought out and organized works, on a monumental scale. In his Bauhaus period, his third phase, he consolidated his pictorial creativity. Exact forms of plane geometry appear: dots, segments of circles, triangles, conglomerations of straight lines. Instead of an irrationally flowing dynamism, we have strict regulation. Clear colors confront each other additively, apparently aiming at a constructivist statement wherein highly individualized visual tensions are achieved. In *Punkt, Linie zu Fläche (Point and Line to Plane)*, a Bauhaus publication (1923 to 1926), he pursued his theoretical experimentation, systematically analyzing his pictorial organization. Here the stress is on the meaningful purity of the elements as opposed to "just painting," which he deplored in his classes. Of course in the writings of an artist one should not always expect art historical logic, but rather one must feel the creative direction that is sought.

From the beginning Kandinsky strove for a synthesis of all the arts as the foundation for a rebirth of human society. This is the reason for his decisive influence on the Bauhaus. He found Constructivism too intellectual, saying, "An unfeeling mind is worse than mindless feelings." He denounced the practical *art engagé*, with its socialist content, as an attempt to "salvage art by forcing it into the service of daily living." "In it I see," he wrote in 1935, "the only artistic crisis of our dismal times." The protest was aimed at the sociologically critical verism of Dix and Grosz, but above all at the "political realism" which grew so powerfully under dictatorships. But Kandinsky knew very well wherein the old and the new remained joined. "The basic law that governs the working method and energies of the objective and nonobjective painter is absolutely the same" (1931). And he had no intention of creating a conflict between the nature surrounding us and his radical transformation. "The abstract painter gets his inspiration not from any random piece of nature but from nature as a whole, and from its diverse manifestations which are summed up in his work" (1935).

When the National Socialists closed the Bauhaus in 1933, Kandinsky emigrated to Paris, where exhibitions of his work made him internationally famous. In France he contributed significantly to the development of every aspect of abstract painting and furthered its continuous enrichment until it gained world acceptance. In 1944, at the age of seventy-eight, he died in Paris, working undiminished until his last breath. In his final period we see large, irrationally playful forms, bold color contrasts, and radiant symbols that seem to stand on an infinite plane. Once more the echoes of the folklore of his west Siberian homeland may be heard, as if telling a story, but caught now in glasslike clarity. Shapes are constructed and organic; subtle and elementary colors meet in an ambience of purity. His last painting, like the swan song of a very old man, he called "L'Elan temporé."

The art of *Paul Klee* (1879–1940) developed entirely on German soil until the year the National Socialists banished him and he withdrew to his native Switzerland. He spun a dreamlike web, gathering his threads from the most remote sources. He began with subtle, extremely representational drawings and somewhat satirical prints. But this phase was followed, under the influence of the ideals of the Blaue Reiter, by a visionary transposition of form. After his journey to Tunis in 1914 his work became more colorful. This development was followed in the Bauhaus period by the introduction of an abstract play of forms, leading to a subtle and systematic dissection of the structure of his paintings through flat spatial areas, linear concentration, and a kind of pointillist technique. At the end of his life, during his final illness in Switzerland, a somber, symbolic sign language emerged.

In a mysterious way he managed somehow to reconcile all contradictions, to juxtapose unrelated, grotesque forms in pleasing harmony, to transform anxiety into reverence. "Investing creation with permanence," as he himself put it. Whereas Surrealism aims at alienating us from the world we know, Klee makes us feel at home in an unknown, perhaps traumatic, world. He wrote, "The visual, in its relationship to the world as a whole, is but one isolated example, outnumbered by other latent truths." With this statement he comes mysteriously close to the sphere of nonobjective painting, although, he rarely entered it. Again and again he hovers on the line between the expression of organic life and of abstract art, holding both fields in magnetic conjunction. A special magic lies in his titles, which we should read while viewing the pictures. The letters seem to twitter mysteriously, like little birds on a telephone wire. They indicate a mood: *Unstable Equilibrium*, *Fugue in Blue and Red*, *Three Notes Squared*, *Active Line Circumscribing Itself*, *Limits of the Intellect;* or they signalize remote constellations: *Growth of Night Plants*, *Pessimistic Allegory of Mountains*, *Countercurrent by Full Moon*, *Revolution of a Viaduct*.

Klee was born in Bern, Switzerland, in a household that cultivated music and cats. His mother's family came from the south of France; from her he may have inherited his dark hair and large Bedouin eyes. In 1898 he began his studies at the Munich Art Academy. On a journey to Italy he was excited by early Christian mosaics and Gothic art; in Naples by the life of the aquarium. In the Munich Kupferstichkabinett he discovered Beardsley, Blake, and Goya, and his ironic–realistic, early graphic style was formed. But already he wrote, "Bound only very indirectly by the impressions of nature, I dare to give shape to whatever burdens my soul." Moving away from Kubin, he wrote that the latter "could not extricate himself from the tough slime of the world of appearances."

His second period began in 1911, when he joined the Blaue Reiter group. A brief visit to Paris in 1912 was of minor importance for him, but through the Berlin *Sturm* he became acquainted with Delaunay and the Futurists, who led him to use more intense colors. After the short trip to Tunis with Macke, he was suddenly jubilant: "Color and I are one." At the Bauhaus Klee's third period began. All imitation was expunged; his intimate communications now became exquisite color miniatures. A subtle order pervades his pictures, the effect partly of his teaching glass painting and weaving, and partly of Kandinsky's influence. For at this time these antipodes were united through their work–Klee's pantheism was joined with Kandinsky's ordered dualism. Their teaching methods differed correspondingly: Kandinsky emphasized construction; Klee fostered his pupils' inner growth, although he too racked his brains over formal problems, as we know from diaries, his *Pädogogische Skizzenbuch*,

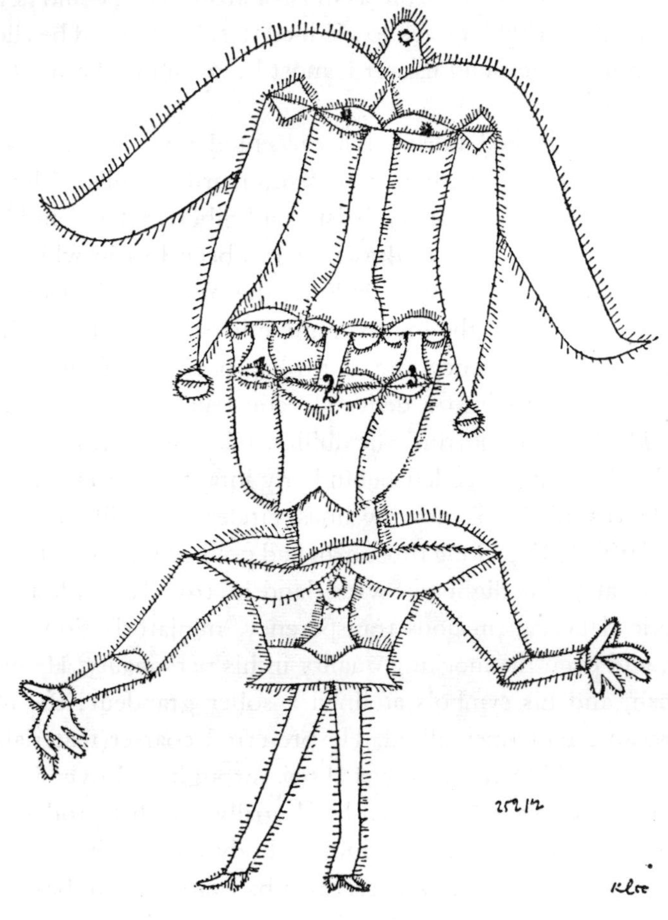

Paul Klee, Three Gentle Jesters, 1925

his essays and lectures. But reason, as in Leonardo's case, could never obliterate the mystic in him. "Evil," he acknowledged darkly, "should be allowed neither to conquer nor to confound us, yet it must be recognized as part of the whole creative process."

After Gropius left the Bauhaus, Klee accepted a professorship at the Düsseldorf Academy (1931–1933), but he was summarily dismissed by the National Socialists, who saw this visionary artist as a "Siberian Jew" and "a dangerous culture-Bolshevik." A series of drawings has been lost in which the banished artist articulated his fury, comparable to the *Songes et Mensonges* with which Picasso protested against the Franco regime in Spain at almost the same time. With ever greater consistency, the world had been transformed for Klee from a frail correlated web into a delicately constructed scaffolding, without his colors' having lost their intrinsic flexibility. Klee's gestures, forms, structures, and parables had long since left behind any infantile aspects. The veins of his unfurling leaves, his loops, flowing lines, circles, the grillwork of his crystals, were now clarified. For a long time, man had not been for him the measure of all things. Soon after his flight to Switzerland in 1933 Klee's last period began. All aesthetic delicacy, precious transparency, miniaturization of the sublime, disappear, and even the mocking quality in his personality. He worked with a broad brush, and his symbols attained a sober grandeur; the format of his pictures became monumentalized. He preferred coarser materials; the cross-threads of the sacking-cloth canvas show through and over it flow doughy, pasty colors. Often we see a leaden black grillwork that produces an effect of threat and obstruction; when the human body appears it is not infrequently dismembered and inert, as if its massive limbs were never to be rejoined. Forms overflow in a swollen effervescence; heavy outlines dominate even his pastels. Sometimes he uses crayon on cotton or jute, or chalk is pressed down into a wet, heavy, absorbent surface. It is not my intention to probe too deeply into the secrets of this last phase of his work. Klee the magician was still not without hope and had not stopped creating pictures in joyous colors; in these, yellow and orange-to-terra cotta, or yellow-green and dark green are closely related, or certain dark symbols are outlined in lighter tones. But now we find oppressive titles: *Demonism*, *Outbreak of Fear*, *Monster in Waiting*, *Death and Fire*. Much of what he did in these last years of illness and banishment now has the effect of a weighty *memento mori*. He died a lingering death, inexorably wasting away. On his grave is inscribed one of his profound confessions: "In this life I am no longer to be grasped. For I live with the dead as well as with those not yet born. A little nearer to the heart of creation than usual, yet not nearly near enough."

Lyonel Feininger (1871–1955) joined the staff of the Bauhaus in 1919. With his soundly constructed, spring-blond, gold-brown, or delicate blue canvases, he turned Cubist principles towards a uniformly ordered transparency. Feininger's paintings are dominated by a smoothly polished elegance that does not always escape the pitfalls of virtuoso design. In his luminous landscapes we find visionary edifices, their surfaces self-reflecting or faceted like crystal. A glassy stillness lies over everything. When Feininger places transparent vessels against the shimmering surface of the sea, he is able to condense the reflecting atmosphere so that it enters into every element of the encompassing fugal structure on which his composition is based. All growing things–trees, for instance–are assimilated to the architecture, yet his straight lines always remain dynamic. Reality and unreality are meant to permeate each other. One could call his seascape and architectural paintings polished dreams of light, from which he either eliminates the human figure or inserts it as punctuation.

As a child Feininger lived in New York, where he saw the crowded forms of that metropolis shoot up out of the ground. At sixteen he crossed the ocean to study music in his parents' native Germany, and also to become a student at the Academy of Applied Arts in Hamburg and at the Berlin Academy. At twenty-one he saw Paris, after which he settled down in Berlin and made a living by contributing drawings to German, French, and American comic magazines. In 1907, with the advent of Cubism, he turned to more abstract forms, and in Paris in 1911 he met Delaunay, whose transparent-color Cubism, "Orphism," had also made a great impression on Marc and Macke. Macke invited Feininger to join the Blaue Reiter and to exhibit at the first Berlin Salon d'Automne in 1913. In 1919 Gropius asked him to come to the Weimar Bauhaus. With Kandinsky, Klee, and Jawlensky, he founded the *Blauen Vier* group. Even Feininger was unable to escape National Socialist persecution; his noble works, which never evoke the demonic aspects of Expressionism, were considered "degenerate." In 1936 he accepted a professorship at Mills College in California and later settled in New York. The circle was closed.

Some of Feininger's statements characterize his position as an artist: "For years I have wanted to present too much of nature, and for this reason have become increasingly popular with those who see a progression in my painting corresponding to their idea of closeness to nature." But everything had to pass "through a process of transformation, through a crystallization" (1907). About his feeling for color he writes, "It could be that in this respect I am poor when compared with others." And in 1950 he speaks of "the will for law and order and the elimination of all traditional accessories."

Oskar Schlemmer (1888–1943) stood a little apart from the Bauhaus because basically he carried on the tradition of monumental figure painting of Runge, Marées, Puvis de Chavannes, and Hodler. However, his figures were more abstractly handled and presented at unusually close range, and Schlemmer, who was after all a contemporary of the Constructivists, turned his figures into columns rising up in imaginary spaces as if to achieve a system of coordinated forms. He rejected all improvisation and subordinated everything to the strict laws of geometry. His color areas were severely composed; not until later did he give them a more abrasive and warmer character. He developed rhythmic parallelisms in terms of towering verticals or extended horizontals that corresponded to one another; at most he admitted an occasional diagonal thrust. Any effect of motion was harnessed in a way that congealed its living quality. He stated, "Runge's sentence has always appealed to me: 'Severe regularity is indispensable above all in those works that spring from the imagination and out of the mysticism of our souls, without external matter or content.'" Even when he employed chiaroscuro, his figures did not soften, but seemed to stand out more independently than ever. Most rarely did he resort to abstract paintings. All techniques were subservient to his intentions, whether oil on canvas, watercolor, pastel, *Hinterglasmalerei*, or lacquer.

Schlemmer admired his friend Meyer-Amden, who died prematurely in 1912. In a muted and smaller format, Meyer-Amden had realized that tense stillness which Schlemmer heightens to monumental proportions. Schlemmer was also a sculptor, and in his sculpture the human figure is abruptly reduced to a mere construction of limbs and signs. He executed reliefs on the stairwell of the Art Academy in Weimar, but Gropius's successor had these reliefs brutally obliterated. In his final years Schlemmer painted a cycle of small "window pictures," in which the human figure is magically captured on the cross of the window frame. At one time during the last years I commented to him that his whole life would be devoted to the human figure; he denied this and pointed out that now he also wanted to subject pure landscape to the mysterious order that he had in mind. His death prevented this dream from being realized. His idea of the human body was founded, he said, on the Apollo of Tenea. His favorite colors were, "in the earlier years, black, gray, silver, pink; later–orange, blue, pink, gentian blue, semper vivum."

At the Bauhaus he directed the workshops for murals, for wood and stone, and for the stage. In this last he created androgynous human and machine creatures who performed sometimes majestically, sometimes in a burlesque style. The geometrically masked bodies were supposed to move as mutely as possible–mime, therefore–and on no account were they to lapse into verbal expression. Varied spatial tensions were his aim. His *Triadic Ballet* made use of completely new, anti-realistic means. His ideas on the dance were the exact contrary of the expressionistic style which Duncan, Wigman, and Laban had developed. What he had in mind was motion governed by laws almost akin to those of classical ballet.

In 1928 Schlemmer painted large murals for the Folkwang Museum in Essen. He left the Bauhaus shortly after Gropius and taught first at the Breslau, later at the Berlin, Art Academy. He was dismissed from his teaching post as "degenerate" and spent the last years of his life in the country, isolated and broken by the regulations that had outlawed him and forbidden him to paint.

For a time *Johannes Itten* (b. 1888), a Swiss who worked chiefly in Germany, brought his own individual method of teaching to the Bauhaus. His art is uneven, but sometimes a healthy, plastic vitality breaks through his structure and color. His teaching, however, seems to have been more effective than his painting, from which he was often distracted. As pedagogue he sought irrationally to combine the ancient Persian religion, Mazdaism, the wisdom of Zen, and a futuristic mystique of motion. Gropius had invited him in 1919 to the Bauhaus at Weimar; there Itten gathered around him the disciples of anthroposophy. The basic teaching he offered was interspersed with studies in hygiene, nutrition, breathing exercises, and psychic concentration. Such aberrations led to conflict because the Bauhaus was also under the influence of the Dutch *Stijl* group, and its leaders wished to devote it to more rational and severe activity in the world of modern industry. After Itten's departure from the Bauhaus in

1926 he founded his own school in Berlin; it existed until 1934. In the large facsimile edition of his diary one finds, with many examples, his ideas on the various types of mankind and their structure. In 1938, he took over the School for Applied Arts and the Applied Arts Museum in Zurich, and devoted himself to the Swiss *Werkbund* at the time the German unions were being liquidated by National Socialism. Itten then organized the Rietberg Museum (Zurich) which was largely devoted to the Oriental art that had always fascinated him.

His own art developed typically. At first he absorbed the representational world in the spirit of Cézanne, then color and mechanistic abstractionism became increasingly important to him, following which he returned occasionally to objective representation. But in the end he devoted himself to geometric abstractions and worked in "variations" that tried to fix rhythmically the "logical" sequence of related forms and contrasting colors.

Of the Bauhaus masters, *Josef Albers* (b. 1888) was the one who devoted himself most rigorously to the teaching of color and form. He worked out a kind of physiology and psychology of the picture itself, making a study, for instance, of optical illusions: how, by changing the disposition of lines, surface, and color, an illusion in depth could be created. Since Constructivism had made a strong impression on him, his pictures of the Bauhaus period consist mainly of straight, rodlike forms which are intended to have an impersonal effect through the arrangement of varied materials or of unmixed, structureless, warm or cold color areas. In his glass painting we find a Venetian-blind effect. In his purest works he shuns all romantic flourishes. But when one takes a closer look at his dispassionate drawings and paintings, one finds irregular relationships between ground and figure, even spatial and temporal attractions that seem to contradict the outward appearance, so that the work does not become boring. Nevertheless, Marcel Breuer called him "a frustrated architect." In Albers we find no trace of the cult of the subconscious which the Surrealists and the Tachists favored. In such pursuits he saw only "sick individualism and wild confusion," as he wrote to me in 1956. "Let us face clearly the fact that no hand, no tool or medium could possibly be quick enough to follow the bare currents of the subconscious." In his teaching his attitude was like an engineer's, in that he tried to solve visual problems with a minimum of material outlay.

Albers came from the Ruhr, was first a schoolteacher, and then studied at art academies in Essen, Berlin, and Munich. In 1920 he came to the Bauhaus, where he stayed until its dissolution. He went from there to Black Mountain College in North Carolina, and from 1950 until his retirement in 1960 taught at Yale University. He has written extensively on art education, on the teaching of form and abstract painting, and for a time he lectured at the Ulm Hochschule für Gestaltung. In recent years his color studies of the square in both painting and lithograph have been his major original contribution.

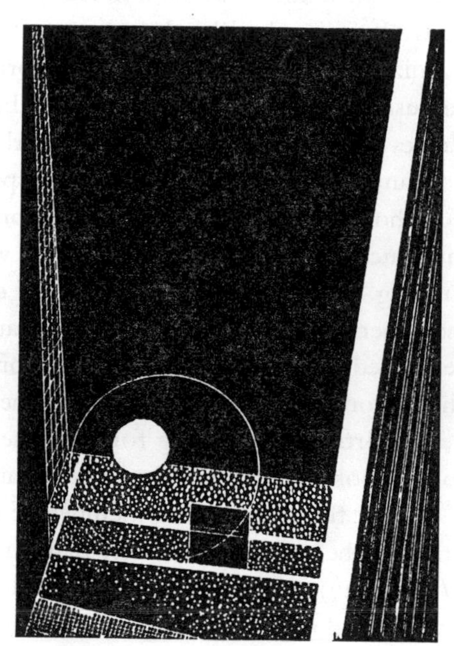

Ladislaus Moholy-Nagy, woodcut, 1924

Ladislaus Moholy-Nagy (1895–1946) was a richer "purist," a source in many ways of our visual attitudes during the second quarter of this century. Like Van de Velde in 1900, Moholy wanted to influence our life as a totality, through an essentially visual cultural education. He was active as painter, graphic artist, sculptor, typographer, photographer, stage director, theoretician, teacher, and organizer of exhibitions. With astounding agility of mind he grasped every idea that was in the air and systematized it. At the end of his much-too-short life he compiled his thought in the abundantly illustrated work, *Vision in Motion* (Chicago, 1947), a book that should form the basis for every school of fine or applied arts.

His life was dedicated ceaselessly to work until he died of leukemia at the age of fifty-two. He came from Hungary, where he had studied law until it occurred to him that one might lead mankind out of the chaos of empty conventions through a new sense of vision–and the first step toward it would be to wipe the slate clean. While he was still in Hungary he founded the group *Ma*. He seems to have been inspired by the master of the black square, Malevich, and by the organizer of the simplest rectangular forms, Mondrian. After he left his country because of the Communist revolution there, Moholy lived in Berlin, in poverty. However, he was able to exhibit his early abstract works–which did not go beyond an elementary organization of space–in the Sturm Gallery. From 1921 foreshortened lines appear in his work, as in the Constructivist Lissitsky's, introducing spatial problems. Moholy wanted to arouse awareness of the surrounding space while limiting himself strictly to plane geometry. From 1923 he experimented with transparent materials such as rhodite and plexiglass. He created reliefs in which the light from the exterior casts delicate shadows within. From this he later developed the space modulator. All this was abandoned for irrational, curving forms at the end of his life.

In 1923 Moholy took over the metal workshop at the Weimar Bauhaus. As a propagandist he was the most active member of the Bauhaus, and Gropius published with him the series of fourteen Bauhaus books. Moholy's *Malerei, Photographie, Film* (1927) was one of these. For Moholy the hunger for objective reality finally was stilled not in painting but in photography. And it was also in photography, to which he devoted himself almost exclusively from 1923 to 1927, that he conquered new visual territory. By changing accents or viewpoints, by photomontage or photogram, he departed from the mere reproduction of nature to a free construction with light.

Moholy's first pictures showed only a few contrasting, smooth color areas. From this stage he turned to spraying paint in thinner, more iridescent chromatic effects, or he introduced greater differentiation of the surface. In abstract sculpture he coupled artificial materials with polished elements, with the intention of dissolving matter drastically by reflections from the work's surround-

VII August Macke, View into the Greenhouse, 1914

VIII Werner Gilles, Bird Cape, Ischia, 1952

ings. Finally he wanted to "paint" almost exclusively with light from a reflecting agent, that is to say, with the screen. Painting might be replaced by a transparent play of light that would either radiate statically–in which case the painter's original would be the slide itself–or would set everything in motion, as in an abstract rhythmic film.

In 1929 appeared his Bauhaus book *Von Material zur Architektur*, an excerpt from his Basic Teachings lectures. In 1928 he left the Bauhaus with Gropius and lived in Berlin where he worked for the State Opera, for the Piscator Theater, and in advertising. It was here that he created the rotating "light requisite" for an abstract play of colors. National Socialism drove him from Germany, first to Amsterdam, then to London. In 1937 he founded the New Bauhaus in Chicago, and after that his own School of Design, in which he was active until his death. In 1946 *The New Vision* was published, a revision of one of his earlier works. *Vision in Motion*, which he was not able to complete, he called his last will and testament. In it he related the study of optics to life, always envisioning a universal rejuvenation. He summarized his aims with the following theses: "An emotional education must go with an intellectual one." "A passionate preference for transparency is one of the most characteristic signs of our time." "Not a life founded on metaphysical miasma, but on a fair balance... culminating in justice and the capacity to express oneself, is the best security for social harmony."

Herbert Bayer (b. 1900) was master of publicity and typography at the Dessau Bauhaus. These were to remain his fields of activity. Exhibitions organized by him were artistic achievements, as for instance his contribution to the Pressa Exhibition in Cologne (1929), and the Paris Trade Unions Fair (1930), on which he collaborated with Moholy and Breuer, and the Architects' Fair in Berlin in 1931. In 1938 he came to New York; he moved from there to Aspen, Colorado, where he acted as adviser on questions of design for the Container Corporation's Aspen development. There was little time for the creative art of painting, but because of his activity in the service of the more pedestrian aspects of life, he was able to contribute much to the cultivation of the new vision. The special attraction of his work lies in those sustained, sleek, melodic qualities that are so often lacking in Germany.

Georg Muche (b. 1895) was teaching at the Bauhaus at the age of twenty-five, but he was not really suited to the constructivist ideas favored there, at least not in painting. His first paintings were abstract, and as early as 1916 to 1919 he was exhibiting works in this vein at the Sturm Gallery in Berlin. But then he turned to swelling forms and a turgid palette. Some paintings and drawings from this period, in pleasant delicate tones, succeed very well, but every now and then he lowered the value of his work with an over-lyrical sweep and too-feminine colors. No other master of the Bauhaus was carried so far from the original program. Morning mists, as if filtered through Venetian blinds, wide-open calyxes, delicate spider webs amid leaves are some of the themes of his recent pictures. A pinkish-red, a curious yellow modified by muted black, remain characteristic of his tonality. Brownish nuances, lilac, leaf green, delicate smoky tones, and a dusty mortar-gray float over many of his pictures. His subjects and palette are surprising in view of the fact that as a teacher of the Sturm Art School he had assimilated an abundance of invigorating modern methods which he passed on to his students–at the Bauhaus, later at Itten's Berlin Art School, and after that at the Breslau Academy and the Krefeld Textile School. In 1939 he wrote a fine book, *Buon Fresco*, and in 1950, *Bilder, Fresken, Zeichnungen*. In 1954 he wrote a bold article confuting the feeble notion that the advance of technical science would destroy art.

Max Bill (b. 1908) was a Swiss pupil of the Bauhaus, of a younger generation. He spent decisive years of his life in Germany, where he carried on the Bauhaus traditions and to some extent tried to reform them. In 1951 he was made director of the Ulm Hochschule für Gestaltung, which he built up and organized; in 1957 he was dismissed and returned to Zurich. Early in his career as painter, sculptor, architect, and theorist he was won over by the constructivist principles he hoped to apply in every field. He belongs to the category of those who like to explain as rationally as possible exactly what they are doing and how they manage to do it. Like Moholy, he has always viewed our visual habits as a totality and sought to lift us from our habitual inertia and guide us toward a disciplined and rational order. His austere paintings consist of simple cellular forms repeated over and over again, the color of a single one accentuated to bring tension into the arrangement. Or he creates sweeping curves in a blended, transparent polychromy. His sculpture tends to be large in format; his smaller works often have a decorative effect, in spite of the precise realization of surfaces. Sometimes his rationalized lyricism achieves a degree of grandeur, for instance in his *Continuity* of 1947, the now famous "bow" that turns in upon itself which has been installed on the shores of the Lake of Zurich. Bill and a few others have demonstrated the fact that some mathematical models may also strike the layman as beautiful and harmonious–for instance those in the Paris Salon Poincaré, which are symbols of mere equations and were certainly invented and installed there for rational purposes only. Here we touch upon the "prestabilized harmony" between intellect and emotion, and experience a new sphere of artistic enjoyment. To call such creations unhuman would be as foolish as to describe as inhumane our astonishment when faced with celestial equations.

Bill's activities should be judged like those of Moholy, in the context of a whole vision with which he seeks to expunge our preconceptions of form. Whereas the individual arts constantly display tendencies to diverge. Bill tries to find the significant and beautiful form of our time for everything and to shape it as rationally and nonegocentrically as possible. This idea corresponds to his "understatement," by which he declared he no longer intended to educate anyone to "art." Here certainly lie healthy anti-elements against the highly subjective thinking in depth with which so many pompous abstract neo-romanticists like to work. Bill's publications have also been effective. He wrote studies on the bridge builder Maillart, on Swiss architecture, on Mies van der Rohe and Kandinsky.

Bill was responsible for bringing to the Ulm Hochschule für Gestaltung *Friedrich Vordemberge-Gildewart* (1899–1964). This painter had remained faithful to the ascetically severe form of expression the Constructivists had made prominent in the twenties. He worked with strictly defined surface tensions and pure color contrasts more consistently than the Russian Constructivist Lissitzky. Vordemberge called himself an "elementarist" and was more radical in his reduction of all pictorial methods to a puristic minimum, but he knew how to put his "nothing" into the picture in a manner that immediately gave a delicate, expansive effect. With a very few upright shapes, some highly original colors and a minimum of clean textural contrasts, he could conjure up a sure, asymmetrical equilibrium that went beyond mere decorative effect, even when it was intended to give an impression of beauty. In the beginning, like his friend Schwitters (whom we shall treat under Dadaism), Vordemberge would sometimes mount a plastic form on his painting. In such cases Schwitters would have toyed with the decadent beauty of aged material, but Vordemberge always sought precise accents that had, one might say, preserved their youth. He placed his few lines and immaculate colors on the picture surface cautiously, as if he feared some disaster might enter the field of action if these elements were to touch each other too soon. One must keep in mind all the things that such purely constructive painting denies because, from the constructivist standpoint, they would have a garrulous effect: improvisation, profusion, gushing color, vital-dynamism, personal calligraphy, density of structure, any suggestion of real space. In 1948 Vordemberge wrote, "Wherever one seeks bravura or virtuosity, one comes up with deception." For Vordemberge, any system that could produce a rich effect with a minimum of means was superior to a system that required more complex means to get the same effect. He wanted to transfer this thesis from theoretical and economic spheres into the realm of beauty.

He divided the picture as simply as possible, never, however, arranging it in a banal way. For instance, he avoided a centralized composition, undeviating symmetry or static progression. If two straight lines converge, they do not meet at the edge of the picture. When he grouped several panels together to form a unity, he was not in any way aiming at a straightforward equilibrium. Although in some respects related to the Dutch *Stijl* group, he does not belong with them; yet he was a founding member of the geometrically oriented group, *Abstraction-Création* (1952). During the Nazi regime he lived first in Switzerland, later in Amsterdam. In 1952 the Rotterdam Art Academy appointed him to teach "color as a space-forming element in architecture." Arp praised his work, somewhat extravagantly, as "a withdrawal from confusion, from frenzy, from the love of filth."

Hans Richter (b. 1888), who was a decade older, is introduced only now because his inclinations and experiments led in the direction of the modern film. But he came to the film from painting. In 1915 he was already working cubistically. He then developed his *Rollbilder* (scroll pictures), long horizontal strips on which abstract motifs were painted and diversified in stages. Here he created a new type of picture which unfortunately, in his opinion, functioned only as an intermediary development toward the abstract film. In fact it actually possessed a special faculty, allowing the single picture to remain static and the eye to jump forward and backward. Within these works he shifted with great precision from the vehement to the delicate. While still in Germany he published with Mies van der Rohe and Werner Graeff the periodical *G (Gestaltung)*, the foremost German publication on abstract art from 1923 to 1926.

In 1918 the Swede Eggeling, the most important innovator of the abstract film, became his friend. In 1921 Eggeling created his *Diagonal Symphony* and Richter his *Rhythm 21*. Richter produced some thirty motion pictures in New York, to which he emigrated in 1941; he became director of the Film Institute and taught at City College.

The development of the fine arts in the twentieth century was regarded in Germany and elsewhere as a progressive alienation from the object, as a crescendo in the transformation of forms and in the autonomous life of color. Nevertheless, as early as the First World War a counter-movement developed, one of those retardations which history likes to throw in as a breathing spell when we have experienced too many innovations. The charm of the object was rediscovered. In opposition to Expressionism, the autonomy of the objective world around us was once more to be enjoyed; the wonder of matter that could crystallize into objects was to be seen anew. In an article written in 1924 I coined the phrase *Magischer Realismus* (magic realism)–"magic" not, of course, in the religious-psychological sense of ethnology. In 1925 the expression was attached as subtitle to my book, *Nach-expressionismus* (Post-Expressionism). The same year Hartlaub organized the important exhibition at his gallery in Mannheim with the title *Neue Sachlichkeit* (New Objectivity, or New Realism) –a formulation I had avoided–to imply that we were not dealing here with a repetition of the more neutral realism of Courbet or Leibl. This New Objectivity was aimed in quite a different direction, seeking an approach to the autonomous sharpness of objects, as in the late Middle Ages, the quattrocento, or to the revolutionary, form-hardening classicism of David or Ingres. Moreover, the emphasis in relation to the objective world implied abstraction, not empathy.

This new direction, however, included too many restorative components; too many expressive structural styles which had been successful were now thrown overboard. To succeed, restorations must include, transformed within themselves, almost the total wealth of the period being broken up–and thus of the preceding revolutions; otherwise, as soon happened in this case, they are swept away by the impact of new revolutions. At this time the usual efforts were made to build a bridge to science in self-defense: if all matter consisted of minute abstract particles instrinsically in motion, then it was declared to be astonishing, even miraculous, that given such fluctuations, matter should crystallize and solidify into what we can call things. Hence, the thing, the object, must be formed anew. In way of explanation, the static, anti-dynamic pictorial form was considered a coordinate of the "rigid fourth dimension" with which modern physics can reduce everything dynamic to states of being.

The original features of this new direction came from the Italian *arte metafisica* (metaphysical art) or from related aspects of Constructivism, which sometimes made use of the objective. However, as soon as these premises were abandoned, the banal realism that was soon to flourish in the Third Reich appeared. The New Objectivity is best understood in contrast to the Expressionism that preceded it.

Expressionism:	*New Objectivity:*
Ecstatic subjects	Sober objects
Suppression of the object	The object clarified
Rhythmical	Representational
Extravagant	Puristically severe
Dynamic	Static
Loud	Quiet
Summary	Thorough
Close-up view	Close and far view
Monumental	Miniature
Warm (hot)	Cold
Thick color texture	Thin paint surface
Rough	Smooth
Emphasis on the visibility of the painting process	Effacement of the painting process
Centrifugal	Centripetal
Expressive deformation	External purification of the object

The painters who stressed anew the objective approach fall into three groups. In north and east Germany, George Grosz, Otto Dix, and Kurt Günther were aggressive social critics. In their opinion the social order could be changed also by a new kind of painting: *art engagé*. In the south, in Munich, the artists were more melancholy and were associated with the Italian *arte metafisica*, which, like the work of Germany's nineteenth-century "Nazarenes," sought a link with Italian art of the early Renaissance. However, the new Italian style, in the early work of di Chirico, was permeated and enriched by surrealistic constructions, whereas the corresponding movement in Munich was simpler and more decorative. A third group, which included Georg Scholz and Walter Spiess, favored the detailed, fussily painted idyll, similar to some paintings of Henri Rousseau.

As a young man, *Alexander Kanoldt* (1881–1939) lived with the paintings of his father, who worked in the tradition of the heroic landscape style of the nineteenth century. But his son, influenced by French Post-Impressionism, soon adopted a simplifying, stylized method with dark contours, a style not unlike that of Jawlensky. At first glance it could be called expressionistic if it were not so strikingly quiet and impregnated with such heavy, hyper-naturalistic colors; Kanoldt's empty interiors and mute landscapes were painted accordingly. In 1909 he was active in the founding of the revolutionary *Neue Künstlervereinigung*. Gradually, however, he developed a more graphic style, hardening all individual objects and covering them with a smooth metallic surface. In schematic modeling, houses, trees, and figures were now severely "objectivized," as precisely rendered as if photographed. As in the quattrocento, all personal calligraphy disappeared. But the characteristic richness of the fifteenth century was never equalled because the later artists were too obviously bent on a decorative, closely knit, oversimplified composition, and a smooth, lacquered surface. Ingres–misunderstood–increasingly became Kanoldt's standard of perfection, with the result that he produced frigid, lifeless portraits and still lifes (characteristically, he often painted the rubber plant). A few landscapes give an inkling that Kanoldt possessed at least a certain stature. He was excessively bitter over Expressionism and made a "purifying" pact with the National Socialists, who gave him a professorship at the Berlin Art Academy. There his style became increasingly torpid.

Georg Schrimpf (1889–1938) also strove for a quiet, purified form. He started as an amateur painter and never entirely lost a certain naivety. A deliberate structural monumentality is found in his best paintings. In Schrimpf's early works figures are distorted, but lack any dynamism, so that it is immediately evident that he was actually striving for a calm solidity. This period was followed by some quite beautiful paintings of big peasant girls resting on the grass, of statuesque cattle and sheep. He gave a new direction to the old theme of the pastorale: passive color areas and solid close-up views with clear silhouettes. He succeeded once more in salvaging the old native German landscape for contemporary art. Some of his pictures exude simplicity and a silent grandeur; others are much too insipid, for something of the amateur painter remained in this sincere man. His naive insights often hit the nail on the head, and at the time he was particularly popular–surprisingly–with the complicated intellectual. His smooth-surface paintings held their own artistically as long as they were supported by his peculiar, ascetic colors; later they became more balanced and conventional. Some of his landscapes are too reminiscent of the minor painters of 1800.

Carl Mense (1886–1965) painted in this Munich style. He tried to combine the New Objectivity with a rather sultry Italian romanticism, less pure in color but with a certain decorative finesse. While Schrimpf preferred matinal tones, Mense's taste ran to the twilit colors, sometimes deeply glowing.

A shimmering palette and acute perspective foreshortening are characteristic of *Heinrich Davringhausen* (b. 1900). He placed his figures in seemingly airless hollow spaces, boxlike constructions in precise linear perspective of the kind developed by di Chirico in his early period. This type of space formation will recur with the Surrealists Edgar Ende and Mac Zimmermann. From 1936 Davringhausen lived in France, and following the trend of the times, painted in a calm, nonobjective, surface style, while others of this group remained true to the emphasis on representation.

Kay Nebel (1888–1954) and Franz Radziwill were the northern representatives of the New Objectivity. In his animal paintings Nebel strove to emphasize objective delineation. His paintings look as if the color had been brushed on as an afterthought. But his understanding of animal life was not deep enough to counterbalance the beautiful, formal schematic arrangement which he gradually established for himself and consolidated in his north German murals and in his teaching at the Cassel Art Academy. *Franz Radziwill* (b. 1895), who grew up in the harbor city of Bremen, discovered German romanticism in Dresden. He reproduced the world around him with painstaking precision, albeit with a rather unusual palette, but he saw our humble human existence as something uncanny and experienced the world as eternally alien. Because of this the Nazis objected to him, in spite of the naturalistic definition of his paintings. The silence of the grave dominates his miniaturelike pictures, in which strange events are always taking place against a darkling sky.

Carl Grossberg (1894–1940), who lived near Würzburg, represented the more idyllic wing of the New Objectivity, sometimes with a slightly ironic undertone. He combined the entangled wire structures of modern technology with small rural houses with their ells, ledges, and eaves, as if everything had been forcibly arrested, immobilized, like a clock stopped beneath our astonished gaze.

An aggressive painter of the New Objectivity was *Otto Dix* (b. 1891), a Thuringian of proletarian origin. Just as Caravaggio had brought down to earth the transcendental proclivities of Mannerism in 1600, Otto Dix wanted to lead an overpathetic German Expressionism back to a mercilessly realistic conception of life. But for him reality was a gruesome thing, never to be glossed over idealistically. He exaggerated this almost timeless type of Expressionism with a pessimistic force and inflexibility never seen before. His horror of war was inextinguishable. He expressed it in flat, spaceless paintings of war cripples and match sellers. In one of the former, as in a Dada montage, four huge men with artificial limbs are pressed life-size onto the surface, like broken marionettes of death. A monstrous scorn exudes from these pictures, which have an effect somewhat akin to our macabre modern ballads, and they were more powerfully constructed than the famous painting of the trench which came later (in 1923), provoking controversy for years. In *Trench Warfare* terrifying figures appear in panopticon style, but a too-detailed description of swollen foxhole corpses makes a comprehensive appeal, an overall effect of horror, impossible. To express the most extreme of his grim statements, Dix employed the graphic arts, to which he remained passionately devoted. His youthful period in Dresden (1919–1922), and the four years immediately following in Düsseldorf and Berlin, produced his strongest work as a painter. At the Dresden Art Academy, where he taught from 1926 to 1933, he painted religious subjects and pure landscapes that are very capable, yet not so convincing as his earlier works because they run counter to his aggressive personality. Now he began to use too many old-master techniques. When he was outlawed by the Nazis, he settled down rather opulently, thanks to a wealthy marriage, on Lake Constance. There he made a forced peace with society and devoted himself to pure landscape painting in which influences of Cranach, Breughel, and the later Dutch painters may be felt, paintings in a clear-cut, mixed technique of oil and tempera, with a fine glaze. After the Second World War Dix seemed to tire of this painstaking style and threw himself into a belated, superficial Expressionism which gave the effect of a repeater course, since he only rarely succeeded in letting his colors speak with primary force.

The merciless verism of his early works remains his major contribution. In them he functioned as social critic, in spite of his bleak acknowledgment of all forms of life. Behind his milieu of prostitutes and profiteers of night and bar life, glowing in poisonous colors, a *memento mori* leers at us. In 1928 he painted *Metropolis,* a kind of negative altarpiece of Satanism, a triptych of lascivious appetites. One shudders when he poses a gray, starving proletarian woman in front of a poisonous-red factory, or when he places a rich widow–like a reverse image of an angel annunciate–in front of a voluptuously padded wall. These moments are much more convincing than his purely symbolic efforts, as in the *Seven Deadly Sins,* which impress one as melodramatic. He lacked the symbolic imagination for themes of pathos, for, as he wrote to me once, he never dreamed. On the other hand, he was successful in preeminently naturalistic, if somewhat caricaturizing portraits; in 1921, he painted the portrait of his parents–an ironsmith and his wife seated on their proletarian sofa; the enormous hands of the laborer, the careworn faces, and above all the iron-hard color scheme are overwhelmingly expressive. He depicted the art dealer Flechtheim, deliberately evoking the effect of a pantherlike animal; and Silvia von Harden, with monocle, looking like a bloodshot snake. The painter gave children the animal-like quality and sharpness with which childhood charges into life. His early uncompromising verism was also recognized as something unique by the French, who had nowhere succeeded in so fearlessly nailing down the horrors of modern life. Their art was dominated essentially by the form and color problems that were missing in this German draftsman; with his powerful, provocative subject matter he simply pushed them aside.

Dix and his friend *Kurt Günther,* both from Gera, were the chief Thuringian contributors to the aggressive verism of the twenties. At first Günther organized his pictures in Dada style: in the background of an ironic painting of a young salesman telephoning, we see his whole world of screws, keys, and gadgets, individual photographs simply pasted on. Günther went on to pure painting, and he too experienced the descrescendo that seems to go with this veristic style. His sharply characterized graphic portraits are his best works. At first carnal woman seems to be his favorite theme; a self-portrait revealing his subjugation to her powers remains a freak example of his painting.

Between Dix and Grosz stands *Karl Hubbuch* (b. 1891), a significant graphic artist, also full of accusations against our civilization, but with more expressive tension in his outlines and his unfolding perspectives. He could transform a twilit city scene into a primeval landscape. In 1931 his book *La France* was published. In it he lashed out at the social misery in France: gluttons, so-called patriots, evil women, and the plundered proletariat swarm in front of the voluted facades of the nineteenth-century. Later he switched to the woodcut and since 1951 paints in oils, sometimes coming very close to the style of Max Beckmann.

While a somewhat idyllic form of the New Objectivity was expressed in Munich and a more aggressive version in other parts of Germany, a third tendency emerged among those painters who saw their world as if contained in a toy box. This trend was a reaction against the summary, monumentalizing aspect of expressionist painting, whose effect depended on distance from the observer. For the new style closeness to the picture was necessary, as if viewing an ant hill with a magnifying glass. On the other hand, some landscapes showed the use of aerial perspective.

Georg Scholz (b. 1890), from Baden, dealt ironically with small-town life, in appropriately intimate paintings and lithographs–trim little houses, adults looking warlike yet going about their business like dolls. A village is laid out as if on the curvature of a globe, or the living room of a station master is depicted as a miniature idyll, satirizing the familiar joys of the petty bourgeois. Thus, from a pathetic expressionism, Biedermeier genre rose again, quite unintentionally, and now with a satiric sharpness.

Walter Spiess (1896–1947) gave this style a dainty-exotic turn. His *Farewell* seems to be viewed from the nearby moon, and it has the tone of a music box of Mozart's time, of a silvery melody heard from afar. In his *Folk Festival*, Spiess shifted the dimensions of his miniscule description in such a fashion that something of the fantasy of Chagall, whom he loved, enters into the picture. Spiess was a musician and a supple dancer. He emigrated to Indonesia, collected its gamelan music, directed the orchestra of a prince, and built himself a curious house in his tropical paradise. In 1938 he published *Dances and Dreams in Bali*, with B. de Zoete.

One could call this branch of the New Objectivity "the Rousseau complex," for many of its disciples had this strange "amateur painter" in mind. *Gyorgy*

Stefula (b. 1913) repeatedly acknowledged the association. Stefula, self-taught, also transforms the art of Rousseau into Biedermeier genre. He is an articulate painter who, with faint irony, is in love with the small happinesses of everyday life, which he describes meticulously. All the outdoors is turned into a trim park for our Sundays, and the people in it look like tiny toy figures. In storybook style he shows us what life in the country and intimate family life can be, and all the time he is smiling at himself.

Anton Räderscheidt (b. 1892), from Cologne, is a lonely figure. Since he possessed a lurking tendency toward Constructivism, he gave the New Objectivity of the twenties some relentlessly geometric features, so that even a man like Moholy could admire him. Räderscheidt portrayed the human body with a cold verism, subordinating it to a system of rectangular coordinates. He gave the ancient man-woman theme a provocative new turn in paintings like *Nude on Parallel Bars*, in which the woman, naked, with moonlit, shimmering flesh stands beside a man in raven-black evening dress, with a bowler hat on his gruesome head; both figures are placed as rigid parallels in hollow space. After Räderscheidt turned his back on Magic Realism, something very strange took place: he tried his hand at practically every style and method of modern painting, one after the other, without ever losing the peculiar Räderscheidt tone. From icy polished surfaces he switched to a furious brushstroke; from strikingly simple themes to complicated cityscapes (Rome, Naples, Cologne); then, after emigrating to France, he began painting heavy, baroque, abstract colossi, and went from there towards nonobjective art.

Dadaism came into prominence during the First World War in Switzerland, the United States, Paris, and Germany, only to disappear a few years later. It was given many different evaluations. It was a link between Italian Futurism, which had existed since 1909, and French Surrealism, which appeared in 1924. One can probably trace back to Futurism and its mystique of motion the Dadaists' pleasure in the tumultuous event, which they used to shock the bourgeois. Their delight in fantasy, which must also be contained in art as explosive material, led eventually to Surrealism. The elementary, said the Dadaists, lives in us repressed, held down by rules and "style consciousness." Futurism had a political aspect in its shameful glorification of war, whereas Dada aimed at more playful effects. The low humor lurking behind some of their projects differentiated them also from Surrealism, which had a clearer program and felt life as a more mysterious entity. For the Dadaists, the museums were cultural graveyards, Expressionism was sentimental, and patriotism and the church mere apron strings constraining all the spontaneous impulses of life.

In 1920 young Dr. Hülsenbeck, poet and philosopher, signed a manifesto of Dadaism. In it he said, "The bruitic poem describes a streetcar as it is: the *essence* of the streetcar, with the yawning of bourgeois Mr. Schulze, and the screeching of its brakes. The simultaneous poem teaches the meaning behind the confusion of events: while Schulze reads, the Balkan express crosses the bridge near Nisch, a pig whines in the cellar of butcher Nuttke... The static poem turns words into individuals."

During the First World War, in 1916, when artists and writers of all countries assembled in the security of Zurich, Dadaism was directed against a union of art and life with politics. From Germany came Dr. Hülsenbeck, the painter Hugo Ball, the film innovator Hans Richter, and Hans Arp, who was Alsatian, at the time writing in German. But between 1918 and 1922 in Berlin, which was in turmoil from the deprivations caused by war and politics, Dadaism assumed a character that was partly political, leftist in its orientation. (The same schism was later to develop in Paris, to form two opposing camps among the Surrealists.) The Berlin Dadaists included, besides Hülsenbeck, the graphic artist George Grosz, the painter Raoul Hausmann, the brothers Heartfield and Herzfelde, who were famous for their political montages, the "nature philosopher" Baader, and the poet Mehring. But the Berlin Dadaists were not absorbed solely by political problems; they also fought constantly over questions of life and art in general. In 1918 Hülsenbeck held a Dadaist meeting with the New Secession; Friedländer wrote about "creative indifference"; Grosz, Hausmann, and the Herzfelde brothers started revolutionary attacks in *Der Dada*. This was followed by tumultuous evenings in Dresden, Hamburg, Leipzig, and Prague. In 1920 the manifesto was issued and a Dada exhibition was held, in which provocative works by Max Ernst, Schlichter, Citroen, Arp, Hausmann, Hannah Höch, and Picabia were displayed. In 1922 George Grosz and the Herzfeldes defected to the Communist Party, into the circle of *Aktion* and the Malik publishing house; with this step the artistic freedom of the movement was buried.

In Cologne the poet Baargeld, Hans Arp, and Max Ernst, who called himself Dada Max, were active. An extreme magazine, *Der Ventilator*, was banned by the British occupation forces. Max Ernst and Baargeld projected ideas for mutual participation to counteract the bombastic individualism: *Fatigaga* was a witty abbreviation for *Fabrication des tableaux garantis gazométriques*. But soon Hans Arp stopped coming to Cologne, Max Ernst moved to Paris, and the Cologne Dada spoof disintegrated.

In Germany the outstanding Dadaists are Raoul Hausmann, Kurt Schwitters, and Max Ernst. *Raoul Hausmann* (b. 1886) was a painter, writer, and photographer, whose inspiration and experimentation were influential immediately. It was probably he who first practiced photomontage with intellectual content, that graphic art with pasted fragments that became meaningful through the creation of plastic tension between its segments. It was an offshoot of French Cubism, but it employed cubist idiom more formally and colorfully–that is to say, nonobjectively. Hausmann hit upon this procedure in 1918, before George Grosz, Max Ernst, and Hannah Höch took it up. It was not only an abbreviated method of composition, but an expression of the feeling that our existence was a contradictory assemblage of compartments forcibly joined together with the joints showing. Hausmann used similar possibilities in language: in his *Manifest von der Gesetzmäßigkeit des Lautes* (*Manifesto on the Rules of Sound*, 1918), he took language beyond its logical connotations, treating it with complete freedom as a structure of sounds and associations. Independently of Hugo Ball, who preceded him, Hausmann wrote poems consisting of sounds only, and read them at a Berlin Dada soirée as early as 1918; these inspired Schwitters to his *Sound Sonata*. Hausmann fled from National Socialism to Spain, Paris, Ibiza, Zurich, Prague, and again France. (I mention this only to indicate how far afield some of the spokesmen for the new values in Germany were driven in that period.) He wrote an essay on the history of seeing, one about the optics of early cultures, another on Mediterranean peasant settlements, and a novel, *Hyle*–but most of his work was unpublished. Hausmann also invented something called psychomorphology, in which he tried to modify psychoanalysis.

George Grosz (1893–1959), a true Berliner, was a Dadaist from 1918. In 1920 he produced some exceptionally terrifying collages consisting of slogans; they aroused furious opposition but could not be obliterated. His painting in these years was influenced by Futurism: in *Burial of the Poet Panizza; Germany, a Winter's Tale*, and *Adventurer*, all completed before 1920, he succeeded in uniting through a kaleidoscopic frenzy of motion events that actually lay far apart. Soon Grosz was excelling in series of graphics that pitilessly unmasked the gluttonous, lewd petty bourgeois, brutal militarists, and the inhabitants of a garish prostitute world. An unsparing verism is carried out with cubist changes of viewpoint and splintered abbreviations, while elements of childlike drawing cut like a knife through the explicit meaning of his forms. Militarism and religious hypocrisy were the chief objects of his scorn.

The Nazis would have hanged him if he had not already left Germany and taken a position in 1932 at the Art Students League in New York, where he later established a private school. Gradually he turned to an anecdotal and gruesome romanticism. In 1955 his autobiography was published in German, with the characteristic title *Ein kleines Ja, ein großes Nein* (then in English as *A Little Yes and a Big No*).

Kurt Schwitters (1887–1948) "participated in the successful campaign of Dada against the armies of the Golden Section" (Arp). He drew his own drastic but sensitive conclusions from the phantasmagoria of Dada, producing true works of art universally valued today. A resounding lyricism restrained the aggressive quality of his dreams, and the startling effect he intended for the petty bourgeois

IX Oskar Schlemmer, Boy with Red Vest, 1928. Bayerische Staatsgemäldesammlungen, Munich

is now lost. But at first the public was enraged because he went beyond the accepted materials of art: "I simply could not see any reason why old streetcar tickets, driftwood, coat checks, wire and wheel parts, buttons, junk from the attic, and heaps of refuse should not be used as material for paintings, any less than colors made in a factory." The visual meaning of the banal fragments, used as whole or completed units, was transformed by their being placed in new and unexpected relationships. His diverse material was often connected

George Grosz, Café

by nothing more than a few dim passages of color. Under his hand the opposing sections seemed to respond to each other. In his combinations of materials he went far beyond French Cubism, for he sought a more aggressively plastic effect. The perishable aspect of broken-down, decrepit forms was the message of his pictures, through which he interjected what we might call a sense of historic time. He mumbled a play on his own name and the word weathering:

X Wassily Kandinsky, Big and Tiny, 1937. Bayerische Staatsgemäldesammlungen, Munich

"Verwitterung, Verschwitterung"–which one might render as "Withered by Schwitters." In a typical Dada christening he called his works of this type *Merz* pictures, inspired by a successful example of this type of painting which had been built up around the graphic symbol MERZ, part of the word KOMMERZ, or commerce; moreover, he realized that these creations belonged to neither Expressionism nor Cubism, nor could they be called paintings, drawings, or reliefs. Later he used this designation also for his poems.

I-Bild (I-picture), from *invenire*, was the name he gave to another category, in which a complete element of nature (like a "found object") played a decisive part. Consequently he occasionally ran around with a small empty frame through which he would focus on something specific in the sense of the "ready-made," a concept that also interested the Dadaists and Surrealists. All one had to do was to alienate a symbolically attractive piece of nature from its surroundings and put it in a different context in order to give it "artistic" significance. The achievement lay in the correct detection. "Tell me what you stop and stand before and I'll tell you what you are."

There was also something of the sculptor in Schwitters. In a gigantic cubist Merz-construction, *Cathedral of Erotic Misery*, an "open sculpture" which he gradually built up through the stories of his house in Hannover, all life was to be mirrored. In it he puttered with and put together the strangest finds: Barbarossa's Kyffhäuser mountain, dog enclosures, Nibelung treasure, art exhibit, sex murderer's lair, Goethe relics, and "many almost-worn-out-by-writing-poetry pencils." In 1943 a bomb reduced it to ruins, along with many other works.

Everywhere he went he fought for a new freedom in art. For a while he had a stimulating effect on typography and on the Bauhaus, whose architects he warned against the pitfalls of mere functionalism. As poet, in accordance with his principles of montage, he used scraps of chlichés and assembled them in new relationships. In his *Sound Sonata* Schwitters was experimenting with a nonobjective, i. e. wordless, literature. Short or long sounds, staccato or legato, were produced, high or low, in gurgling or cutting tones, connected by vowels or consonants, but arranged in counterpoint. Here one was faced with a totally new art form which was neither speech nor music, nor song, nor mere noise, but included elements of them all. In his paintings Schwitters developed an astonishing feeling for material and color contrasts. In the middle and late twenties his works became simpler and a little more severe. He was always in touch with international trends: a few of his works appeared in *Esprit Nouveau*, *Transition*, and *Cercle carré*. His fate in his last years was typical of many exiled artists in those days: in 1935 he emigrated to Norway; in 1940 he fled to England, and after a period in an internment camp, eked out a living painting portraits in London; from 1945 he was busy again with efforts to revive his great Merz structure; at times he was crippled and blind.

While Magic Realism turned daily life into eerie form, Surrealism, which developed only a few years later, set out to smash our existing world completely, inspired by the extremism of Dadaism. Surrealism constructed a new world, a world never seen before, not even, perhaps, in our fantastic dreams. The ordinary things of life were bewitched; constellations, ideas of space and the function of gravity were transformed. Without this transformation we are still in the realm of Magic Realism, and many artists shifted from one area to the other and back again (especially the Belgian painter Magritte). Typical surrealistic themes are a burning tree or a giraffe tumbling out of a window; a creaking ox-cart rumbling through a Louis XVI salon; the fastidious study of a scholar resting on the damp bottom of the sea; a slaughtered steer lying on an open grand piano. First, therefore, we are shocked, but to be effective the desired tension must rest on structural unity. The Surrealists sought to emphasize in a sublimated fashion the mystery and insecurity of life as we know it really is if we think beyond the order we accept in everyday life. Their conception was a variation of the demonic vision with which one can at all times confront the harmonious view. Since comparable conceptions arise in our dreams, the Surrealists admired Freud and the subconscious, spoke of "trance" and the *expression pure*, and were against all "enlighteners."

It is not surprising that the genesis of German Surrealism occurred in the Lower Rhine regions where it was developed mainly by Max Ernst, from Brühl. This was not far from the area–one of the most civilized in Europe–that had produced Bosch and Breughel, who had also lived in an epoch of social and religious upheaval. The result, then as now, was a pictorial form that no longer strove for a stable overall composition but indulged in a type of compartmentalization that was to make evident, even in its formal structure, the ambivalence of all appearances and values. But Bosch and Breughel had an easier time, because for comprehension of even their most bizarre pictures they could rely on their contemporaries' familiarity with the strange customs of the time, sectarian ideas of a general nature, or the wisdom of traditional proverbs. The twentieth century Surrealists had a harder task because they were driven by purely individualistic fantasy.

The art of *Max Ernst* (b. 1891) is extraordinary. His unprecedented compositions make superb use of the latent possibilities of all nonobjective art. He has created new technical procedures which not only allow a shortening of the painting process but also create fantastic surface textures and effects (Plate XII). He has invented beings and objects and produced a commensurate pictorial universe–a terrifying Utopia.

The harmony-seeking artist creates his Utopia by transcendentalizing his world. His demonic counterpart descends to the unfathomable depths of being. To condemn or reproach the latter as meaningless would be a failure to recognize the entire sequence of development from Bosch, Arcimboldi, and Goya to Max Ernst. The historian of art must exert greater effort to penetrate the meaning for mankind of what we call "black humor."

Max Ernst gave Surrealism its greatest range, appealing to us not only with his ludicrous themes but also through form. Phantoms appear–hybrid creatures, part animal, part plant, gesticulate in front of nocturnal mountain shapes. A forest becomes a jumble of human limbs, creatures are ejected, creatures resembling us but with insect eyes and bird feathers. In a night sky, where alien suns circle, a huge cosmic symbol glows. The most precise representational quality is interspersed with abstractions of which the object forms a part, and thus seems ruled by a comprehensive order.

Like all the great painters of our century, Ernst was an experimenter. In his montages he revealed a strange world, one also found in his writings *(Répétitions, La Femme 100 Têtes, Rêve d'une petite fille, Semaine de bonté*, etc.). Concerning the montages, he wrote to me in 1926, "It was less important to me to construct new entities than to create electric and erotic tensions by relating elements which until now we have felt were alien and unconnected. This resulted in explosions and high voltage, and the more unexpected the associations (for instance: gun barrel, beetle mimicry, lace skirt) the more surprising was the flashing spark of poetry." Another technique he revived was *frottage* (rubbings), which he employed in 1925 in his *Histoire Naturelle.*

In painting also Ernst developed new procedures, which he interpolated in his pictures in fascinating contrast to the parts that were freely painted. In 1953 he isolated strange micro-effects in his *Sept Microbes*, which was composed of nothing but colored structures in miniature. His large picture, *Father Rhine*, displays the same qualities. Many small pieces are united in a large composition, yet remain separate from it. Both are meant to exist in a state of tension with one another. Microcosm and macrocosm are not intended to merge. In such later works Ernst moves away completely from objective Surrealism, although the early paintings are in a pure narrative style, transmitting a representative phantasmagoria.

The private life of this painter has been equally turbulent. As a child he was tormented by hallucinations. He studied history of art, wrestled with philosophy, then, self-taught, groped his way to painting; he was harried through the First World War; in despair and scorn he became the leader of the *Dada W 3* group in Cologne; in 1920 he was already exhibiting his strange collages in Paris. He moved there, and in 1924 he and his friends founded the Surrealist movement. Already in 1922 he had painted the original group of Surrealists in the numbered portrait that has since become a historical document. In it the artists are seated on the edge of a glacier, between Raphael and Dostoevsky. In 1941, Ernst went to the United States to live, but finally returned to Paris. In 1953 he returned to his birthplace in Brühl, where a truly surrealist "happening" was created to celebrate his sixtieth birthday: the trim little rococo castle of Brühl was filled with his terrifying paintings and drawings. Ernst is also a sculptor and the author of poems and essays; his book, *Beyond Art*, is well known.

At the time Dadaism erupted in Cologne and Surrealism was already being heralded, *Heinrich Hoerle* (1895–1936) lived in that city. In his *Factory Worker* of 1921, he does not give us a nature-picture, as the Magic Realists would have, but presents a ghostly robot composed of metal cylinders, crane joints, and hookhands, standing ready to start any machine, a pressure meter in his limbs, on his head a metal boiler with a zero on it, and, where we would expect to find the face, a needle for reading pressure–a symbol of our frightening affiliation with the machine age. Later he developed similar themes in a more felicitous style. *Franz W. Seiwert* (1894–1933), like Hoerle, died young. Seiwert felt close to the radical workers' movement, and with constructions similar to Hoerle's tried to express the meaning of solidarity and the masses in the turmoil of modern life.

Rudolf Schlichter (1890–1955) fell between Surrealism and the New Objectivity. In 1922 he entered the highly charged cultural climate of Berlin, where he moved in the politically inflamed circles of Berthold Brecht and George Grosz. In his drawings he ridiculed the times or elaborated on sex. He illustrated books, carrying on the tradition of the nineteenth century. In 1932, after having turned his back on the sin-ridden Tower of Babel that was Berlin, he withdrew to his home province of Swabia and then in 1939 moved to Munich. He finally embraced Roman Catholicism, as the Dadaist rebel Hugo Ball had done before him. In his paintings, Schlichter increasingly stressed surrealistic inventiveness, but because his powers of artistic transformation were inadequate, his work remained overly objective and for the most part unsatisfactory. At times his paintings seemed to depict nothing more than nightmarish dummies in a state of petrefaction. Fearful visions of childhood were consolidated in strange landscapes in which he erected abstruse symbols of brutishness or of cultural barbarism–"a materialized mélange of chthonian and daytime reality," as he put it. He was the author of *Das Abenteuer in der Kunst (An Adventure in Art*, 1949), a polemic against all abstract art, in which he saw cultural ruination, or at best a merely ornamental value. If Schlichter had at least experienced these possibilities of expression, his considerable talent might have achieved greater freedom. Certain landscape drawings remain gripping. In these, he said, stone should call to mind muscles; the bark of the tree, the texture of animal hides–"all deformations and monstrosities included."

Mac Zimmermann (b. 1912) was renowned in Germany as a Surrealist. He came from the north; hence, no doubt, the emphasis on lowlands and monotonous beaches in his pictures. Gesticulating dream figures are manipulated rhythmically; fantastic inventions give an intellectualized effect; strange spectral women haunt a combed, striated, half-tone world. Gigantic, but drawn with a netlike transparency, they fill the foreground. Dead trees stand on a glowing earth as if they were receiving stations for distant radio announcements. Some of his human bodies look like gigantic insects on a dead star. Whereas his delicately tinted, transparent, enamel-like style of painting is not always convincing because he does not give his color full play, as a draftsman he was completely successful. A highly spirited *Skizzenbuch* by Zimmermann was published by Piper in 1955.

Edgar Ende (1901–1966), like his fellow Surrealists from the north German lowlands–Zimmermann, Battke and Lüdcke–tended to emphasize the surface plane of his paintings, allowing his figures only to perch on the top, without spatial penetration. His perspective construction was derived from the early workof di Chirico, and accentuated the emptiness of space. Dreamlike pavilions stand upon this surface, helpless cripples somehow emerging from them. A boat, pale as death and overloaded with frightened passengers, hovers in the sky. Ende's interiors, again reminiscent of di Chirico, are represented as separate sealed-off rooms–frames, as it were, for the inevitable loneliness of mankind. Ende was drawn to anthroposophy, which he interpreted in a passive form, from a sense of unavoidable destiny. The specific difference between man and woman disappears. We find none of Dix's social protest, none of the products of engineering which Ernst introduced as contrasts to organic life; hence no support for the pictorial structure. A discreet, sometimes dull, sometimes glowing, color scheme prevails. Fear and longing cry out in harmonious stagnation. Some pictures reveal a schism between the source of the will and its bizarre results. It is as if a mystic order is to be founded, and is subsequently negated.

Unlike others of his generation *Joachim Lüdcke* (b. 1922) proves that Surrealism lives on into the present generation, even if rarely. Lüdcke's brushstroke disappears entirely. Enamel-like compact surfaces are created in a type of oil-resin painting. With uncanny precision he depicts gruesome, dreamy landscape happenings. *Heinz Battke* (1900–1966), best known as a graphic artist, was a late convert to Surrealism. Whereas the fashion of our time has dictated preservation of the surface, objective Surrealism, since the early di Chirico, surrendered to the magic of space. Battke worked with deep perspective thrusts which are cut off in the distance. The human figure, in fact all nature, was oriented toward mysteriously divergent vanishing points on the horizon. Perspective is introduced as magical construction, just as certain quattrocento masters used it, not solely for scientific pictorial construction but also as an element of expression. Battke's spatial structure is based on a subtle linear order, apparently electrically charged, which encompasses the energy of all matter.

THE REGRESSION OF NATIONAL SOCIALISM

Many new artistic impulses were developing in Germany when the devastating storm of National Socialism broke, sweeping everything before it. In the most varied fields of development the clock was drastically turned back. Not only were democratic achievements of communal life destroyed, but freedom of the arts was lost in a way never before experienced by any culture in modern history. To be sure, earlier ages have sought to throttle new stirrings of expression, for an inertia of the soul, an intellectual sluggishness, rules a majority of observers. In my book, *Zur Geschichte des künstlerischen Missverstehens (The History of Artistic Misunderstanding)*, I have been able to show that the average educated man usually requires several decades before he is able to assimilate new intellectual creations.

To a certain degree, the National Socialists produced art of their own, but on close view one finds nothing but a repetition of the attitudes of the nineteenth century, a stereotyped imitation of external nature interspersed with a declamatory pathos, either in the cause of heroism or for "Blood and Soil." Strange how similar in this respect were National Socialism and Bolshevism, however much they professed to hate each other. We are dealing here with the artistic ideals of the ever-culturally-retarded petty bourgeois, who is always opposed to the new and unwilling to respond to the intense cultivation of formal values. In 1945 German art could do nothing but pick up where it had left off in 1933. All in all, the art that was created on order by National Socialism is a foreign body; it would be a waste of time to illustrate it here. I shall therefore limit myself to summarizing the basic attitudes of that time and pointing out the results.

Even before the Nazis came to power, reactionary cultural forces had arisen which would have been incapable of following any of the progressive developments. One has only to recall the Werdandi Bund at the turn of the century, Theodor Alt's protest against Impressionism (1911), the "flaming protest" of the Munich representatives in the *Reichsverband* of Creative Artists against the acquisition of paintings by Van Gogh, or remember the "Protest of German Artists" by Karl Vinnen. But heretofore all such views had remained in the background, whereas now the obscure artists could surge to the fore and take over the leadership.

In 1923 Hans Günther published his *Rassenkunde des Deutschen Volkes (Racial Science of the German People)* in which he mixed scientific information with pure superstition. The aggressive myth of the unique superiority of Nordic Man gained ascendance, a racial belief that was now to form a decisive foundation also for the arts. In 1925 *Die Drohung des Untermenschen* was published;[1] in 1928 L. F. Clauss moved into the limelight with his work *Die nordische Seele*, founded on the grotesque polarity "Viking or Bedouin." Schultze-Naumburg, who wrote about "heroic man," seconded Clauss from the aesthetic side. Thus were assembled the various sources of National Socialist teaching of art. Alfred Rosenberg's *Mythos des 20. Jahrhunderts* (1930) closed the cycle: according to him, one had arrived at "impressionistic and expressionistic impotence." What Van Gogh, Gauguin, Signac, and Picasso had created "emerged boldly and openly after the [First World] war: mestizoism [mongrelization] demanded the right to present, as expressions of the soul, its bastardized abortions, created by the syphilis of intellectualism and painted infantilism. The Kokoschkas, Chagalls, Pechsteins, etc., were worshipped by Jewish writers as leaders of the painting of the future... Lovis Corinth gave evidence of a certain robustness, but even this butcher of the brush descended to clayey, corpse-hued bastardizations in a Berlin gone Syrian." Rosenberg's *Kampfbund* was soon talking about art that was "cheap and degrading... a fist in the face of Germany, its heroic army, and the Führer." Bauhaus methods, in Italy called *stilo tedesco*–German style–were considered foreign and were branded by their own countrymen as "cultural bolshevism." One heard criticism of Paul Klee's "foolish scribblings" and Kokoschka's "daubing." "We see cultural bolshevism in the subhuman style of Kollwitz, Zille, Barlach, the technical bungler Nolde, Schmidt-Rottluff, Chagall, and in the ethical nihilism of Dix, Hofer, and Grosz."

In 1933 the Nazi news agency *Deutsche Korrespondenz* demanded: 1. All work giving any indication of foreign influence should be removed from museums

[1] *The Menace of the Underman*, a translation of selections from *The Revolt of Civilization, the Menace of the Underman*, by the American Theodore Lothrop Stoddard.

and collections. 2. All museum directors falling under the same heading should be dismissed. 3. The names of all Marxist and Bolshevist artists swept along by this tide should never be mentioned publicly again. An "Abominations Exhibition" *(Schandausstellung)* was organized under the heading of "Government Art from 1918 to 1933," in which Liebermann, Slevogt, Corinth, Marées, and Munch were dispatched too. Karl Hofer in Berlin and Paul Klee in Düsseldorf had already been dismissed in the spring of 1933. At this time the *Deutsche Kulturwacht* wrote: "What we are being offered in the Berlin Kronprinzenpalais as young modern German art is Jews, nothing but Jews." Actually the Jewish contribution was two per cent. Barlach, Nolde, Schmidt-Rottluff, Kandinsky, and Klee were considered especially nefarious. Rosenberg attacked Nolde as "negroid, impious, crude, and lacking in any formal inner powers." The art historian Schardt was arrested when he delivered a speech on the twentieth anniversary of Franz Marc's death.

In 1934 Hitler spoke out on the subject for the first time, rendering the situation even more acute. When a few sensible people made efforts to save what they could, the *Völkische Beobachter* wrote, in 1935, "The rats are coming out of their hiding places and are trying to spread themselves out again in the sacred temple of German art." In the same year Hitler declared that art must be comprehensible to the people, although he had to admit that the nation's masses could not share in the achievements of science "or any of the other loftier expressions of life or philosophy." In 1936 Count Baudissin, the director who had been forced on the Folkwang Museum, wrote, "The most perfect form, the most glorious thing constructed in the course of the last epoch, did not originate in the studios of our artists; it was the steel helmet which our storming gray columns wore." The time had come "to ferret out the most important works from their private hiding places, to confiscate them and to arrange for their disposal, and to make their previous destruction punishable by law." The Racial Political Bureau brought to the attention of the Reich Cultural Chamber the fact that pictures were still cropping up which "regrettably depicted the German family with only one or two children." And in 1937, at the inauguration of the House of German Art in Munich, Hitler forbade painters to use colors that the normal eye could not apprehend. Whoever did so in spite of this edict was either sick, in which case a doctor should see to it that he left no heirs, or he was a fraud and should submit to the law.

At the same time the exhibition "*Entartete Kunst*" ("Degenerate Art") was opened in the House of German Art; twenty-five German museums were plundered for it. There one could see hanging, alongside their imitators and followers, the finest painters of the nation, all the masters who today enjoy international fame. One hundred and twelve artists were "disgraced" in this exhibition. The loss for the Berlin National Gallery alone ran into more than a million gold marks. In the plundering of the Berlin Kupferstichkabinett, the vandals went back as far as Van Gogh and Munch. In a Berlin lecture course in 1937, Matthias Grünewald was attacked as a psychopath and Rembrandt denounced as a portrayer of ghettos. The opportunist Franz Hofmann announced triumphantly at a "Cultural Convention" that approximately 12,000 drawings and 5,000 paintings had been confiscated. In 1939 the famous Lucerne auction of these precious German art treasures took place. Hofmann suggested that "the remainder be burned in a bonfire as a symbolic propaganda action." 1,004 paintings and 3,825 drawings were reduced to ashes in the courtyard of the Main Firehouse in Berlin in 1939.

Germany's Loss in Artists

The position of National Socialism had catastrophic results. The most productive and courageous spirits either retired into a silent inner emigration or escaped to freedom abroad. That Germany had not bled to death artistically by 1945 is a miracle. We cannot touch here upon the effect on German literature caused by the exile of writers and poets like Thomas and Heinrich Mann, Arnold and Stefan Zweig, Franz Werfel, Jacob Wassermann, Leonhard Frank, Hermann Kesten, Joachim Maass, or of a theatrical producer of the caliber of Max Reinhardt–men who were dependent on the German language in which they had thought, felt, and created. For those who worked in an international idiom, banishment was less tragic: the language of composers, architects, painters, and sculptors was comprehensible in any country, even if it bore the impress of Germany. A few artists perished in concentration camps: the architect Paul Meller, for instance, an important associate of Oud and Bartning; and Friedel Dicker, an immensely gifted weaver and sculptor. The following artists fled: Kandinsky, Klee, Feininger, Moholy, Bayer, Molzahn, Itten, and Albers

–all the important masters of the Bauhaus–as well as Beckmann, Kokoschka, Schwitters, Scharl, Adler, Reichel, and Vordemberge-Gildewart. The highly original graphic artists T. Heine and George Grosz, were also among the exiles, the sculptors Belling and Gabo (who lived in Berlin until 1933), and the typographer Jan Tschichold. Max Ernst had left Germany previously, a disappointed artist. Every one of these men enjoyed international fame at the time. Painters such as Nolde, Schmidt-Rottluff, Heckel, Hofer, Baumeister, Nesch, and Fuhr just barely managed to survive total isolation in their own country. Schlemmer and the sculptor Barlach perished, forlorn and in misery, broken by Germany's "new culture." German architecture was also robbed of its most productive forces. Gropius, Mies van der Rohe, Mendelsohn, Marcel Breuer, Hilberseimer, Ernst May, Bruno Taut, Rading, all managed to get out. Important art theoreticians and critics were also lost to Germany. It was above all those German art historians who emigrated to the United States who were able to bring to fruition their comparatively new branch of scholarship.

Fundamental Errors

Now that we have given a brief résumé of the proclamations and measures of National Socialism, let us consider, *sine ira et studio*, the reasons which made it impossible for the National Socialists to accept the new formal methods of their day. Here we find two levels of prejudice which we should separate from each other. One is the result of the special demands of their political attitude, the other is of a more general nature and still exists in the attitude of the middle class today. We should discuss both of them if we want to understand the very core of modern creative methods.

The National Socialists demanded that where art should conform to the values of the Nordic race, it must include some sort of moral ideology, and, above all, it must be beautiful. Twentieth century artists rejected all these criteria, although they have remained popular with the public of today.

Taking them briefly:

1. Today's creative artists seek to express their inmost feelings, without regard for either biological or historical normative demands. The study of races, still very obscure, has come up with certain hypotheses, but has drawn

no compelling conclusions from them. It recognizes that Germany does *not* constitute a unified race, and that the relatively small area where the race is relatively pure happens also to be the least fruitful artistically. In addition one recognizes that modes of expression have changed radically in the course of history in order to give adequate form to the prevailing emotional needs of the time. Furthermore–and this is a sensible aspect of art today, in Germany too–there is a spontaneous search for elements that bring people together and do not stress national and consequently divisive idioms. The situation is in fact similar to the internationalism of artistic expression of the Middle Ages or the Baroque period, and therefore in this respect hardly new.

2. It is a mistake to try to make the fine arts an instrument of political ideas. This has been proved in today's Russia, where such a bond has resulted in the atrophy of painting and sculpture. National and political bonds insofar as they are necessary at all, belong in a *civilization*, in which it is necessary to work through organization, rule, and prescription. But they are not a part of a culture. On the contrary, twentieth-century art opposes the innumerable pressures arising from today's collective life, seeks to present an outlet for the free flowing of our inner being, and thus to counterbalance the political control.

3. The precept that art must be generally understood is also highly dubious. The artist hopes, in due course, to become comprehensible to as many people as possible, but he wholly rejects any idea of working deliberately toward such an end or of making any concessions; in this such disparate painters as Hans Thoma and Picasso agreed. This attitude of the artists is also nothing new, for it accords with the trend in all recent intellectual history. All comparatively new, unexpected, or truly original creations were at first unpopular. Only later, like a stone dropped into water, did they leave behind them ever-widening circles of effectiveness. Abstract painting, when it is good, may be expected to find a growing response among the public, after the usual delay.

4. Fidelity to nature may be demanded of realism, but not of today's creative procedures, which aim to project the artist's spiritual condition with or without reference to a prescribed world; in this respect, therefore, contemporary art is akin to absolute music. According to Willi Baumeister, when "abstract" art no longer deals with the world of things in finished form, it turns its attention to and re-forms *other* manifestations of nature, such as rock or lava-like substances, the bark of trees, even microscopic structures whose

individuality may be recognized as infinitely variable. It may well be impossible for the artist to find a form that does not already exist somewhere in nature.

5. There is no need for a work of art to illustrate an idea, much less a moral. Those who expect some kind of message (the eternal question: What does it mean?) are too rational in their approach to art, for its essential function is the manifold expression of feeling, not the transmission or illustration of thought. Such mistaken demands arose from the nineteenth-century conception which assumed an early convergence of the lines of development in art and science. The contemporary view relegates this moment of merging to some time in infinity.

6. The last demand is perhaps the most sensible one: every work of art should somehow or other be beautiful. But this makes sense only if one interprets it as the expectation that a formative process has occurred that of itself uplifts and carries us beyond the mere imitation of nature or any indiscriminate piling up of abstract elements. Behind this common demand, however, always lurks an antipathy to the enigmatic and profound, to the mysterious intensities that might shock us. The works of Bosch, Breughel, Goya, Daumier, Ensor, Picasso, and also comparable works of literature, were not beautiful, but they were profound. Beside the harmonious, there is a demonic world view and form of expression. To prove its exceptional importance in our life as a totality is one of the most difficult questions of aesthetics. Because the nineteenth century tended to be overly harmonious, it is not surprising that in the twentieth century the pendulum has swung the opposite way. Since time began such historic contrasts have taken place within the dialectic development of the human spirit.

In twentieth-century art, *Oskar Kokoschka* (b. 1886) occupies a place all to himself. Landscape, figure compositions, and portraits were his special domain; the rarity of his still lifes is indicative of his inner restlessness. In landscape and human beings he felt fiery-fluid forces. His work is more nervous and improvisatory in effect than that of the masters of the Brücke, with their cumbersome and heavy combinations of form and color. Kokoschka did not seek a firm scaffolding for his pictures; one could say rather that he carried on the Slavic-Austrian tradition of the late Baroque painter Maulpertsch. One could also link him with Corinth, for both stress the quick, intuitive creative process: the painting should be experienced *in statu nascendi*. In his last years Kokoschka returned to a new Impressionism, and although his brushstrokes and color were livelier and more pulsating, one could say that finally he approached Slevogt.

Kokoschka was born in Austria, but many decisive years were spent in Germany. His first style was developed in Vienna. As early as 1897 a strange, decadently nervous atmosphere had been created there–by the Secession under Klimt and Schiele, then by the publication in 1900 of Freud's dream theories, and by the intermingling in this atmosphere of waves of emotion from an echoing Jugendstil. In 1907 Kokoschka began painting portraits that give a trancelike effect. The Viennese critic Karl Kraus and the Swiss psychiatrist Professor Auguste Forel are depicted as if seen from within, made tensely transparent, in a few muted, faded, yet somehow phosphorescent, colors. Beside such works even the mysterious personalities portrayed by Munch, his predecessor in this field, seem stable. Take Kokoschka's *Still Life with Dead Sheep* (1909), his *Dent du Midi* (1910), and the drawings that appeared in the Berlin *Sturm*: in all of them his agitated strokes whirl out from a vital sensitivity. Subsequently he painted with oilier pigments. The spots of color were more saturated, became heavier, and blended more naturally with the object. But the pressures of life also increased constantly, producing Kokoschka's most

XI Paul Klee, Riverbed Landscape, 1934

intensely dramatic period. He totally disregarded the formal problems which the Cubists were working on at this time. Everything was wildly thrown together, sometimes in burlesque, sometimes in apocalyptic style; *The Tempest* is filled with a passionate unrest.

In 1917 Kokoschka moved to Dresden, and in 1920 his work entered a third phase, taking on a lapidary quality. His color areas developed even more sweep and were more specific, glowing in purer contrasts of green, red, and blue. The spacious splendor of nature overwhelmed the psychology of the subconscious; neurasthenic traits, evident at the beginning, began to recede. The more expansive color areas with which Nolde and the Brücke masters were painting had probably made an impression. Powerfully burgeoning colors now appeared in the picture as constructive elements. In these years Kokoschka achieved his most enduring results.

In 1924 he left Dresden suddenly for Switzerland, Vienna, and Paris. Now, ever more uninhibitedly, he mastered the infinite space of landscape. In the series of cityscapes that followed, the handling is broadly spacious and at the same time infinitely complex in that it presents a number of spaces. He painted Bordeaux, Rome, Marseilles, Toledo, Madrid, Paris, London, Venice, Constantinople–an *orbis pictus* was created, the old post-medieval theme of views of the world, with high horizons to permit the widest possible view, as had been customary since Patinier, Breughel, Merian, Canaletto, and Guardi. (These pictures should be brought together sometime as a cycle illustrating the great centers of man.)

In 1934 Kokoschka, declared "degenerate," moved to Prague and then to London. In a fourth phase his painting became even more strongly impressionistic. Beside fully realized works we find others that disintegrate in soapy colors, and the frequent allegories do not always come off. In recent years, with a total lack of understanding, he has polemicized against Picasso and against the progress of art in the same manner in which voices were once raised against him.

Another great master, *Max Beckmann* (1884–1950), stands in isolation, not connected with the exuberant experimenters of the Blaue Reiter or with the expansive Brücke painters. The virile Beckmann was a direct contrast to his contemporary, the more feminine Franz Marc. While the creations of the latter seem to rest in the lap of Mother Earth, Beckmann's are stubborn, lusty

Max Ernst, Grasshoppers' Song to the Moon, 1953. Wallraf-Richartz-Museum, Cologne creatures that deny pictorial space. (Plate III). The same applies to his landscapes–with Marc all seems to swing in spherical harmony; with Beckmann trees and rocks block each other in a threatening manner.

This broad-shouldered, sturdy man with the powerful head came from Leipzig, studied briefly at the Weimar Art Academy, and paid a fleeting visit to Paris, which made little impression on him. It was in Berlin, where he lived from 1907 to 1914, that he began to shape his world. The horrifying years of World War I were followed by a first period of affirmation in Frankfurt. From 1925 to 1933 he taught at the art school there, and then he fled from National Socialism, never to set foot on German soil again. He lived in Amsterdam from 1938 until 1947, when he accepted a teaching position at Washington University in St. Louis; he died three years later in New York.

He painted mysterious orgies, bold circus scenes, lewd women, but also Greek mythological themes in powerful triptychs. Already in his early period he dared to approach majestic symbolic themes: *The Bearing of the Cross*, *Rape*, *The Sinking of the Titanic*, *The Night*, *Resurrection*. Death and life seem interwoven in these pictures. He repeatedly outlined or caged his sensually turgid colors within dark tones. In his compositions the figures press forward as if their vitality would burst the frame asunder, yet they are crowded together within the limits of the picture as if imprisoned. He tended toward compact, oblique compositions, or narrow rectangles, vertically placed.

Beckmann emerged from the gloomy, flowing, late Impressionism of the Corinth school, inevitably attracted by its bleak vitality. Then, from 1917 on, cohesive, almost stereometric, forms appear in his pictures, most probably through the influence of German late Gothic masters. At the same time he touched upon themes of social criticism in paintings akin to the Magic Realism of Dix at that time, distorted pictures of a sordid world, reminiscent of our more macabre modern ballads. The figures, with their over-lifesize heads, seem clamped together by some kind of bizarre mechanism. Rigid forms, as if masked, press against the picture plane, often glassy and cold in color, sometimes looking almost like random daubs of paint. In this period Beckmann also produced many drawings.

During the twenties, in his third period, his innate color-drive breaks through, inspired perhaps by renewed visits to Paris. His segments of reality are more natural and free; the graphic aspects of the picture have been sucked up by a new richness of color. A luminous yellow, a rich green, and a deep blue dominate, interrupted by night-black. Some figures give the effect of fruit, ripe to bursting, but everything is pictorially linked. The structural power of his painting gradually reaches a high point of effectiveness, even if here and there occasional free-flowing areas of color are permitted. He created nine huge triptychs–one thinks of the nine symphonies of Beethoven, Schubert, Bruckner, Mahler–worldly altarpieces, yet fraught with meaning. The period in which he had ridiculed all structural approaches and had slandered the paintings of Franz Marc as primitive "Siberian-Bavarian *Marterlplakate* (votive tablets)" lay far behind him. Now he wrote, almost exaggerating the opposite viewpoint, of a necessary "mathematics of expression." In translating the three-dimensional space of the objective world into the two-dimensional space of the picture plane, he was moved above all by a passionate desire to compress the multiple substance of life. He chose to steer clear of nonobjective art, but he declared, "In principle every alteration of an object is permissible, provided the necessary capacity to create form is demonstrated." To the end he shaped things out of an inner demonic passion. "I would worm my way through all the sewers in the world, suffer every humiliation and disgrace, to paint."

Karl Hofer (1878–1955), Beckmann's contemporary, started his career from more serene premises. In his southern landscapes he sought to construct an idyll, doubtless influenced by impressions of Rome–by the "relentless clarity of this city, which not many can withstand," as he put it. Favored by fortune in his early years, he was supported by a rich Swiss patron, Dr. Theodor Reinhardt, who made it possible for him to live in Rome, Paris and India. In the twenties and thirties he painted groups of young girls, in which harmony of existence was bound up with monumentality of form. His landscapes of the Ticino combined melancholy loneliness with a conciliatory harmony of color planes: violet, pink, green, and a curious shade of brown or gray. Despite the apparent placidity of his temperament, however, he was disturbed by the First World War and the revolution that followed it, and he gives us also a world of drummers, lemurs, nocturnal ruins. Gradually he included curious forms and abstractions in his paintings, which became flatter and chromatically duller. Partly as a result of the destruction of many of his paintings during the Second World War he began to repeat himself, copying the lost compositions. In addition, as Director of the Berlin Art Academy from 1945, he had little time for new works. And Picasso's deformations seem to have influenced him in a way that did not suit him. In Picasso he admired "that so rare *unio mystica* of form and color which determined his unique personality." But Hofer's figures increasingly resembled masks. Only Beckmann, with his richer powers of observation, was able to avoid the weakening of age.

Anton Kerschbaumer (1895–1931), a somewhat younger painter from the Alps, developed a style based on the broad rhythms of Expressionism, but he adapted them to his own ends. He aimed to clarify the picture structure, stressing the continuity of lines. He used colors harmoniously, although he thereby lessened their tensile quality. Quiet chords of dull green, matte red, blue, brown, or yellow are united in his landscapes of city and harbor, with houses massed in cubic fashion. "Now expression is the fashion, form is derided," he said in 1919. "Why can't we have both side by side?" In this connection he often stressed that he was "a southerner in Germany," a barb aimed probably at the northeastern Brücke group. He painted only from memory. His pantheistic confession reads, "With a landscape one must sleep, with a river glide, with the clouds float, with bridges leap over the water."

While some painters chose only the superficial aspects of expressive painting, *Werner Scholz* (b. 1898) developed it further. He paints close, threatening figures flowing over the picture surface. Frightened communicants, anxious nuns, strange animal creatures, gesticulate in colors that could denote life or death. All life is filled with affliction, even in his summer landscapes. During the twenties in Berlin, Scholz developed a grayish Expressionism filled with sharply angular, flattened figures of beggars, cripples, orphaned children. In the thirties this style changed when he moved to the Tirolese mountain village of Alpbach. A little more color and feeling for space now permeated his pictures, but he continued to throw in some black and white. He painted ponderous peasants, oversize flowers and butterflies, but above all biblical themes, some of them in large triptych form. Recently he has tended more to abstraction.

An astonishing painter who has unfortunately been forgotten in Germany was *Jankel Adler* (1895–1949), a Pole who developed as a painter in the art circles of the Lower Rhine. His art lies somewhere between Léger and Chagall: the former influenced him to produce oversized figures; the latter, who was of the same faith, inspired him to paint Jewish types. At the international

Hygiene Fair in Düsseldorf, the *Gesolei* of 1926, he established himself as a monumental painter in his decoration of the planetarium. His paintings from this period look as if they had been molded in viscidly flowing clay, yet his tonality remains varied. His figures seem imprisoned by their own weight. Everything is developed in a soft, hushed gray-brown. His later works were influenced by Picasso and are more radically abstract in the treatment of objects and exhibit stronger color contrasts. But strong contrasts were not his forte, for his chromatic scale is less convincing than his tonal gradations.

Adler's life was filled with oppressive unrest, which never succeeded, however, in deflecting him from his course. The seventh child of a Jewish miller who lived near Lodz, he was trained to be an engraver. He moved to Barmen in western Germany; then, during the First World War, he was under police surveillance, and his parents had to flee. Following this he lived precariously in Berlin, Düsseldorf, and Spain. Klee had just created working quarters for him in Germany again when he had to escape. He vegetated in Paris, Italy, the Balkans, Russia, finally again in France. When at long last he had found a place of rest in London, he died of a heart attack.

Xaver Fuhr (b. 1898) was a unique figure, self-taught. The impressions of his youth in Mannheim affected his painting: reddish stones, bridges, tow barges on the river, and the harbor. Everything has an exotic air, although Fuhr never left Germany. When he paints mountaintops, graveyards, caravans, a laboratory, or figure compositions, he seems to have a realistic point of departure, to be pinning down a fleeting observation of a banal event, but he proceeds simultaneously to spin it into a web of lines and color strands curiously inimical in their effect. His color scheme reminds us of a defoliated autumnal world in which flashes of color and pallid tones alternate, wherein fragments of nature crop up, which he tries to overcome by transforming them into energetic lines. In all, a strong linear structure underlies his color; painting and drawing are deliberately opposed to create tension. His forms are placed on a slant, as if everything were teetering on volcanic soil. The way he is able to combine daubs of color and firm drawing with a certain realism is often astonishing. The small formal matrices are fragments between larger thrusts.

Fuhr, who has taught at the Munich Academy since 1946, is an enemy of abstract art, but his own work could not escape the trend of the time. Recently, the objects he paints look as if they had been melted; extension into depth by means of perspective is reduced, the scale of individual elements is larger, and at the same time they are more abstractly rendered and stretched out over the surface of the canvas. The object represented is hardly recognizable any longer. The sharp, significant bits of reality, like things turned to stone, with which he interspersed his early pictures, have disappeared.

In the work of *Rolf Nesch* (b. 1893), from Württemberg, a German Expressionist style was also shot through with a network of drawing, but Nesch went farther than Fuhr in abstraction. An innovator in the graphic arts, he drilled through etching plates, and the holes thus formed left gleaming spaces on the print. He soldered wires onto the plate which pressed deep grooves into the paper; he also used wire netting of various sizes and tin cutouts that could be shifted around. These processes, when he did the printing himself, resulted in remarkable graphic effects. Suddenly he saw the intrinsic value of the plates themselves as reliefs, and he painted them with oil or tempera. With the fantasy of a tinkerer he playfully produced attractive pictures with new materials and fresh structural techniques. Schwitters, an abstract tinkerer, would have enjoyed them. But Nesch, unlike Schwitters, continued to relate everything to particular objects, whose strange quality he sometimes used to create a mood of oriental splendor and sometimes to develop toward caricature. At one time he had been strongly inspired by Munch and Kirchner; in 1924 he worked with the latter, who split his color areas more vehemently than his friends in the Brücke. Nesch also produced gouaches, oil paintings, and numerous print cycles, some of them permeated with grotesque humor.

Werner Gilles (1894–1961), a Rhinelander, was a less flamboyant personality. In his Italian landscapes he had no intention of being merely imitative, but brought together diversely constructed color areas and enclosed them with a minimum of color outline. Sometimes he came close to figurative symbols, especially when he was dealing with mythical Mediterranean themes. In these he fell somewhere between Klee's later period and Picasso, even if his abstract lyricism never attained the floating quality of the former or the vitality of the latter. Occasionally he produced something poetic in narrative cycles–*Rimbaud* (1933–1936), *Orpheus* (1947), *Tibetan Death Book*. In such series he was at his best, since he sometimes tended to oversimplify his single sheets so that they resembled heraldic emblems. His early works at times display a deeper sensitivity.

After a short period of study at the Bauhaus under Feininger, Gilles went to Paris and profited by exposure to the French formal heritage. Subsequently, his experience of the southern landscape in Italy was similarly enriching. Later he spent his summers in Ischia and his winters in Munich, surrounded by a peaceful circle of friends who revered him as a prophet.

Although *H. A. P. Grieshaber* (b. 1909) is known primarily as a graphic artist, he may be mentioned briefly. He raised the color woodcut to the status of a mural, creating prints that may be hung as rhythmic articulation of the largest walls, but never abandoning graphic structure.

Several German painters who went beyond the technique of Impressionism as early as the first decade of the twentieth century come under this comprehensive heading. Each in his own way came in contact with the new French feeling for form, since all of them lived in Paris for some time, beginning around 1908. Here in the Café du Dôme they met other painters–from Vienna, Warsaw, St. Petersburg, Bucharest, and the Scandinavian countries. Under the leadership of Matisse they raised color and form to autonomous pictorial values, thus effecting a relatively smooth transition from pleinairism, unlike the contemporary Brücke painters. This absence of violent contrast with the recent past also explains their success with the general public, which was achieved much earlier than was possible for their more radically deforming colleagues in Dresden. But the latter produced a more profound caesura in the history of art.

Rudolf Levy (1875–1943) at first studied in Germany, then from 1903 to 1914 lived in Paris, where he studied with Matisse from 1907. Levy painted colorful landscapes, still lifes, human figures, and he developed a pulsating palette. For the most part he carried on the tradition of opulent bodies and the pliant lyricism of his master; sometimes he reminds us of Derain. Since the plastic volume of his figures gradually became his chief concern, he tended to concentrate his colors on them, whereas Matisse let his colors sweep more freely across the canvas. Of the styles that followed, Levy admired Franz Marc, but shied away from the distortions of Klee and Kandinsky. He moved to Berlin, where the art dealer Flechtheim became interested in him because, in contrast to German Expressionism meanwhile grown so powerful, Levy's culture was more French. From Berlin he went to Düsseldorf, but made constant visits to Paris. In 1926 Matisse turned his school over to Levy. During the period of National Socialism Levy lived in Italy, painting harmonious Mediterranean landscapes, until he was captured, deported, and later put to death in a concentration camp.

Hans Purrmann (1880–1966) was also a Matisse pupil. Purrmann's paintings are broken down into smaller parts than those of Matisse, with rust-red tones intervening between deep green and blue, as if all were glowing under a setting sun. (Plate II.) His landscapes and portraits are threaded with interlinear drawing, as if old Germanic elements–from Dürer's time, for example–were trying to unite with the teachings of Matisse. In 1906 Purrmann moved to Paris, and with Levy, Moll, Ahlers-Hestermann, and the writers Uhde and Heuss became one of the Café du Dôme set. "In my personal contact with Matisse, I noticed how strictly he examined and judged the effect as a whole. He always seemed to ask himself how he should fill his canvases in order to create something expressive, clear, and penetrating, without any superfluous ballast." In 1935 Purrmann became director of the Villa Romana in Florence. After World War II he lived in Montagnola, painting in pithy colors with a close feeling for nature. He was still very vital in his later years; at the age of seventy he took a positive view in the dispute over modern methods, pointing to the fact that the arts are constantly subject to change: "They are based neither on a yearning for destruction nor on sensationalism."

The third painter in the Matisse group was the Silesian *Oscar Moll* (1875–1947), who joined it in 1907. More delicate and lighter in tonality but more nervous in his composition, he was the only one in the circle who went beyond Matisse and squarely faced the problems of Cubism. "I fight against Nature, yet I try to construct something unified and new with her means." However, with his rather feminine sensitivity, he was unable to carry through the dialectics of Cubism. The inexhaustible theme "View from a Window" was his favorite, often repeated; the treatment in later examples bordered on nonobjectivity. When the romanticists cultivated the same theme a hundred years ago they caught an actual landscape view within the window frame. Moll, however, especially in his later, increasingly abstract paintings, imagined nothing much more in the picture square than a contrapuntal play of summerlike color areas. After his return to Germany he lived in Berlin and owned a choice collection of French paintings. In 1918 he was called to the Breslau Art Academy and eventually became its director. He rejuvenated the institution by bringing in prominent architects, and the painters Kanoldt, Schlemmer, Molzahn, and Muche. His academy, Dessau, and Düsseldorf were the three art schools in the border regions of Germany that at the time were offering good

H. A. P. Grieshaber, Autumn, colored woodcut, 1951

instruction and producing fine work. But everything he was striving for was eliminated by National Socialism as "degenerate." According to Moll, every effort should be encouraged "that moves away from the view offered by nature. One forms an equivalent for it by constructing a new visual experience with one's imagination."

Ahlers-Hestermann (b. 1883) was not actually a member of the Matisse group, but he was allied to the German circle in Paris. He devoted himself to a poetizing style in dreamily veiled colors as if seeking a lyrical union with old romantic motifs. In *Pause vor dem dritten Akt* he told the story of his life in art historic terms, and in *Stilwende (Turning Point in Style)*, conveyed the enduring importance of the Jugendstil.

One of the first artists to encounter the new art forms introduced by the Fauves and the Cubist painters in France was *Rudolf Grossmann* (1882–1941), a casual, somewhat vacillating painter and graphic artist who was constantly improvising. But his landscapes give little evidence of any new methods, and in his drawings and etchings he is closest to Cézanne. With thinly drawn strokes, more often than not in a pointedly ironic tone, he takes aim at all the questionable aspects of cultured man and strangely enough manages somehow to convey the same type of message in his landscapes.

Helmut Kolle (1899–1931) was a member of this group. Self-taught, he moved to Paris in 1924, but died of a heart ailment there when he was only thirty-one. He painted in subdued gray values, contrasting them with black, brown, and red areas, thereby bringing movement into his pictures which increased as time went on. Kolle's friend, Wilhelm Uhde, extolled him in a monograph.

Albert Weisgerber (1878–1915) belonged to this Paris circle for a while, although he was not happy in it. After that, in Munich, he sought to develop a sweeping, more malleable variant of early Expressionism, but he died too soon. He seems to have been inspired by Cézanne and Greco. As a disciple of the new endeavor to overcome the realism of pedestrian painting, he made less use of the modern pictorial methods developed by Marc and Klee, or by Kandinsky (formerly his fellow students in Franz Stuck's classes), but seemed to feel more strongly drawn to the expression of emotional content. He indulged in passionate but very representational effects as, for example, in his many paintings of St. Sebastian, *David and Goliath*, in a pathetic Absalom, or in *Mother Earth*, a gigantic overscaled nude stretched out luxuriously in a typical German landscape. If he had not been killed in the First World War he probably would have adopted the style of New Objectivity, since it laid stress on themes with content.

Munich

Munich was a broad reservoir for the art of painting even after Jugendstil and the Scholle had died out. But the art of the Blaue Reiter group, after its leading members had been killed in action or had scattered, left scarcely a trace worth mentioning on local artists. In the place of this stormy group more conservative painters now stepped forward, picking up a point in the development of style which the Blaue Reiter painters had bypassed. Variations of the possibilities implicit in the work of Cézanne and Van Gogh now appeared in more restrained forms.

Richard Pietzsch (1872–1960), still bound to a more solid, older form of realism, depicted his native Isar valley in muted colors. *Otto Geigenberger* (1881–1946) painted his native city, Wasserburg, with its unusual encircling wall. He favored controlled colors and a loose, free style with which he captured felicitous motifs, and he became very popular with the general public. *Adolf Schinnerer* (1876–1949) produced, besides etchings, compositions with allegorically meaningful figures in which a varied and almost blazing green dominates. *Hans Gött* (b. 1883), painting in a more subdued palette, still and somber in his expression, continued the romantic tradition in his landscapes of his homeland. When he painted figures, he favored the female nude in the attitudes of Marées, but worked out in greater detail. Unlike the painters just mentioned, *Wilhelm Maly* (1884–1943) adopted the stronger colors which Macke had introduced in Germany, but he blended them more gently. *Heinrich Brüne* (1869–1945) painted more lightly. His floating color reminds us of Renoir, whose portrait he painted when the French master sought him out on a visit in the Bavarian highlands. *Joseph Eberz* (1880–1942) absorbed the color theories of Hölzel (see p. 121), but later sank into a sentimental, rather oppressive, one might almost say perfumed, mysticism. *Karl Caspar* (1879–1956), on the other hand, was an artist whose religious painting could be taken seriously. He began with relatively dark colors, then adopted a more modern chromatic key although his tonality remained rather chalky. His religious figures were conceived in blocks of color and worked in with the foreground. At first the church rejected his work, even though he had given a south German twist to Expressionism. Not until his later years did he receive the important commission to decorate the apse of Bamberg Cathedral. He taught for many years at the Munich Academy and was a strong influence on the development of south German painting. His wife, *Maria Caspar-Filser* (b. 1878) was influenced by him, but her work was lighter and remained closer to Impressionism. She moved her figures back towards the middleground, where they merged into colorful space or luxuriant vegetation. *Julius Hess* (1878–1957) translated the forms of Cézanne into subdued, tapestrylike creations, while *Erich Glette* (b. 1896) turned nature into tonal values with strandlike brushstrokes.

Willy Geiger (b. 1878) revealed an attraction to gruesome themes that wat totally uncharacteristic of Munich, where he lived. He also frequently painted anti-militaristic works in an intensely glowing palette.

Max Unold (1885–1964) created small-scale paintings of the ordinary activities of harbor life and cities; now and then he tried his hand at portraits. Everything is painted in strangely subdued, fuzzy, yet harmonious colors. He also wrote, in an easygoing style, about the painter at work. If we say that Unold's work is in a minor key, then that of *Richard Seewald* (b. 1889) is definitely in a major. His favorite subject was the clear Mediterranean landscape which he tried to stylize in simple forms. He was continuously drawn also to religious themes and he painted church frescoes and illustrated many sacred legends. He has also written himself, illustrated books, and actively opposed current artistic trends.

The paintings of *Oskar Coester* (1885–1955) were highly original. A gay pessimist, he described the singular forlornness of the human animal or some unlikely misfortune. In the beginning he favored dark, sibilant colors and a large format; later he painted small green landscapes stretching under a blue sky.

Joseph Scharl (1896–1954) started painting in the manner of the early Van Gogh, with dull, heavy colors, but eventually developed a powerful style with surrealistic, grotesque forms. Everything remained representational, but exaggerated in size.

In his later years, *Carl Crodel* (b. 1894) came to Munich from eastern Germany, bringing yet another style. He was a versatile, imaginative painter and graphic artist, always improvising, subdued in tonality, and versed in all techniques.

Adolph Hartmann (b. 1900) took an energetic part in Munich's art life after the Second World War and organized the avant-garde into "The New Group." He began by painting in the style of Corinth, in a grayed, muted tonality, after which his forms became more colorful and forceful. His later paintings are based on a more precise calligraphy and sometimes give the effect of monumental drawings that have been subsequently colored. His wife, *Babs Englaender* (b. 1922), at first painted lively animal sketches, then adopted the style of the New Objectivists. One might say that both tried to swim upstream against the current of European trends.

Representational, painterly expressions are found in the more conservative, but varied, styles of *Arnold Balwé* and his wife *Elisabeth*, *Thomas Niederreuther*, *Remigius Netzer*, and *Jürgen Kallmann* especially, while a stronger formal composition is sought by *Ernst Weiers*, *Josef Kien*, *H. von Habermann*, and *Christof Drexel* (known for his system called choric drawing), and a kind of graphic painting is often found in the works of *Hubert Distler* and *Emil Scheibe*.

Johanna Schütz-Wolff is more impressive in her figural tapestries, with serene flowing designs, than in her painting. Anja Decker and Irma Hünerfauth, now working in Munich, belong to a later chapter. Baumgärtel, Raum, and Martin are also already part of international nonobjective painting.

Other Sections of Germany

If one looks around South Germany beyond the radius of Munich as far, let us say, as the Main River, one finds no closely defined tendencies, only pleasant individualism, a variety of personalities. Let us select a few painters who present a number of contrasting points of view, and list them just as they appeared. First, those who remained faithful to representational art:

Otto Dill (1884–1956) continued the tradition of Impressionism. *Paul Strecker* (1898–1950), like Dill, had a very light hand, creating an overall effect of a mere impression, approaching the shortland style of Dufy. *Walter Becker* (b. 1893) in his later work achieved bolder distortions and a less restricted color application, connected only loosely with the object. In the landscapes of *Will*

Sohl (b. 1906), representations of a sea and dune world, Fritz Wichert saw "wild, immeasurable loneliness between sky and sea." A disturbing versatility and a unifying lyricism are at war with each other, but his flowing line is more effective than his gushing color.

A bleakness pervades the paintings of *Willi Cramer* (b. 1900) of Nuremberg. He continues Expressionism in his still lifes, painted with a harshly flowing, weighty brushstroke, and in generalized landscapes that have a sinister glow.

In Stuttgart, besides Schlemmer and Baumeister, who will be discussed later, three artists must be mentioned here: *Walter Wörn* (1901–1963) developed further Schlemmer's problem of figures aligned in parallel on the picture plane and united them with a warm color scheme. *Ida Kerkovius* (b. 1879) studied at Adolf Hölzel's school, having followed him from Dachau to Stuttgart, but she was also active at the Weimar Bauhaus. She organizes her paintings and tapestries in wide sweeps of color, combining objective and nonobjective elements. *Hannelore Busse* (b. 1926), of a young generation, created paintings in Schlemmer's tradition, peopled with compressed female bodies in a baffling chiaroscuro. Her recent work is abstract.

Ferdinand Lammeyer (b. 1899), who teaches at the Städelschule in Frankfurt, creates very painterly landscapes, achieving a heavy balance with his tempera colors. Somber colors dominate–heavy ocher, rich red, a darkening blue. Lately he has turned to painting pure signs in color. He is author of *Maltechnik für Kunstfreunde (A Technique of Painting for Friends of Art)*.

Kurt Weinhold (1896–1965), from Calw, was influenced simultaneously by Expressionism, New Objectivity, and Surrealism, and had difficulty in reconciling these contradictory styles. *Karl Kunz* (b. 1905), originally from Augsburg, now living in Frankfurt, is in a class by himself. He paints huge, gloomy pictures on wood, in which structural form and tense colors are combined with fantastic surrealistic fragments. *Rudi Baerwind* (b. 1910) worked first in Mannheim, then in France. He painted large-figure groups and demonstrated his capacity as a muralist with a number of wall paintings for Mannheim. "If possible, let us have once again large themes of universal significance," he demanded a few years ago, but he has since turned to nonobjective painting, aiming for warm, full-toned color, undiluted by graphic elements. *Bernd Krimmel* (b. 1926), from Darmstadt, studied architecture, then turned, self-taught, to painting. Probably inspired by Picasso, he circles around the human body, entangling it in curoius formal tensions. *Curth Georg Becker* (b. 1904), not to be confused with Walter Becker, was a student of Nauen. A fluid movement of color and form flows through his pictures, in which there is a seeming gaiety that can turn into aggressiveness at any time. Becker eludes every "program." In Bopfingen (Württemberg), *Fritz Landwehr* (1897–1966) worked with wall hangings in suitable materials and created small paintings in a dense palette. Around 1956 he turned to abstraction. *Arthur Fauser* (b. 1911), living in Frankfurt, is an autodidact and has attracted attention with the strident construction of his post-Cubist still lifes and landscapes, which are carried out in heavy, luscious colors and diagonally accentuated forms.

Among his generation, *Eberhard Schlotter* (b. 1921) is a representational painter of interest for he seems somehow to succeed, paradoxically, in bringing back the external world with the methods of nonobjective art. He paints southern landscapes in which the walls of the houses overlap like wings on a stage set, with abrupt views of monotonous shores or the lonely sea. He never models anything, yet succeeds in producing depth, a perspective effect which remains strictly on the surface. Time seems to stand still; village squares and beaches are deserted, the whole almost ghostlike, the colors somewhat pallid.

Finally, an artist should be mentioned here who stands alone: *Paul Kleinschmidt* (1883–1949), who lived in Ulm, and later in the wooded heights above the Bergstrasse in the Odenwald. His paintings, in a heavy impasto technique, fall between Corinth and Beckmann. In them we find strange men wearing tight-fitting costumes with puffy, ruffled borders, monstrous creatures who both intoxicated and grieved their interpreter. Had his colors not developed such a monotonous yellow-gray tonality, he might have become a master of the monstrous. But on this account we cannot agree either with Meier-Graefe's evaluation of him as the equal of Van Gogh, or with some favorable comparisons of his work with that of Corinth.

Berlin

Unlike Munich, where conservatives were in the majority, in West Berlin, after the unfortunate division of that city, progressive forces concentrated in the schools. This made it possible after the Second World War to re create an art center there that could play an important contemporary role in modern German painting. Since it is our intention to treat in this chapter only those artists who are still struggling with external reality, we must mention at this point that the painters of Berlin rarely lose themselves in the impressions of nature, certainly not with any passive feeling of delight. Most of them tackle reality as a competitor who should not be evaded, who must be overcome. In Berlin we find cutting straight across the various generations a tendency toward a translation of reality in graphic terms, with intellectual precision and ambiguous fantasy alternately expressed in equal proportions. The so called *art informel* plays a less important role in Berlin than in other parts of Germany.

Ernst Fritsch (b. 1892), a typical Berliner, developed during the period of Expressionism a dry but powerfully simple style, influenced by Henri Rousseau and noteworthy for its plastic clarity of composition. Later he indulged in experimentation and invented Chagall-like fantastic themes. But since this Berliner lacked the dreamlike fantasy and light touch of the "Parisian" Chagall, his later works give a realistic impression. *Dietmar Lemcke* (b. 1930) is related in feeling and just as emphatic, although he is nearly forty years younger than Fritsch. His angular, plastic, cubically constructed landscapes or city scenes are worked out in a naive, drastic stylization, with simple, dense, and thereby powerful volumes. Pictorial architectonics are here willfully crossed with distortion, color, and spatial force.

Hermann Teuber (b. 1894), a Dresdener, comes from the Hofer School and since 1950 has been teaching at the Berlin Art Academy. He loves the peaceful ambience of a room or the serene view from a placid, sheltered spot where a lonely figure or a beckoning structure awaits us. Or he places in his pictures objects of equal size–birds, or tiny riders–letting them rest motionlessly as if on a chessboard, seeming to imply pictorially that all living things are alike, lonely yet dependent on each other.

Several Berlin landscape painters have mastered the architectural picture, and may be compared: *Werner Heldt* (1904–1954) one might well call the Utrillo of Berlin. But he was less concerned than Utrillo with the painterly quality of his mute, white-walled houses. Heldt belongs to another time, and he presents the monotony of a metropolis. Foreground planes dominate bare, curving zones; rows of deserted streets, seen as if from a window, lead into depth, and where the lines of perspective end houses bar the way, as on a stage. Trees and people scarcely enter the picture. The cityscape almost becomes a dehumanized abstraction. *Rudolf Kügler* (b. 1921) has been active mainly as a graphic artist. His color prints–exotic cityscapes or harbor scenes–consist of a network of intersecting and cross-secting lines, between which are compressed towering architectural forms, people, or plants that look as if they had only subsequently been touched by color. The landscapes of the Rhinelander *Ernst Schumacher* (1905–1963), who also lived in Berlin, were quite different. Opulent, colorful nature is alive in his pictures, but the summery vegetation is painted in few blocklike forms and colors. In the beginning he absorbed Parisian stimuli and was associated with the Fauves, though gradually his sense for pictorial order led him to greatly simplified contrasts of horizontal and vertical planes, with relatively few extended diagonals. (Beside him an Expressionist like Schmidt-Rottluff is an extremist.) With yellow, blue, and rose facades and intensely green vegetation, Schumacher sometimes succeeded in achieving a mood all his own in very simplified compositions.

We now come to the painters who "deformed" more freely and who aimed to put reality at a distance. First, *Cesar Klein* (1876–1954), who worked through all the trends of his time, passing through Expressionism, a severely objective phase, and the dreamworld of Surrealism. In his first works we are reminded of abstract surrealism, but his figurines in this style rarely succeed in arousing any profound emotion. Klein lectured at the Berlin Art Academy from 1919 until his dismissal by the National Socialists. He was active also as a scene designer, with the result that the decorative element in his talent was too prominent. He especially favored frescolike color harmonies that were too strongly rooted in brown-yellow. In spite of his failings he succeeded in making a considerable impression. The poet Theodor Däubler wrote a lively monograph on him.

The Berliner *Max Kaus* (b. 1891), a pupil of Erich Heckel, abandoned the virile woodblock style of the Brücke painters, letting it dissolve into a colorful lyricism. Smooth curves converge in his paintings, forming no sharp contours, only amiable guidelines for the embedded colors. In the thirties he was still working with a certain degree of perspective, but he soon began to arrange his color forms over the surface in the fashion of enamel work. Slowly but steadily he arrived at a basic handling of his materials, achieving sweeping bands of color which trail in a subdued, tapestry-like fashion through his pictures. He rarely uses contrasts of complementaries, tending toward paintings carried out either all in gold-brown tones or in twilit blues. A contrasting color may turn up along the edges. His subject matter is frequently the weary, lyrical mournfulness of a convalescent, of a woman, or a landscape.

Hans Jaenisch (b. 1907) as a very young man went through the visual revolution achieved by the *Sturm* group. From the beginning his pictorial forms existed without any realistic space. Everything is spun onto the bare surface and held together by large simplified curves drawn through the whole picture. The result is rather like runic script scratched on a weathered wall. These graven, relieflike figures suggest dream-images of people or animals. Age-old colors are produced by a curious mixture of techniques. Flattened fossils and skeletonized bodies are covered with crackles or scabrously weathered material, as if to indicate that these creatures must remain at the bottom of this surface forever, and that their value is solely symbolic. Lately, his tonality has become more glowing as his style becomes increasingly abstract.

In the work of *Alexander Camaro* (b. 1901) we find a similar attitude, yet his intention is something quite different. A village built on piles evaporates into a dream-grating; a girl at a window into a pale ghost; the slope around a coal pit into a twilit tapestry. With him one never knows whether a recollection of reality has been extended into a dream or whether a dream-symbol has gently absorbed a piece of the real. Camaro is a disembodying poet; sometimes, though, he is little more than an insipid symbolist. More richly creative and versatile, *Curt Lahs* (1893–1958) wove a chain of signs across the surface, switching willfully from painterly to linear areas. He, too, wandered off more and more into the world of abstraction. Self-taught, he lived in foreign countries for many years, was then an instructor at the Berlin Academy, was removed by the National Socialists but called back in 1948. Occasionally the influence of Braque and later of Willi Baumeister are melded into his work. *Hans Thiemann* (b. 1910) has developed a clear style that captures objects in a clean, still-life fashion: they are permeated with veins or parallel hatchings and thus acquire a certain dogmatic uniformity of effect. From his early surrealistic pictures, when he was still working with perspective, he has progressed to an increasingly planimetric surface style.

A few Berlin artists who were born in the nineteen-twenties should be mentioned here. *Alfred Winter-Rust* (b. 1923) has painted expressive, pictorially rich landscapes, which are at the same time puzzlingly simplified in form. He is moving more and more toward nonobjective art, although various mysterious recollections of nature are still apparent in his work. *Harry Kögler* (b. 1921) constructs massive machine and architectural fragments in his pictures, as if to develop further the monumental style of Léger. The paintings of *Otto Herbig* (b. 1890) remain more conservative and are closely allied to the tactile, corporeal world. His themes are the child, the young mother, or rhythmically broken landscapes, usually in pastel. For more than two decades he lived in Berlin, and he taught at the Weimar Art School. *Hermann Bachmann* (b. 1922) came from East Germany and began to paint in a style somewhere between Hofer and Beckmann. Always experimenting, he has probed almost every possibility so that it is virtually impossible to characterize his style.

Manfred Bluth (b. 1926) paints like a Caspar David Friedrich of the twentieth century. In his landscapes the desiccated countryside stretches out in clearly ordered planes from which all human life is banished. Everything is based on a horizontal structure, even where an occasional vertical projection seeks release. Here precise measurements and a geometric plan rule supreme. After he had almost achieved a totally nonobjective pictorial form, he "discovered" Claude Lorrain. "Lately I find myself seeking a greater simplicity in my painting, for to my mind the secret lies more in a realization of concrete images... than in an original or exaggerated treatment of the materials of painting."

Johannes Molzahn (1892–1965) sought a precise, similarly geometric joining of objectivity and abstraction. He emigrated to the United States in 1938 and was totally forgotten in Germany. Using the vocabulary of plane geometry, he created space- and distance-compositions, which give the effect of a grille-like network of repeated and flattened architectural units. One might describe it as a transcendentalized architectural metropolis; there is no above or below. Occasionally, classical and Christian symbols are interwoven. Molzahn's unpublished tract, "Ist die moderne Kunst ein Ausdruck unserer chaotischen Zeit?" *("Is modern art an expression of our chaotic times?")*, is aimed at today's culture-pessimism.

North and West Germany

As in south Germany, we find individual styles of painting that adhere to older traditions dispersed across all north Germany. Although the art we are about to discuss is not strong enough to form the basis for a school of painting, a few of the artists have done work of high quality and refinement.

As an example of solid tradition we have *Tom Hops* (b. 1906), who paints harbors and the shallows around the North Sea island of Sylt. The objects depicted provide the strength of his composition, not just the emotional atmosphere. *Hans Hubertus von Merveldt* (b. 1901) creates harbor scenes with heavy forms in original color harmonies; boats and broad sails are prominent in the foreground.

The more fundamental painting of *Friedrich Karl Gotsch* (b. 1900) was influenced especially by Kokoschka. Dull, minor-keyed tones alternate with broadly glowing areas. The paint is thick, almost doughy. Figures, animals, and landscapes are treated with the utmost freedom. He remains faithful to representational art, but declares. "God alone knows to what point you can drive the object." His watercolors, pastels, drawings, and prints also bear witness to his somber view of life. Almost his entire oeuvre was destroyed during the war.

A north German friend of Gotsch's student days, *Hans Meyboden* (1901–1965), was also first influenced by Kokoschka. With both Gotsch and Meyboden, the color does not flow, like Kokoschka's, but stands in the painting as if congealed, broad and stubborn. Meyboden's pictures give an effect of thickly woven carpets. Again like Gotsch, he speaks a rather clumsy language, as if he had long been isolated from human society. The transcience of all earthly things, allusions to sickness and death, are themes in Meyboden's work, but he has never dealt with religious subject matter. *Kurt Sohns* (b. 1907), who lives in Hannover, paints interiors in warm colors, inhabited by schematic human beings. His quiet compositions are extremely simplified, and forms are distorted, but they never offend; instead they tend to have an appealing, almost helpless effect, amid pleasantly spread, astonishingly beautiful color areas.

Max Pfeiffer-Watenphul (b. 1896) became known for his pictures of Venice, painted in a flaky style adopted from a late-Impressionistic technique. His is a strange Venice, wrapped in fallow light and a woolly atmosphere. Nobody would dream that this artist was a product of the Weimar Bauhaus; he seems to follow the techniques of Bonnard. *Arnold Bode* (b. 1900), who teaches in Cassel, has no intention of breaking down the representational world but seems rather to want to condense it harmoniously in a few suggestive colors, endowing it with a degree of plasticity. He drew attention to himself through his extraordinary installation of the international art exhibition in Cassel, *Documenta*, in 1955.

Finally, two woman painters from north Germany must be mentioned. *Irmgard Wessel-Zumloh* (b. 1907), who lives in Iserloh, is the wife of the painter Wilhelm Wessel (see p. 137). She depicts groups of figures, painted very freely in flat, interwoven color compartments and giving the effect of still life. The younger painter, *Sigrid Kopfermann* (b. 1923), from Hannover, constructs abstract landscapes with heavy spots of color in a more ponderous rhythm.

Hamburg, a city that is often considered indifferent to cultural activity, has produced several quite important objective painters. *Fritz Kronenberg* (1901–1960), a much-traveled painter originally from Cologne, carried on in Hamburg the tradition of Cubism and painted still lifes or figures that derive from the late work of Braque and Picasso. He never took a painting lesson in his life and developed a highly original tonality; sometimes he achieved a weblike effect, with the underpaint showing through; sometimes he used light tones, with much delicate gray; at other times he used saturated colors in which the entire scale of red hues is dominant. A true painter, Nolde called him.

In the landscapes and figure compositions of *Karl Kluth* (b. 1898) form and color as ends in themselves struggle with a more realistic viewpoint, lending unrealistic tension to the pictorial plane, which becomes independent, crowded, and staccato in its color effect. His style of painting, inspired originally by Munch, wrestles wildly with the monumental. *Willem Grimm* (b. 1904) from Darmstadt, now living in Hamburg, sees man in a mask; a clamorous tumult of masqueraders erupts from his paints. His colors are exciting, even when he is only painting still lifes. Kluth and Grimm are temperamental painters, carrying on the possibilities of Expressionism. *Herbert Spangenberg* (b. 1907) seeks a bridge between representational forms and geometric abstractions, working therefore in a borderline area that is very difficult to master.

Eduard Bargheer (b. 1901), of Hamburg, moves back and forth between the fogbound lowlands of the German north and the radiance of Italy, and perhaps for this reason his inner conflicts are not always resolved. Large figures and suggestions of landscapes are linked with more geometrical forms and composition. On the other hand, he also seeks to capture, perhaps under the influence of Klee, a dreamlike quality in a muted, almost evanescent tonality. He calls his pictures *Gewebe* (woven things). "It is a simple word, but I know no better. God knows, it does not mean a decorative problem, but actually a metaphysical one, because *Gewebe*–oneness–is everywhere."

In the Rhineland, when we look at the painting that has remained close to nature and belongs to no clearly defined movement, we find a lively concentration of old and new forces. Conservative artists, some of whom adhere to traditional Rhenish painting, still carry a good deal of weight. On the other hand, in just this region and in the nearby Ruhr area, we find a growing concentration of young talent pressing forward to new areas of expression. Some day, when the freshness of their artistic conception has been accepted, people will speak of a typically Rhenish palette.

Among the conservatives were the painters of idyllic landscapes *Julius Bretz* (1870–1953), *Max Clarenbach* (1880–1952), and *Theo Champion* (b. 1887). *A. Buschmann* introduces intimate surroundings in fragmented color and brings shadows of objects to life. *Carl Barth* (b. 1896) tries to unite old painterly traditions with greater emphasis on structure. *Robert Pudlich* (b. 1905) and *Josef Piper* (b. 1907) are popular for the pleasing sweep of their colors. *Carl Schneiders* (b. 1905), *Felicitas Auer* (b. 1902), *Willi Deutzmann* (b. 1897), and *Oswald Petersen* (b. 1903), press more for expressive organization, each in a different way, of course. *Peter Janssen* (b. 1906) favors multiple small details, mild in color, such as the facades of houses with innumerable windows, or a throng of human figures in a landscape, seen as silhouettes against a coarsely painted ground. In these paintings one senses that Janssen passed through abstractionism. In his monumental still lifes, *Friedrich Vordemberge* (b. 1897) stresses strange colors which are worked out in flat, immobile areas, existing eternally as expectant parallels of their objects.

Finally, we come to two other Rhinelanders who, in their serious concern with human beings as subject matter, hardly fit into our usual conception of Rhenish *joie de vivre*. *Peter Herkenrath* (b. 1900) paints emotionally oppressive interiors or uneasy portraits in which the person seems to be turned into stone and pressed into the surface of the painting. The expression is uncanny, reminding us of monumental caricatures. *Bruno Goller* (b. 1901) does his best work in murals. He arranges his humans in checkerboard zones, using the meagre hues of fresco but clearly delineating his figures. On occasion he chooses only a part of the human body, magnifying it to mythical proportions, as in *The Big Ear*.

ABSTRACT PAINTING

The German "Old Masters"

Our investigation of abstract painting has been confined so far to the pioneering efforts of Kandinsky and the work of his Bauhaus colleagues. Its further evolution as a many-sided and far-reaching movement in the general history of twentieth-century art has occurred only since the second World War, and it is this phase with which we shall now deal. But first some basic principles must be made clear.

Abstract painting, as we understand it, is an approach that rejects any reproduction of the outside world of visual experience, even the freest interpretation. From the very beginning, however, virtually as soon as the public had become aware of the development, there was a quarrel over definitions. The expression "abstract" was at first used also for Cubism and the more radical aspects of Expressionism whenever objects had been transformed into an abstract scheme, but eventually only that which had relinquished every relationship with the object was termed abstract. Then, in an analogy to absolute music, the expression "absolute painting" came into use, a term meaning that line, color, and form were now to be read and experienced for their own sake, without external reference. The expression "nonobjective art" *(ungegenständlich, art non-figurative)* was less popular, since it defined negatively. The paradoxical expression "concrete art" *(konkrete Kunst)*, first used by the Dutch painter Theo van Doesburg, was intended to convey that in this style of painting, line and color were autonomous. That is to say, they were complete and independent concrete realities, in contrast to their status in a painting–in a still life, for example–where they serve dependently to create something else. The expression "concrete" was not generally adopted, however, because Doesburg claimed it for his own constructivist style and consequently for only one aspect of nonobjective art.

The gradual disintegration of the object came about historically as a result of various conditioning factors. Impressionism, in its most radical phase–with Monet, for example–had already dissolved the world into ephemeral nuances of color, and it is significant that Kandinsky should have declared that one of his inspirations for the omission of the object had come from this direction. Then Cubism, radically modifying Cézanne, split the outer world into a system of surface fractures, and Expressionism ignored the confining outlines of its forms to express ecstatic gesture. All three of these currents were able to flow into the waters of absolute painting. When one takes a closer look, they may be followed further. One may speak today of an Impressionism that has become abstract whenever a riot of color predominates–Tachism; and one can recognize an abstract Expressionism when the expressive gesture is paramount and in non-objective reference; and finally there is an abstract Cubism that works today with purely geometric forms–*abstraction froide*. But with this the possibilities of nonobjective art are by no means exhausted. Grown independent, it gives birth to children of its own. Here again are all those possibilities which Heinrich Wölfflin established as polarities for objective painting: centric or eccentric, unified or multiple composition, linear or painterly technique, flat or three-dimensional spaces, closed or open forms; to these must be added all the possible approaches to life, from gay to tragic.

The "grand old men" of German nonobjective painting are Kandinsky, with whom we have already dealt, Hölzel, Baumeister, Ritschl, Hans Hofmann, and Theodor Werner. Each of these men struck out into this new territory in a different way, but the earliest point of departure lies with Kandinsky and Hölzel. Kandinsky's contribution was a spring which gushed forth; Hölzel's flowed in a more leisurely fashion.

Adolf Hölzel (1853–1934) was influential, although less directly than Kandinsky, through his teaching. He was a member of the Dachau group, and as early as 1893 founded a school of painting in that city which for a time included the young Nolde among its students. Since Hölzel belongs to the generation of Klinger, Liebermann, and Corinth, it is astonishing to realize that in 1904, when he published his first theoretical work, he was already introducing an emphasis on broad surface areas and color in his paintings, thus stressing pictorial architecture rather than the object. The Jugendstil had prepared the way with its effective pictorial rhythms and, however strongly Hölzel tended toward compressed forms, his statement remained softly lyrical. In 1906 he was appointed to the Stuttgart Art Academy, and in 1910 he finally achieved non-objective compositions. Yet he was devoted to religious themes and therefore only rarely excluded the representational world. With his friend Theodor Fischer, an architect interested in moderate reforms, Hölzel at first devoted himself to murals; then he became more radically abstract in glass windows, colorfully composed, and, after 1923, in pastels. In 1917 and 1918 he painted compositions on a new theme, *Farbige Klänge* (colored sounds). He was a firm believer in good comradeship and insisted on communal work, as for instance in the banqueting-hall of Pfullingen where under his direction the Swiss Brühlmann and other students created as freely as possible. He painted a mural of a huge crucifix for the Ulm Garrison Church and cycles of glass paintings for the Hannover firm of Bahlsen and for Stuttgart. In Stuttgart, Meyer-Amden, Schlemmer, and Baumeister were his disciples for a time.

But Hölzel's main contribution lay in his theories, in his teaching of the *Farbenschlüssel* (Color Keyboard). He was of the opinion that when a work of art "excites our feeling most, we are in the presence of order. Just as a *maestro di cembalo* has to have full knowledge of the chords for every given note, so must we know the triads, transitions, and other sound effects, and how to use them." Characteristic of the anti-realism of the twentieth century was the fact that he had in mind a science of harmony such as had been developed in music long ago. As early as 1916 he knew that "there exist certain qualities that are justified in their own right and do not require representational supplementation, in fact suffer and atrophy under it." The following declaration was also something quite new: "If anyone believes that he must first thoroughly study nature in order to arrive at a picture, he is greatly mistaken... first we must grasp the idea-picture, in order to take from nature what we require." The artist should work with eight categories of color: the primary colors themselves, with light and dark, cold and warm, and with the complementaries; then with intensity, quantity, the non-colors (black, white, and gray) and the simultaneous contrasts. Under Hitler the eighty-year-old Hölzel was cruelly relegated to the ranks of the disgraced.

Willi Baumeister (1889–1955) also developed in Stuttgart, becoming Germany's foremost nonconstructive abstract painter. The richest contrasts and the greatest powers of transformation were innately present in this artist, whose natural talent for painting was undiminished by strong tendencies toward theory. He established a strange secret connection between the oldest cave drawings and the spiritual explorations of modern man. Artists such as he like to symbolize the mystery of life in opposition to the rationalized order that controls us, and to express it in an irrational sign language.

In the beginning Baumeister was impressed by the monumental forms of Léger and later he was inspired to some extent by the fantastic imaginings of Miró. But he transformed both approaches, even when he was at his most eccentric, into a more appealing play of material and color. After Baumeister had become an abstract painter he declared that this method of painting "is not abstract in the sense of being alienated from mankind and life. The perception of the artist is entirely natural. Certain manifestations of nature, such as the surface of water, waves in the sand, tree bark, geological formations in quarries, branches, everything structural or modulative that is visible in nature, stand very close to the painting of today."

In 1919 he began to paint "wall pictures" that sought their stability in the consolidating wall or were turned into wall-reliefs through an admixture of sand and putty. But soon his forms became less identifiable, more complicated and agitated, and his signs became whispering symbols. In 1938 he painted his *Eidos* pictures, in which appear amoebalike forms, single-cell creatures reminiscent of the mysterious early stages of organic life. These were followed in 1943 by his "African Pictures," which remind us of cryptographs of early cultures and whose puzzling forms attract us. Out of these developed, in 1945, his *Peruvian Walls;* here he again established a unity with the wall, but he now let punctured color forms haunt the surface ("Perforation Pictures"). These were followed by works he called "painted reliefs," in which colorful symbols seemingly floated on a sustained surface. Finally he painted gigantic *Gelände* (territories), black and white continents that filled the entire picture in monotone, emitting glowing color or revealing close details at their outer edges only–delicate jags, specks, twisted lines.

Such forms interpenetrate in his work, at times in a subdued nocturnal light, at others in a matinal glory of color, sometimes spread flat over the picture plane, then again in high relief. "A predilection for immobility is also evident," he declared, "and for perceptions of movement, for a state of floating, and for decompositions. The forms react to each other, create spheres of action or rhythmic chains, which color serves as music." Baumeister remained a man of surprising transformations–the pointed could become cloddish, combed effects are placed beside granular, smooth areas adjoin the lumpy, firmly drawn lines are next to jerky strokes. A gray, murmuring, runic tone could appear beside unexpected signs in saturated color, dull material beside the most beautiful glaze. After sometimes suspecting the painter of a certain caprice, on close acquaintance with the work one realizes that everything is in its rightful place after all. In his book, *Das Unbekannte in der Kunst (The Unknown in Art*, 1947) he declares that "all great results are found casually, through coincidence or in uncontrolled ways." In 1928 he was called to the Frankfurt Art School, but was dismissed as "degenerate" in 1933. After the war, in 1946, he took over the direction of the Stuttgart Academy.

Hans Hofmann (1880–1966), who became a highly esteemed painter in the United States, was inspired originally by the Fauves. Before the First World War this Bavarian artist lived in Paris, in close relationship with Matisse, Delaunay, Braque, and Picasso. In 1915 he founded a school of painting in the Schwabing section of Munich which flourished unnoticed, but taught already the possibilities of abstract painting. After the war Hofmann used to spend his summers in Ragusa, Capri, or St. Tropez with his pupils. In 1930 a friend brought him to the University of California at Berkeley, and four years later he started his school of painting in New York City, with summer semesters in Provincetown. During the first half of his life Hofmann was a teacher; in the United States, however, he developed a chromatic technique of considerable force. American critics have described his powerfully colored paintings as "controlled explosions." He was not dependent on nature–although he did not necessarily eliminate the object–or on the principles of Cubism. He looked upon his colored formations more as "complexes of pressure and forces," barely held in balance. Titles such as *Ecstasy* and *Burst into Life* are characteristic.

With his seemingly improvised, riotously colorful pictures in which life permeates all matter, he contributed the element of complete freedom of non-objective expression which has become so decisive for the development of the most recent American painting. His teaching stressed the difference between tonal painting, with its emphasis on light and dark gradations, and pure painting (to which he assigned his own work) that established "open" elementary color contrasts, with the superabundant color also serving a formal function.

Theodor Werner (b. 1886), with Baumeister and Schlemmer the third Swabian to achieve international fame, was quite different–more the meditative painter-philosopher. He lived for a long time in Greece, Paris, and Berlin. Inspired originally by Cézanne, he moved gradually toward nonobjective painting of space-creating colors and interpretative rhythms. In the 1930's he was still using corporeal forms, shaped like elongated wedges or rising up like bundles of rays. In the 1940's he used ellipses and circles, and passages that give an effect of astronomical tracks. Since 1950 he has been filling his pictures with more limited forms, some plantlike, some crystalline. Between such "psychic signals" we now find pauses, connections are less direct, many possibilities remain open. Sometimes a circle or a staff-shaped form is placed in front of the more amorphous color areas, as if to measure symbolically a specific place in this semi-articulated realm. Even when he resorts to broken–one might even say splintered–rhythms, Werner's tonality remains original and definitely aesthetic.

In 1954 he successfully carried out the commission for a nineteen-meter-wide mural for the Berlin Academy of Music, one of the largest abstract murals in Germany. Here a symphony of forms is developed in three movements, clearly demonstrating–for the first time in Germany–that nonobjective painting, going far beyond its improvisational features, can dominate gigantic surface areas.

Otto Ritschl (b. 1885) has represented a Constructivist-Purist wing of abstract painting. He presents us with stereometric, clearly defined forms designed for large surfaces, severely built color and line structures; they are devoid of all subjective effect and in the most harmonious order possible–a style which today is called, much too disparagingly, *abstraction froide*. "At present I am striving for a picture that shall be formed completely on the surface, without the dual effect of a ground on which the forms rest. I also no longer want anything more than form, neither expression, therefore, nor mood... To me it seems contradictory to use in an abstract painting a color that has been developed for a representational subject, that is to say, a color that possesses material, spatial, or atmospheric qualities." If one compares such a "program" with the words of Baumeister, one senses the antithesis of commitment.

Hilla von Rebay (1890–1967), born five years after Ritschl, passed through Expressionism and Cubism to arrive earlier than he at abstract painting–in her case of a loosely rhythmicizing nature. She was a fanatic exponent of nonobjective art. She emigrated to the United States and in 1937 took a decisive part in founding The Museum of Non-Objective Art in New York City (now the Guggenheim Museum) which was focused chiefly on Kandinsky and Rudolf Bauer. *Rudolf Bauer* (1889–1953) grew out of the Berlin Sturm group, where he met Hilla von Rebay. In 1929 in Berlin he founded Geistreich, a private museum for abstract art. In 1939 he emigrated to the United States. He painted monumental pictures with geometrically firm color forms.

Construction or Expression?

At this point I would like to remind the reader that as early as the second decade of our century, nonobjective art had already split and become polarized around two possibilities, even though many of the artists involved developed hybrid forms of the two approaches. Beside Kandinsky's vehemently expressive, irrationally affecting configurations, Malevich, Mondrian, and Doesburg were stressing the strictest order of simple, undifferentiated painted surfaces which allowed no calligraphy with the brush. Beside flowing improvisation, therefore, stood the rationally restrained effort; beside a vital abundance of form and color, a purist, Platonic order. At the Bauhaus both possibilities existed side by side, Kandinsky and Klee beside Moholy and Albers. In the 1920's geometric clarity as propagated by the Dutch Stijl group was highly esteemed, especially since it conformed with the new, purely constructive, functional architecture of the time. After the Second World War, however, this geometric approach was forced definitely into a defensive position. As *abstraction froide* it was considered schematic and lifeless, as if in the arts only the intensely warm and intoxicating were of value. However many exciting events may have taken place in the meantime in the field of the new *élan vital*, one should not condemn the opposite principle. We must cease rejecting as old-fashioned the idea that there exists in art a masculine principle of control which is opposed to a feminine principle of dynamic expression, for this polar tension, this contrast in attitude, is necessary for the completeness of life.

Such a contrast develops in most periods rich in art. Beside the iron of Piero della Francesca appeared the vital motion of Pollaiuolo; beside the strict order of Poussin, the overflowing vitality of Rubens; next to the reserve of Ingres, the exuberance of Delacroix. Beside an organizer like Seurat, Monet worked in his own evanescent style; and a figural, almost constructive painter like Schlemmer worked side by side with a visionary, playful Klee. In poetry and music we find the same polarities. To some extent they are connected with the difference between the power of abstraction and the capacity for empathy (Worringer[1]), but also with the eternal archetypes–classicism and romanticism. However, such axes incline obliquely toward each other in the globe of possibilities. The contrasts in today's art, like everything else in a period devoted increasingly to the specific, seek to reach an extreme, an exceptional, purity. Thus some put their faith in the stability of Vordemberge or Bill, others in the whirlpool of Pollock or Wols.

An association of German Constructivists that is too little known was formed in Hamburg as "The Group" of 1948. Prominent among them were *Hildegard Stromberger* (b. 1904), *Max H. Mahlmann* (b. 1912) and his wife *Gudrun Piper* (b. 1917), *Joachim Albrecht* (b. 1916), *Hans Hermann Steffens* (b. 1911), *G. F. Ris* (b. 1928), and *Günter Frühtrunk* (b. 1923).

German Innovators in France

Hans Hartung and Wols developed two specific forms of nonobjective art that were destined to create schools of painting: Hartung with a rhythmic linearity, and Wols through an equally uncontrolled manner of expression which was termed "*informel*" or "tachistic." Both developed their art after they went to France. The Leipziger *Hans Hartung* was born in 1904, the year the Brücke was founded, which may be considered symbolic, for he was to become one of those who overthrew Expressionism (Plate XIII). Raised in eastern Germany, he at first accepted Expressionism–certain of his early drawings resemble those of Nolde–then he gradually turned away from anything that recalled reality. He is primarily concerned with the projection of broadly swinging forms in front of a shimmering, transparent ground plane, as if he were writing a message in the sky. Dark arcs floating in colorful space take on grotesque grille shapes, fine lines are overpowered by crossbars, the elastic spring of linear dynamics is blocked by heavy beamlike forms, quick curves are braked by inert black passages. Ever more strongly he developed into a master of rhythmic balances. Man's simple, psychomotor basic energies were his concern,

[1] Wilhelm Worringer (1881-1965), whose *Abstraktion und Einfühlung, ein Beitrag zur Stilpsychologie (Abstraction and Empathy, a Contribution to the Psychology of Style)* was published in 1908.

and he proceeded from an entirely physical feeling to develop them in broad, sweeping forms. With increasing intensity he submitted his monumental, autonomous, expressive motion to harmonious pictorial controls. During the last years his paintings have become simpler. Individual sweeps of the brush rest on a greater harmony of form, even the shimmering ground from which the latter unfolds is becoming more monotone.

Hartung's steady stylistic development is based on a highly unstable exterior life. He studied philosophy and history of art in Leipzig, then abandoned his studies and lived on Minorca; he moved from there to Paris, where, as a passionate opponent of National Socialism, he joined the Foreign Legion in 1939 and fought in North Africa. After the war he resumed painting. Then, in Paris, he began to work furiously, soon becoming internationally famous.

Wols (Alfred Otto Wolfgang Schulze, 1913–1951) brought something quite different to the art of abstract painting–the unpredictable whirlpools of totally irregular line and color motion that are to be experienced as symbolic of the unfathomable wealth of life. Within the realm of abstract painting it is impossible to conceive of a greater contrast than that between the Constructivists and Wols, who was hailed by many, in Germany as well as France, as the prophet of *Tachism*. This vague name (blot-painting) meant in those days–the mid-forties–a turn toward an irrational, dynamic experience. In Wols's paintings an abundance of linear and color particles dart, whirl, and are knotted together. An ambiguous but comprehensive form of being was to be made perceptible–not, however, an existence that could be distinguished in stone, plant, animal, or human being. And in this the agony and the humor of this remarkable personality was captured.

His short life was even more of an odyssey than Hartung's. He worked in Paris in Frobenius's Africa Institute, then, in Berlin, under Mies van der Rohe and Moholy. For a time he lived in Barcelona and in the Balearic Islands. The outbreak of war found him in France again. When he fled from the German troops, he left all his works behind to be destroyed but took with him a heavy sack of beloved shells and little stones. These were the things that let him forget "the meaning of man and the chaos of his actions. Eternity is demonstrated in these harbor trifles." After he was freed he remained in France, starving. Suddenly he found support in Sartre, and illustrated his works, as well as those of Kafka, Artaud, Paulhan, and Solier. In the course of this

XIII Hans Hartung, Picture, 1948

XIV Heinz Trökes, Staccato

detailed work his eyes began to suffer, all light became painful and he left his room only at night. He began to drink and, unable to buy an easel or paint, he resorted to the smallest format. He died accidentally of food-poisoning at the age of thirty-eight. In the end, he who had never wanted to exhibit found his way to a free, irrational painting that skyrocketed him to fame.

Munich

In 1949 a number of painters working in the vicinity of Munich formed a group that called itself ZEN. It was the first important association of mutually sympathetic artists to be created in the German post-war era, and in the following five years almost all the abstract painters of significance joined the group.

Fritz Winter (b. 1905) had studied at the Bauhaus, but from the beginning he worked in a style all his own. His early paintings are dominated by dully glowing and twilit colors. Other pictures remind one of crystal formations that have been raised out of the depths. Through the Second World War and his captivity in Russia (1939–1949), his creativity was largely interrupted, but after this period he worked in Diessen on the Ammersee, painting in richer colors and fuller forms. At one time he gave titles to his work–as in a series of oils painted in 1944, *Triebkräfte der Erde (Driving Forces of the Earth)*. Winter's dark forms are laid somberly, like inert beams, over shimmering foundations in yellow, red, or greenish tints, and are locked together with a certain grandeur. The two-layer effect sometimes achieved a maestoso quality. In 1955, at the Cassel Documenta exhibition, he showed a gigantic painting in rhythmic forms which extended across an entire transverse wall, dominating the whole room. Here was another proof that solely through color and form, abstract painting could articulate and enhance a large-scale architectural assignment, and do it equally as well as any of Léger's representational compositions. It is, in fact, just this kind of art that needs the opportunity to go beyond the movable easel picture.

Lately Winter has been incorporating more luminous color areas, without, however, abandoning the somberness of his forms. Since 1955 he has had a chance to develop his pedagogical capabilities at the Cassel Academy. "Greater faith and greater strength are needed," he says, "to make visible the invisible in a free formation than is required simply to confirm the visible and tangible as such."

Conrad Westpfahl (b. 1891) expresses himself more lightly. He turned from objective painting and drawing to a passionate endorsement of the new art, rather as a poet might turn from narrative to lyrical writing. In his early paintings and drawings youthful female figures were spun across the surface in a lively shorthand, sometimes in a painterly fashion, sometimes with the stress on linearity. A line would take its course so willfully that one could already sense this artist's future development as an abstract painter. He began with a muted palette but with the most extreme freedom of rhythm, later using more intense colors in order to strengthen the pulse of life inherent in them. He has taken part frequently in philosophical discussions on modern art, has written articles, and in 1948 a brochure, *Zur Deutung des Bildhaften (Toward an Interpretation of the Pictorial)*. "The visibility of the representational world is not arrived at through the visible world but by way of the surface that has been made to vibrate through color and form. We are not portraying the dead fruits of detached observation, we are rendering the event itself." He believes that "the use of perspective makes things rigid. Solely decisive for the essence of the picture is the tempo of the line determining the direction; the modulations of the transitions of haptic motion; the power of color, radiant or dull, bearing a transcendental message." But pessimistically he adds, "All this can be followed only by those who can feel music in form."

Rolf Cavael (b. 1898), who came to Munich from the north, was able to develop his potentialities only belatedly because of the war and the National Socialist ban on his work. His aim is the freedom of motion and dynamics of color and line that result from a feeling of physical relaxation. His tonality is not based on striking contrasts of complementary colors but on a differentiation of cold and warm. Working with small formats, he began as a linearist whose forms, derived from handwriting, rarely went beyond a tinted calligraphy, remaining essentially self-contained. Later, however, everything became expansive and free. Yellow, red, and green glimmer between a tracery of lines which are now more dynamically extended. The foundations are enhanced by a variation of transparent and opaque colors, and improvised lines dip and dart like the flight of a gull before an approaching thunderstorm. They seek to become increasingly unified with the picture ground, which in its turn also vibrates.

The result is a fluid, sensitive, but also rather nervous style. As a teacher at the Munich *Volkshochschule*, Cavael succeeded in creating in simple working people the desire to express themselves abstractly by discovering their own inner rhythm and learning to project it with pencil and brush. It is encouraging that many people were willing to indulge in such a very private adventure.

Gerhard Fietz (b. 1910) came to Munich from eastern Germany. His paintings are quiet and fine-meshed, and avoid all gestures. They are best seen close to, whereas those of Soulages or Schneider, to name two somewhat comparable French painters, achieve their effect from a distance. Around 1949 Fietz began to construct geometric pictures that gave evidence of a rational and spatial tendency and in which color was nothing more than a delicately balanced afterthought. But in 1950 he seemed to find this type of organization constricting and began to seek more lapidary symbols. This resulted in vitally streaming forms out of which one can rarely wrest a single event.

Karl F. Brust (1897–1960) lost all his early paintings in the war. He worked at many professions and only took up painting again much later. He too was a disciple of nonobjective art, and stressed a specific painterly style, but used fewer lattice-structures than Fritz Winter. A warm red, a richly modified blue, and a deep green glow on his canvas, the colors running in broad tracks that travel diagonally through the picture, becoming more loosely organized as they approach the edges. The color is intended to flow, yet the dissolution of the pictorial organization in a tachistic sense is avoided.

Fred Thieler (b. 1916) an abstractionist of the second generation, began to create nonobjective pictures around 1950. His colors do not ebb at the outer edges, and the effect is less painterly than that of Brust; also he leaves fewer interstices, since it is his intention to fill the entire surface with a hammerlike motion of color. Here organic and mechanically rigid forces seem to plough through each other. Whereas Hartung or Winter would have let a black latticework emerge with something white shimmering through, Thieler explodes these contrasting non-colors within his mosaic of motion. His tonality denies the naturalistic implication that blue has a cosmic meaning or green a vegetative one; the colors react "abstractly" to each other, but some dominant note still rules.

Ernst Geitlinger (b. 1895) was appointed in 1951 to the Munich Art Academy, where he is surrounded with young painters. In the important yearly exhibition in Munich's Haus der Kunst, he made ever-increasing room for the abstractionists. Before Geitlinger turned to abstract art he painted pictures with objective content. Numerous decorative commissions may have contributed to his shift from an intimate fantastic genre to comprehensive abstractions.

Rupprecht Geiger (b. 1909), son of the famous graphic artist and painter, Willy Geiger (see p. 109), began by painting large still lifes with a southern luminosity in a style similar to his father's, after which he turned to rectangular abstractions. Out of varied mobile forms he developed geometric compositions, until he finally arrived at constructivist painting. His style differs from that of Mondrian or Doesburg, later continued in Germany by Vordemberge-Gildewart; Geiger does not place evenly colored planes against each other but instead lets the color within each compartment swell, from the most delicate transparency to the bleakest glow. The introduction of drastic chromatic modulations produces imaginary distances and an appearance of space, without, however, perforating the surface. An intangible stratospheric stillness is contained in these mute canvases. There is an effect of silent energy emanating from the tensions that arise between varied overlapping horizontal layers with a supporting framework of off-angled verticals.

Hans Platschek (b. 1923), who belongs to a younger generation, concentrates more irrationally on color in motion, letting it glow transparently or darken blackly, as if he did not want to disturb its intrinsic life at any point. His braidlike forms swim away lyrically; scarcely born, they seem to want to vanish again, and it is hard to tell whether motion or quiet is intended. Every picture is based on a sustained color harmony of a subtle ochre, an atmospheric blue, an autumnal red, or a sensitive gray. He published *Dichtung Moderner Maler* and was an editor of the journal *Blätter und Bilder*. *Rupert Stöckl* (b. 1923), Platschek's contemporary, tries to immerse a multiple abstract play of form and color in illusory space.

North and West Germany

From Berlin came Theodor Werner, whom we have already discussed, and *Hans Kuhn* (b. 1905), who also painted first in a representational style with surrealist content. In a second phase, spectral humans and vegetation were interwoven as objective recollection gradually disappeared. After 1950 objects were entirely eliminated; one finds only colored planes in a rather somber rhythm. Harmonious connections prevail; shrill colors are taboo. A dreamy phlegm is common to all phases of Kuhn's development. Lately he has turned to enamel painting; color is given a new luminous power and an extremely fluid mobility. This results in detailed, spongelike, and trickly structures which invite the viewer to take a closer look.

Heinz Trökes (b. 1913) also developed his art in Berlin and turned to abstract painting from Surrealism. At first he created imaginary, yet identifiable, ironic monstrosities. These landscapes were first worked out with perspective, but then gradually flattened, so that the monsters were suspended in the picture in a relieflike fashion and took on an illusory existence somewhere between corporeality and mere symbol. In a third phase these aspects also disappear. Now only gay color planes, stripes, drips, and meshwork appear on the picture surface. Certain spectral elements have been preserved, but they no longer represent objective recollection (Plate XIV). With Trökes we see how the strongly fantastic style also may eliminate everything representational. This procedure would once have been considered impossible, although for a long time it has been customary to speak of "fantastic ornament" or "fantastic music." Trökes described his working procedure in a way that is valid for most painters of the irrational: "I have no definite plan... I let myself be driven... begin in one corner or other... then I am often surprised. Involuntarily something attracts my attention... and from there I spin on. I interweave and connect, until it gives off a whole sound. Every drawing, every picture, is in its conception full of adventure... much of course doesn't come off and finds its way into the wastebasket... It is the spontaneous ideas which astound me, not the dreams."

K. R. H. Sonderborg (b. 1923), who now lives in Paris, creates rich and exciting effects. A merciless linearity tears diagonally through his pictures as if it had no beginning or end but led out into the universe. These trajectories with astronomic effect, seemingly produced by meteors, suck up small particles as they whiz by. *Überschallgeschwindigkeit (Beyond the Speed of Sound)* is the title of one his pictures. Speed of motion here seems to correspond with the speed of work. *17:03–18:34* is another title, indicating the exact time in which the work was painted, an hour and thirty-one minutes. Sonderborg says that he does not work regularly but stores up his dynamic impressions, which shoot out of him when the time is ripe. For the present he has eliminated color and compresses all decisive statements into black and white; at most red is sometimes added. He works into the black with knives, occasionally also with a cloth, as if it were necessary to stop the merciless tracks and provoke them. Sonderborg is a dramatizing agitator; in his pictures the agitating forces at times take on something of the compulsory character of machines.

Whereas the cultural climate of Berlin has not proved exceptionally attractive for abstract painters, this art form has developed exuberantly in the Rhineland, as if the proximity of Paris had a vitalizing effect. One of the strongest personalities was *Ernst Wilhelm Nay* (1902–1968), distinctively a creator of rhythms in the new art form. In 1936 he painted his Lofoten pictures, pictures of fishermen and boats on these lively Norwegian shores, in which the influence of E. L. Kirchner is still effective. These were followed by freer but still representational work in a diagonally plunging, zigzag rhythm. Objective memories were still being interjected, but we also find rhomboid forms and atactical splinters and stops. Passionately glowing colors rub against muted colors. After 1946 the scaffoldings are independent and linearly taut, autonomous formations bordering occasionally on the decorative. But after 1950 Nay's colors become very light and spread out; all graphic outlines melt away. Now nothing but loose circular color areas flow through the picture, filling the surface atmospherically like blossoming globular clouds. They give an effect of loosened, coloristic improvisations, yet they produce a rhythm in which the white, empty interstices can swing right along. Concerning the "relief" of his paintings, this painter said, "The picture is given depth and space not through its structure but in the change from cold to warm, from light to dark color." He gave color no value besides the structural one, and believed in excluding "other values, as for instance those of a symbolic, associative, or psychic nature." In 1955 he published an indicative work: *Vom Gestaltwert der Farbe (Of the Structural Value of Color)*.

Georg Meistermann (b. 1911) stands alone in that he tries to bring the new art of abstraction into the church. Stubbornly he puts his faith in the idea that the transcendental should not employ any realistic pictorial means. Content that is not of this world can only be grasped through abstraction. At the same time he is well aware that whenever artistic expression has changed, the church has inevitably opened its doors in the end to a new *Zeitgeist*, from the rigidity of the Romanesque to the swinging rhythm of the Baroque. One senses his spiritual conflict in his paintings, in which highly ambitious overall planning is crossed with extremely individual motion. "Earlier times," he said, "presented the observer with pictures of the values and ideals which bound him. Are we doing anything different? We are bound to freedom, but we don't say that it is easy to achieve." Since 1937 Meistermann has created numerous windows, at first ecclesiastical, later also secular, in which he transformed the tradition of Johann Thorn-Prikker. Between cool gray glass and winding strips of lead lie glowing color areas. In the 1940's most of his paintings looked like abstract, multiramate treetops or rich ribbon patterns. Processes of growth were symbolized and soaring formats therefore appear. From 1950 his color areas extend more to the sides and become larger; everything is more broadly and thoroughly rhythmicized, but diverging life forces come up constantly against cosmic enclosures. Lately he arranges his color areas more geometrically, and the colors are no longer active, but contemplative, as in Rothko.

For quite some time *Hubert Berke* (b. 1908) painted both naturalistic illustration and nonobjective work. In the latter there are no luminous rhythms of the kind we find in Nay, but softly modulated, restful courses of color which seem to float side by side, separated now and then by black areas. A gentle melancholy is expressed. Sometimes we hear echoes of an autumnal day in blue, brown, yellow, or green, then again of a winter night, in black, dark blue, and white. With this painter the summers are not hot or the winters bitingly cold.

Josef Fassbender (b. 1903) fills space in a more varied way. Wide stretches look as if they had been knitted with big stitches, rich colors alternate with flatter washes, quieter sections with others in a restlessly scribbled calligraphy. Interior planes alternate peculiarly between reminiscences of technical and floral forms. Everything serves to create a highly unexpected, extremely irregular ensemble, yet, strangely enough, the effect is balanced. The colors remain soft and close to each other. In certain pictures everything is based on various nuances of red, in others on green and black tones. From 1956 until he was called to Düsseldorf in 1958, Fassbender was in charge of the graphic arts department of the Werkkunstschule in Krefeld. He demonstrated (in the Arndt-Gymnasium, Bonn, 1954)–like Werner in Berlin and Winter in Cassel–that abstract painting is also suitable for great mural decorations.

The works of *Hann Trier* (b. 1915) were dominated at first by an energetic network of lines that seemed determined to destroy the abundance of color that shone between them. For a long time everything seemed permeated with rebellious forces, as if the painter wanted to make clear the perverse complexity of life. His choice of format was already proof of the energy of his statement: he did not choose the balanced square but preferred the rectangle, either rising up determinedly or lying radically on its side. Lately, though, his linear nets are spread more stably, and the color ground shimmers through more restfully.

Carl Buchheister (1891–1964) proceeded from subtly perforated, nervous compositions, transparent beneath a veil-like overlay. After the First World War, in Hannover, where he still lives, he and Kurt Schwitters founded a group of abstract painters. Later he joined the *Abstraction-Création* group. His experiments with "oil-reliefs" are unique. *Marie-Louise Rogister* (b. 1901) belongs to that northwest German circle whose members like to crowd the canvas as richly as possible with toothlike and crustaceous elements in which the graphic effort is dominant.

For the Ruhr area we must mention the group "*Junger Westen*" (Young West) which was formed in 1953. Its premise is the working out of the inner tension resulting from the polarity between the modern technical world and irrational creation. The leader of the group is *Thomas Grochowiak* (b. 1914), the self-taught son of a Recklinghausen miner. Today he mixes constructive and organic forms in his nonobjective pictures. A versatile man, he has for years been in charge of the exhibition at the Recklinghausen Ruhr Festival and of the museums in that city, and has done much to further the visual education of the working man. One of the most talented members of the Junger Westen is *Hans Werdehausen* (b. 1910), a Westphalian. He developed slowly, beginning with firmly constructed figures, then turning to geometric abstractions. Finally he arrived at free, imaginatively mobile, nonobjective "landscapes" made up of "suction and gravity, of whirlwind motion, of pressure from above and below"–all this on well-painted, sometimes transparent foundations which still allow certain suggestions of space.

In Düsseldorf the situation of the young painters became increasingly lively. In 1952 a spark from the flame of French Tachism ignited a passion for subjective expression. "Group 53" was formed. Very few of its members were over thirty-five. Recently *Gerhard Hoehme* (b. 1920) has become known for a kind of series of swarming pictures with small, calligraphic forms, and *Winfried Gaul* (b. 1928) and *Peter Brüning* (b. 1929) for unstable bands of color which extend the lighter areas. Also part of this group were Herbert Kaufmann, Rolf Sackenheim, Gerhard Wind, and Peter Royen, and the quieter K. F. Dahmen and Hermann Dienz.

Outside the circle, but bound in friendship to this young western-oriented group, we find the older painters Emil Schumacher and Wilhelm Wessel. *Emil Schumacher* (b. 1912) has a special talent for extracting the essence of color and material by setting them against each other. He alternates surfaces cracked by twisting streams of color with the resulting ridges raised above these color beds. The possible threat of chaos is ruled out by his personality. The palette is composed of gray or various shades of brown, and all matter comes to life when a little sienna turns up beside cobalt blue, some white beside an earthy green, a dab of crimson lake beside a strip of ochre. Lately the many accents show a tendency to unite mysteriously, becoming "continents" which vanish into empty space as they approach the frame, rather like his *Tastobjekte* (Tactile Objects). Under this heading Schumacher creates compositions of fluid masses of paper, wire, and color, resulting in something resembling a relief map with elevations, furrows, and ominous craters where the shadows collect.

Wilhelm Wessel (b. 1904) started off conventionally as a graphic artist and only in recent years has given himself up completely to painting. "Earth mould, the substance of my cigar ash, the patina of a stretch of asphalt, excite me today..." In these, he believes, there may be "more general metaphysical content than in the portrait of a person or in the material of our culture." Wessel feels himself part of what was called in France *un art autre* (Dubuffet, Fautrier, Tapies). Substance demands form in its own right. Often he uses synthetic resin as a binding medium, a material which thickens to a barklike consistency, and he covers it only very sparingly with color, achieving curious relief effects.

While anti-constructivist painting had one focal point in Westphalia (the Junger Westen group) and one in Düsseldorf (Group 53), another center developed in Frankfurt, around the painters Götz and Schultze in particular. In his best pictures, *K. O. Götz* (b. 1914) confines himself mainly to black and white but succeeds nevertheless in unfolding broad, space-creating movements. These are painted with brushes of various widths, rubber erasers, and cloth, spontaneously swelling and diminishing, yet always balanced. His spatial swirls sometimes achieve a melancholy expressiveness, almost balladlike in tone, and should not for a moment be categorized as Tachism. After most of Götz's work was destroyed in the bombing of Dresden, he published a highly stimulating journal, *Meta* (from 1948 to 1953), and subsequently worked on a similar publication, *Cobra*. He also edited *Das Bräutliche Antlitz* by René Char, and *Behaarte Herzen* by Hans Arp, and designed a *Fakturenfibel*, whose manuscript was also destroyed.

Bernhard Schultze (b. 1915) was influenced by Wols, but transformed his ideas into a more colorful, romantic form of expression. In his pictures we find no active convolutions of form but painterly, muted colors. However, the "material process" demands expression: "Matter wants to stream, to flow back and forth." Some of his paintings look like topographical maps, the land seen from the air. "The more technical the world around us becomes, the more vehement grows my desire to burst it asunder and seek the amorphous base of form." As long as the painter sought to reproduce the visible, he often tried to hide the working procedure; now, however, the abstract painter delighted in revealing all his strokes, thickening, streaking, and dissolving the color. The procedure itself had become expression and picture. Since Schultze works without any strong specific color contrasts but does employ priming and glaze, he strengthens the appearance of his work with relief effects. Cloth rags are laid on the surface and covered with so much paint that they look melted in, without the sharp play of contrasts seen in earlier work of this kind, such as that of Schwitters. Recently Schultze has arrived at a new, panopticon-like naturalism.

In the extreme southwest, on Lake Constance, nonobjective painting was first represented by Ackermann and Bissier. The paintings of *Max Ackermann* (b. 1887) derived less from expressive precepts than from Hölzel's system of color harmonics. For a long time Ackermann was overshadowed by Baumeister. His forms and colors were coarser and less balanced, yet often sensuously fresh. His pictures had a certain gaiety. But in recent years they have grown more severe in composition; the planes are larger and more even in color, and his early, rather drastic expressiveness is being replaced by a luminous stillness. But he says, "The dominating color always demands a good position because it is the one that does the talking, and a reading of the picture begins with it."

Julius Bissier (1893–1965) began with landscapes in the style of the New Objectivity; then, through his friendship with Schlemmer and Baumeister, he progressed farther afield. Of his development he said, "In my youth I thought I could best capture the essence of things in the beliefs and forms of the old masters... but many years of struggle with nature led only to my defeat before the schism existing between the power of the object and the intrusive, unavoidable demands made by the law of the picture... Since 1933 I have concentrated on a play of entirely private symbols. I repeated these symbols over and over again in wash, in the style of the oriental painters, clarifying and improving them with graphic calligraphy. In 1945 I decided to use color instead of wash... These objects have nothing to do with external nature, not with water, earth nor air; yet somehow they contain all these elements."

Boris Kleint (b. 1903), who began to paint under Itten's influence, taught at the School of Art and Handicrafts in Saarbrücken, and has worked on a systematic *Bildlehre* (Pictorial Science). Although he paints nonobjectively, he also explores new possibilities for objective presentations with his students. In these explorations he sometimes succeeds, "but for the most part my efforts fail because the great interest of the young painter lies in abstract painting." Kleint creates in various ways–geometrically, with freely scattered forms, in small format, or on large wall areas.

Several young painters in southwest Germany are directly or indirectly connected with the activity of Willi Baumeister, who taught at the Stuttgart Academy. His inspiration radiates in many directions. *Klaus Bendixen* (b. 1924) came via Cubism to a division of his pictures into large planes which move back and forth in reaction to each other, thereby creating an effect of overlapping, but always preserving the picture surface. Dissociated textures lend irony to the composition. Forms, at first definite, then dissolved, confront us with mysterious symbolism. *Claus Jürgen-Fischer* (b. 1930) seeks an intermediary path between organization and irrationality, between the specifically drawn and the painted parts of the picture. He became prominent as a result of an article he wrote attacking the philosopher Martin Heidegger, and, filling the triple role of artist, critic, and philosopher, edits, together with Leopold Zahn, the journal *Das Kunstwerk*. The paintings of *G. K. Pfahler* (b. 1926) frequently remind one of densely filled geological formations, whereas in the work of *G. C. Kirchberger* (b. 1928) and *F. Sieber* (b. 1925) we are faced with magnetic fields of tension. *Heinrich Wildemann*, who teaches at the Stuttgart Academy, is trying to develop a style in which the paint itself will be expressive solely in terms of shifting color planes.

PAINTING IN GERMANY SINCE 1955
by Juliane Roh

Afterlife of the Art Informel

The continuation of *Art Informel* is clearly established in Germany. This was demonstrated in an exhibition of German painting arranged by Franz Roh for the Salon Comparaison in Paris in 1964 of which Restany said, "Recent German painting has not yet had its crisis of abstraction." In this representative exhibition every variety of abstract art was included, through every stage, culminating in what may be called Phantom Painting that juggled with fantastic recollections of reality. However, it completely overlooked the recent stylistic innovation dealing with the consumer's world and life in a megalopolis, a development that has exploded *art informel* and left it looking like a mass of broken eggshells.

Collage and *décollage* were differently interpreted in Germany. In these the world of reality was not regarded as antagonistic to the *informel*, as, for instance, it was by the French *nouveaux réalistes*, but, on the contrary, as a part of it. What had been purely abstract structure now incorporated broken elements of the representational world. What had fallen into ruins could be assimilated, and that which had served formerly to symbolize the transitory by its construction alone was now given expressive implication through the injection of "the ruins of technology."

K. F. Dahmen (b. 1917) arranges rusty iron, rotted rope, torn canvas, and old scraps of writing to form a poetry of ruin. Until 1965 he stressed the informal structure, but in his 1966 montages, objects take control. Pieces of once-functioning practical apparatuses are here arranged like prehistoric fossils. The articles of civilization have, as it were, outlived man. Now they appear as diagrams, the signs of which can no longer be deciphered. An informal Nature-Romanticism has become a romanticism of the decayed artifact. A glimmer of immaterial color, no longer connected with any object, asserts itself as the last existing force.

In Germany, Action Painting has developed along lines of its own, different from those of other countries. We find the grand gesture expressed freely only by K. O. Götz (see p. 137). With painters like *Gerhard Baumgärtel* (b. 1924),

Walter Raum (b. 1923), *Ernst Wild* (b. 1924), *Dieter Stöver* (b. 1922), and *Hans Joachim Strauch* (b. 1930), all of whom live in Munich, a motor gesticulation becomes inhibited and is interrupted by elements of order that seek to arrest these motive energies. Raum confines all black-and-white contrasts in a powerful script, whereas Strauch tends to force symbols and gestures into a serial order. Wild tames his *élan informel* with a geometric framework or a strong chromatic base. Baumgärtel reduces impulsive movement to primeval gesture in which "the buried mathematical core will reveal itself again." The spontaneity of the gesture is preserved but limited to a definite form. The struggle between pictorial antagonists takes place on the abstract white surface. The colors do not glow sensuously but with a cool fire. *Irma Hünerfauth*, also from Munich, belongs in this category. She proceeded from the creation of a graphic scaffolding in space, which she has subjected to *informel* accents. In her latest works, "radiograms" of objects haunt this spatial tension as if held and drawn by invisible powers.

Beside this dramatic style we find a quieter wing of the *art informel*, which includes Schreiner, Schreiter, and young Bernd Völkle. *Hans Schreiner* (b. 1930) modulates dark earth colors into suspended masses; compact layers float in a sluggish stream. *Johannes Schreiter* (b. 1930) has developed a process with which he achieves subtle color transitions. He ignites white paper at the edges and the smoke creates the finest color nuances, from dark brown to white. He arranges these scraps of color on black cardboard in groups and rows, a process which results in a fascinating play of dark and light that could not be conjured up with any method of painting. The strength of *Bernd Völkle* (b. 1938) lies in a completely varied palette which becomes unified in a single grandiose free formation.

Abstract Expressionism and Phantom Painting

In contrast to *art informel*, in so-called Abstract Expressionism a strong unbroken tonality and a form-world somewhat akin to the painting of children play an important role. Here two German centers emerge–a Munich circle, formed by the group *Spur* (Track), which owes a great deal to the Dane, Asger Jorn, and a second group in Karlsruhe, less closely knit. Spur put quite a few of Jorn's aesthetic theories into action, for instance the unconditional adherence to teamwork and the acceptance of experiment and play as necessary for the realization of a new art form that was to permeate all life. The results are basic aesthetic experiences in the elementary use of form and color, which are intended to enable man to endure life in the city and in the consumer world. To this end Spur developed playful forms which deal with modern life more naively than Pop Art, at the same time also more artistically. Here the painters *Heimred Prem* (b. 1934), *Helmut Sturm* (b. 1932), and *H. P. Zimmer* (b. 1934) play leading roles. They have developed their individual styles yet are not averse to bringing their personal research back into the collective effort. Together, in 1963, they painted a huge hall in the Palazzo Grassi in Venice, and at the *Biennale* of Youth in Paris they showed their original *Spurbau* (Spur Structure). *Anja Decker* transforms stimuli of the Spur group into large-scale encounters of color. The group *Geflecht* (Interweave), which grew out of Spur, tries to combine sculpture and painting in an expressionistic fashion by dynamically intertwining strongly-colored wood and metal strips.

Among the Karlsruhe neo-Expressionists we find the former Grieshaber pupils *Walter Stöhrer* (b. 1937) and *Horst Antes* (b. 1936), and also *Herbert Kitzel* (b. 1928), who comes from East Germany, and his pupil *Hans Baschang* (b. 1937). Kitzel has let his figural motives become increasingly absorbed in a whirling maelstrom. For a while *Stürzende* (Falling Things) were intended, but soon nothing was left but the motion in the paint itself of falling and plunging. Baschang at first followed Kitzel with his frenzied diagonal brushstrokes, but he succeeded in arresting this motion and ordering it in fields of bright color. With powerful streams of color Stöhrer creates an extensive field of pictorial action. In the work of Horst Antes, a mythical figure slowly emerges out of a basically informal shifting of color. One-eyed monsters with powerful heads and long, trunklike noses are perched on massive columnar legs, and on a close-up view threaten the observer. Later they appear as precise, plastic forms placed in front of abstract color signals. At present his development flows in the direction of an almost "classical" tranquillity–the colors have always been radiant–and the monster becomes an emblem of burlesque.

Phantom Painting offers further varieties. *Piet Moog* (b. 1932) lets grotesque figurations issue from a dark world of color. *Jan Voss* (b. 1936), who spends most of his time in Paris, employs the scribbling style of children for a more narrative expression, and *Siegfried Kischko* (b. 1934) invented a fabulous creature with which he fills long narrative strips. *Herbert Schneider* (b. 1924) started off with a lavish language of informal signs, then connected them in strictly-observed rows. Lately he has been enlivening these rows and compartments with a personal variation of Pop Art, inspired by the fresh colors and the naive script-and-picture language of peasant ex-votos, which he connects humorously with everyday events.

The works of *Reinhard Pfennig* (b. 1914) and *Peter Schubert* (b. 1929) border sometimes on Surrealism; this applies also to the ghostly world of signs of *Edgar Schmandt* (b. 1929) of Mannheim.

New Surrealism

Surrealism has many faces. If one includes under this heading work which emphasizes the fantastic and supra-real, then Surrealism can "happen" in every style. In Abstract Expressionism, phantomlike formations sometimes crop up which are difficult to interpret. The open form of this style does not allow a more precise definition. For the true Surrealists, however, it remains characteristic that dreams and visions necessitate detailed reproduction. Most Surrealists are virtuoso draftsmen who transfer their anxieties to paper with great accuracy. Frequently perversity and cruelty are presented with so much aesthetic charm that one feels the artist was bent on finding, via a detour through beauty, a *modus vivendi* that would make it possible to endure life in a world of demons. If one compares the voluptuous depictions of the terror of hell (Dante above all) in the Middle Ages with contemporary versions, the only difference is that the surrealist artists of today paint their own private hells.

Two older Surrealists should be included here. Both became well-known to the broader public comparatively late–*Hans Bellmer* (b. 1902) because he has been living as a recluse in Paris since 1938, and *Richard Oelze* (b. 1900) because he lived in a painters' village near Bremen from which he only recently emerged. Both have a compulsive fixation on their themes. Bellmer expresses a witchlike pansexualism in his drawings; in Oelze's pallid-tone paintings, his fantasy circles around an ogling ground figure from whom issue cloud formations and entire landscapes. Herbert Pée wrote about Bellmer, "His drawings are labyrinths... everything flows. A hell of passions, as with Hieronymus Bosch, a worship of the body combined with lust and horror." And Wieland

Schmied wrote of Oelze in 1964, "With Oelze the forest has gone through many metamorphoses.... At twilight all appearances move so near to each other, the woods seem to come so pressingly close that there is no escape."

The fantastic sculptured surfaces of Bernhard Schultze, discussed earlier (see p. 138), also seem somehow connected with a forest-experience. He calls them *Migof*. Sweetly decaying colors wind through space and are linked to form an impenetrable weave, conjuring up memories of spectral roots from the legendary woods of Nordic prehistory.

Most of the German Surrealists come from the north. *Horst Janssen* (b.1929) and *Paul Wunderlich* (b. 1929) live in Hamburg. Janssen is exclusively a graphic artist. He began with large woodcuts in which space was transposed into a willful linking of planes. In his etchings (since 1958) his themes become more eerie, his invention more grotesque. Everything is first neatly skeletonized in thin strokes which are then drawn together into crinkly light-and-shade areas that are interwoven in a labyrinthine way. Wherever his form-dissolving luminosity does not penetrate, a gnawed face, an animal or human skull shimmers through.

Wunderlich also celebrates a macabre world of death. Transparent bodies are laid on top of vials and retorts so that they seem to be suspended in space, transformed into homunculi and arranged in an almost heraldic fashion. Painting in precious iridescent colors on dark grounds, he achieves an overall effect of clear solemnity. If sometimes Janssen is in danger of a supra-sensibility that could lead to total disintegration, Wunderlich is threatened by an aestheticized posture in his meticulously arranged *mementi mori*.

The borderline between Surrealism and a fantastic style of painting that uses signs and symbols is fluid. Whereas the true Surrealists exist to some extent under the dictatorship of their neurotic fantasies so that their creatures make themselves independent, rather like the sorcerer's apprentice, the symbolists among them connect their signs with a rich association of ideas. In *Rainer Küchenmeister* (b. 1926), who lives in Paris, ideas of root, seed-germ, and shell are joined in a kind of *Keimgestalt* (germinal figure). In his watercolors it appears in delicate linear branches and precious blendings of color; in his oil paintings it is more powerfully abstract and raised to monumental proportions. In *Konrad Klapheck* (b. 1935) some of the discreet object-magicality of *arte metafisica* recurs, applied now mainly to technological subject matter. Appara-

XV Horst Antes, Large Family Picture

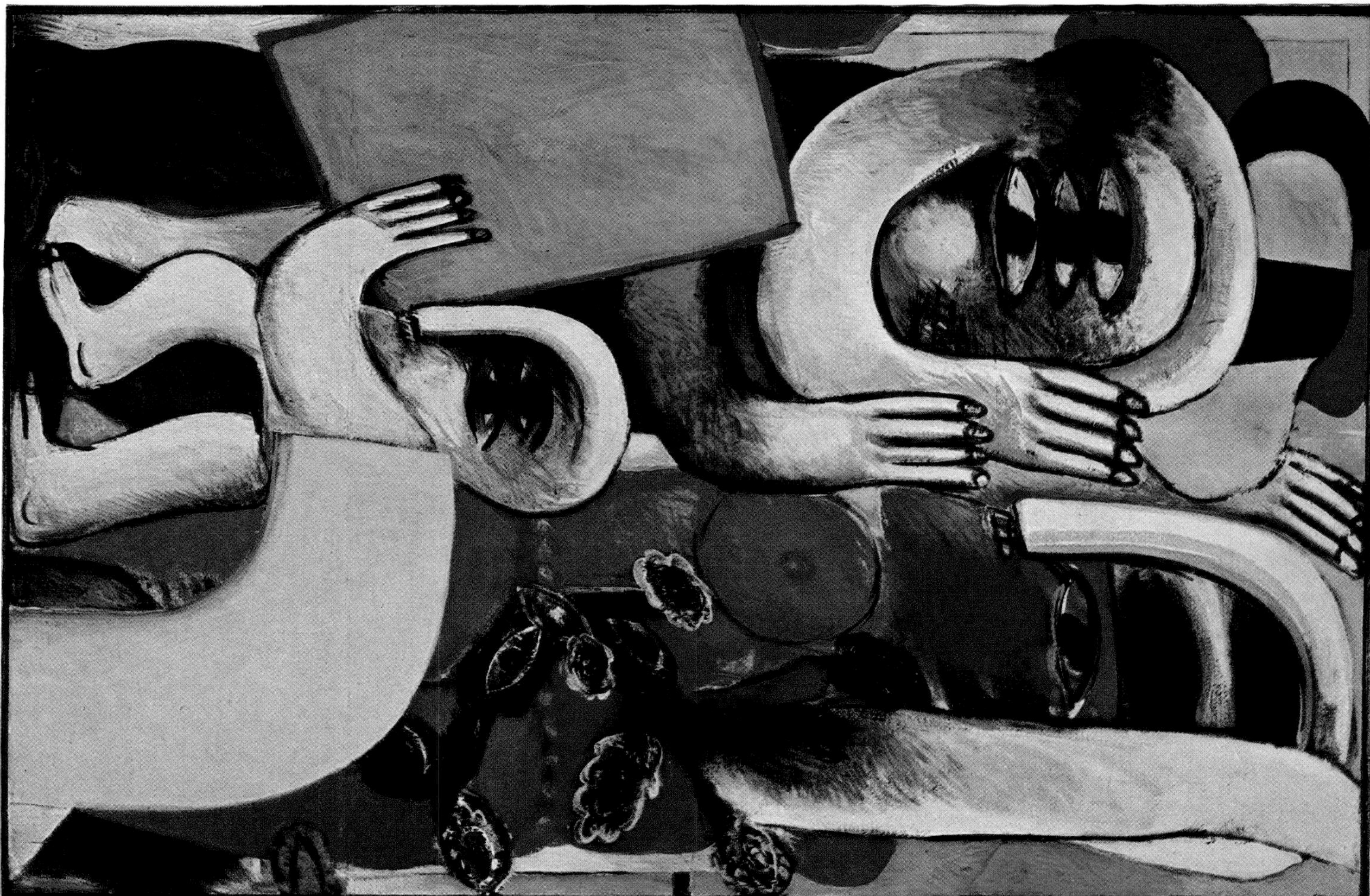

XVI Herbert Schneider, Panopticon, 1967

tuses stand, big and still, in a close format. One senses the invisible powers emanating from them. Suddenly they are personalities with human attributes. The Portuguese *Costa Pinheiro* (b. 1932), who lives in Munich, assembles abstract and objective signs in dreamlike pictorial riddles. Their color refinement is just as persuasive as their formal structure. *Dieter Krieg* (b. 1937) finds his symbols in the sterile perfection of today's hospitals. People, bundled and bound up in white mountains of cushions, surrounded by cold bars or hidden behind towels, die a hygienic, immaculate, clinical death.

Pop, Happenings, and Collage

Pop Art came to Germany relatively late and remained an import for which there was not much demand. A group of artists, gathered around the Grossgörschen Gallery, adopted the "Consumer Style," with its advertising effects and emphasis on sex, often in a highly aggressive, ironic form. The most outstanding of this group seem to be *Hans Jürgen Diehl* (b. 1940) and *Werner Berges* (b. 1941). *Lambert Wintersberger* (b. 1941) of Berlin goes beyond Pop, creating bizarre erotic scenes in which the shock is sweetened by the elegant softness of the color. Others confront Pop elements with expressionist gestures, and create surprise by abrupt changes of style in the same picture. Here we might cite *Uwe Lausen* (b. 1939), who began with a vigorous Abstract Expressionism but was later influenced by the British painter Francis Bacon. A demonic, destructive streak, with convulsively entangled forms, gradually consumed the radiant gaiety of his colors. He subsequently clarified his pictures under the influence of the flat poster style of Pop, but the new pictures, too, are dominated by an oppressive mood.

Sigmar Polke (b. 1941) uses a coarse dot-screen which causes the reality lying beneath to disappear. *Gerhard Richter* (b. 1932) paints fuzzy black-and-white photographs in gigantic format. Here too a diffuse structure alienates reality in a very simple fashion. The simplicity of the procedure is somehow disarming–poetry "off the rack."

Frequently the aim of the Pop artist is to obliterate a reality that has already penetrated the picture, or at least to crowd it back, and this purpose is served by overpainting, tearing, and pasting over. Décollage, on the other hand, is supposed to lay bare something that lies at the bottom. The veil of abstract dreams is torn; behind it, the banality of everyday life becomes visible.

In the case of *Herbert Kaufmann* (b. 1924) the former tendency prevails. In his columnar drums *(Litfaßsäule)*, for example *Hommage à Litfass*, the reality of old advertising kiosks is effective as a dreamlike memory. The whole thing becomes the kaleidoscope of an enticing bygone world. In his décollages *K. H. Hödicke* (b. 1938) strips off advertisements, adding his own painted connecting passages. In his warm colors, crass effects are tranquilized, as if filtered to give aesthetic pleasure. *Wolf Vostell* (b. 1932) is quite different, and his approach is emphatically aggressive. His décollages reveal even when they delete. For the most part we are dealing in his case with scores for Happenings, with a quasi-map of planned events which are corrected by him as he goes along, and also by the Happening itself. Vostell has presented many Happenings in Germany, and made a name for himself in New York with his play, "For dogs and Chinese not allowed," which was presented in the Somethingelse Gallery. The sculptor *Joseph Beuys* became prominent in the Rhineland as a producer of shocking Happenings. That Pop and the Happening are more strongly represented in the Rhineland may be connected with the historic figure of Till Eulenspiegel, as well as with the carnival traditions of that region. *H. P. Alvermann* (b. 1931), also a Rhinelander, combines Pop with a moral involvement. Through shocking found objects which he builds into his pictures, he speaks out against the inertia of the privileged groups.

In contrast, *Peter Klasen* (b. 1935), who lives in Paris, has no intention of shocking anyone with his elegant and urbane collages. He is concerned with "the definition of the individual who has been reduced to the level of a consumer." *Siegfried Neuenhausen* (b. 1931), again a Rhinelander, wants to master artistically the sensational aspects of Pop, its obliteration of the borderlines between reality and illusion, between fanciful and real life. He works with papier maché, which permits him "to remain as amorphous or to become as precise as the work at hand demands." Actually his effects rest for the most part on an ironic substitution of values–a head may be perfectly flat, while a fall of hair is represented wholly three-dimensionally in the foreground.

Whereas Pop has been popular in Germany only since about 1963, everything related in the broadest sense to the "New Abstraction" has enjoyed a longer and more independent tradition. It may be recalled that *Rupprecht Geiger* (see p. 132) was constructing his quiet, colorful walls while the whole world around him was engaged with Tachism. His influence on some members of the young generation is revealed above all in their effort to make color's qualities of light an experience in themselves. Within this trend we can distinguish three different tendencies:

a) Work with unstructured color planes, more often than not in clear contrasts, in which symmetry and decorative harmony are again given an expressive function.

b) A tendency toward monochromy, toward the overevaluation of a single color, which develops a painterly or structural life of its own.

c) Manipulation of lines and the refraction of the surface to achieve instability of form. This may be extended to create a play of real light and motion (Op Art).

Among the painters who follow the first tendency, *Georg Pfahler* (b. 1926), who lives in Stuttgart, has made a name for himself. About 1960 he began to draw colors together to form coordinated blocks, spatially isolated, in an unstable equilibrium but related. Since about 1963 Pfahler has been painting smooth color planes, directly adjoining, across the entire surface. These color areas seem to control autonomously the degree of their expansion, and to keep their balance in suspension, and thereby Pfahler avoids any oscillation of color at the edges. In his case color is not equal to light but an independent quantity. *Bernd Damke* (b. 1939) of Berlin works in a similar style, but his more luminous color areas, which sometimes swell chromatically, create more space. *Gernot Bubenik* (b. 1942) of Berlin connects the life of color planes with forms and formulas taken from seed-germ physiology. Genes and seed-buds are arranged to form burgeoning blossoms. A form-world never used before, culled from medical text books, is here given artistic importance. According to Bubenik, "Where the interest of the scientist stops, my work begins." *Winfried Gaul* (see pp. 136) makes the most of the signaling function inherent in colors. He would like to carry over into the non-utilitarian world of art the accomplishments of our traffic signs. But the bare optic signal alone, with no secret behind it, is quickly exhausted, which is why these superficially sensational objects are closer to Pop Art than to the New Abstraction. *Peter Brüning* (see p. 136) proved that a master of abstract lyricism could also shift to harder colors and technological symbols without losing any of the enigmatic quality of his work. Roads and signs on maps become metaphors of a personal cartography, re-formed into new ciphers for the ancient landscape of the soul.

Werner Schreib (see p. 1925) has turned to using the husks of our consumer world and impresses them as ciphers on a plastic foundation. One might call the results *Tontafeln*, the "clay tablets" of our times–the "accidents" of breakage and rubble are delivered right along with the rest of the record.

Paul Uwe Dreyer (b. 1939) and *Heinz Kreutz* (see p. 288) have revived phases of Constructivism, the former by constructing scaffoldlike supports out of angular elements, the latter by assembling arcs and circles to form a delicate spherical architecture.

Rolf Gunter Dienst (b. 1939), *Jürgen Claus* (b. 1935) and *Arnold Leissler* (b. 1939) are trying to revive the use of ornament. Dienst pulls stripes, filled with so-called logograms, like a scroll across a monochrome surface. Leissler encloses his individual signs with parallel borders that look like neon lights, and Jürgen Claus fills sections of his magical sign-world with symmetrically organized patterns. The ornamental accessory is always brought out of the frame to which it was traditionally confined into the picture where it is transformed into an independent expressive factor.

Monochrome Painting, the second direction followed by some of the younger painters of the New Abstraction, was seen first in an exhibition which Kultermann assembled in 1960 for the museum in Leverkusen. The older *Johannes Gecelli* (b. 1925) used monochromy for objective purposes–with delicate contours a figure took shape out of the independent life of the color. *Bernd Berner* (b. 1930) and *Claus Jürgen-Fischer* (see p. 139) both began with a delicate color weave which created a spatial vibrato that either communicated directly with the color plane surrounding it or was stopped by painted-frame motif. Here the problem of picture and frame is stated anew: a vibration area is the nucleus of an all-inclusive movement which the edge of the picture continues in augmented form, just as sound waves are amplified by a megaphone. *K. H. Graubner* was absorbed by similar problems. *Eduard Micus* (b. 1925) divides his canvases in two, like an open book. The side he keeps empty is pure white, while the other is partially filled with colored stripes. Both sides are given a special stimulus by seams, soft plastic impulses resulting from the material itself.

Lothar Quinte (b. 1923) developed color out of the opposite–shadow. Glazed, painted black stripes become increasingly light toward the center and are suddenly pushed apart by a radiant red. *Reiner Jochims* (b. 1935) sees color as light in space. He too gathers light out of deepening shadows, which change softly but constantly, with many coats of glaze, so that his pictures are not much lighter than the cloudy sky in winter that borrows its light from the reflection of the snow. *Raimund Girke* (b. 1930) used to paint pure, delicately structured white areas. His latest works, however, toy more strongly with the mobile effects of optical illusion.

In our third group we are dealing with Op Art only in a limited sense. Almost all the artists under this heading start with the premise that light and color may change any given form without motion necessarily taking place. One might say that the triumph of light over static form has been reached. In 1958 ZERO was founded, a periodical published in Düsseldorf by Otto Piene and Heinz Mack, who were joined in 1961 by Günther Uecker. The Frenchman Yves Klein was working in the Rhineland at the time. Together they dreamed of breathtaking Happenings, for instance of sculpture made of "air, water, ice, and fire, that would be in a state of constant flux." In the ZERO program one read, "ZERO is silence. ZERO is the beginning... the sky is above ZERO. The night–the eye–silently." Here a longing for quiet and contemplation is revealed which undoubtedly is linked to the tradition of German romanticism.

Otto Piene (b. 1928) lets the sensation of light and dark take place through light itself. In smoke pictures and fire-gouaches, something of the generative process of light actually is precipitated. In the finest gradations and dispersions, luminosity is created, to all appearances out of itself. To achieve this effect Piene proceeds from a dark or light focus which radiates toward the edges, thus repeating in an artistic experiment something that takes place in the cosmos all the time. He has also created a "Light Ballet" in which he sends rays through perforated, rotating sheets of metalfoil. *Heinz Mack* (b. 1931) works with pleated aluminium foil which reflects the light like lightning. Through its own rotations, or through the motion of the observer, a constant fluctuation of light and shade is created which may be rhythmically manipulated. Mack dreams of gigantic reflector walls in the desert or on the sea that could magnify his play of light to cosmic proportions.

Günther Uecker (b. 1930) creates a play of light and shade through a forest of white nails on a white ground. At first he placed his columns of nails in strict, orderly rows; later he let them undulate slightly on a colored foundation. The white structures are made to oscillate by a change of lighting, without making a move of their own. *Hans Albert Walter* (b. 1925) transforms effects taken from Piene's Light Ballet into a skillful light-and-shade painting.

Another group, residing in south Germany, is working with related problems. They achieve kinetic effects primarily by interfering with a given order through black-and-white or colored elements. Symmetrical surface patterns force the eye to see dominant arrangements, which, however, do not remain stable. This results in an illusory, jerky motion which may also be achieved with color. (The phenomenon of the after-image in the eye.) *Klaus Staudt* (b. 1932), *Rudolf Kämmer* (b. 1935) and *Roland Helmer* (b. 1940) are experimenting in this direction. *Ludwig Wilding* (b. 1927) creates net structures which artfully overlap, so that manifold perspective illusions are created. He carries these effects over into the third dimension by shifting a transparent, striped pattern in front of another lying behind (screen effect). *Gerhard von Graevenitz* transfers the principle of instability to mechanically mobile equipment. In contrast to other kineticists, his constructions are extremely simple; the almost magical effect is therefore all the more surprising. In this connection we must also mention *Uli Pohl* (b. 1935) who succeeded in creating the first actual light-sculpture. Whereas most other sculptors use reflected light to dematerialize form, Pohl hit upon the lens effect of cut glass to create illusory forms of light. He bores through a cube of glass, forming an arched hole. This creates, in effect, a lens that produces an image of an enlarged and changeable light form within the glass block.

This severe form of Op Art, which is not concerned primarily with sensations of movement but rather with silent, meditative effects, is very German. Here stimuli of Albers and Moholy have been revived in a different form.

CONCLUSION

The reflections which summarize Franz Roh's review of painting in the twentieth century have lost none of their validity in the past decade. On the contrary, since the recent revival of a new representational style and a refreshed interest in kinetic art, they are more timely than ever. That is why I would like to end with his conclusion from the earlier edition of this book:

To sum up, let it be said that it is not a sign of degeneration if today we find objective and nonobjective art existing side by side, since both satisfy different sectors of our being. The one will never be able to completely replace the other because point of departure and goal are so different. But hybridizations are possible, as is proved, for instance, by the late development of Max Ernst. In abstract painting we enjoy the fact that formal design or a construction in color has at last been freed of any specific relationship to a particular object. The result is that we experience a nonspecific pictorial organization without association or reference beyond itself, just as we experience it in music. In objective painting we are moved, contrarily, by constant reference to the representational world, and enjoy the interpretations and transformations undertaken by the painter. It should be possible for every richly endowed human being to be stimulated by both types of painting instead of bemoaning the fact, as many people do lately, that we are suffering from an impossible multiplicity of the arts.

A comparative investigation should one day be undertaken into this plurality, which various epochs have experienced, for we are being deceived by misleading effects of the perspective of time. When we look down an avenue of poplars, the trees farthest away seem to be closer to each other. Similarly we tend to see the past as more cohesive, the present in which we live as more disintegrated.

Because of the impetus toward motion which has also gripped the latest development of German painting, a big question looms on our horizon, one that was asked by Moholy as long as thirty years ago: Will this frenzy of motion, as captured in the single picture, perhaps be resolved in favor of the abstract film, in the actual motion of a colored play of lights, and like absolute music demand a passage of time? With such an eventuality painting need not entirely lose its specific meaning. The significance of the easel picture would still lie in its traditional ability to arrest and preserve dynamic form.

1 Max Liebermann, Huis ter Duin, 1913

2 Max Slevogt, Village near Höhenreit, 1913

3 Lovis Corinth, Still Life with Melon, 1921

4 Paula Modersohn-Becker,
Birch Trees, c. 1902

5 Christian Rohlfs, Hyacinths, 1925

6 Emil Nolde, The Family, 1931

7 Karl Schmidt-Rottluff, Rising Moon, 1956

8 Ernst Ludwig Kirchner, Berlin Street Scene, c. 1912

9 Max Pechstein Canoe, 1917

10 Erich Heckel, Girls by the Bay, 1924

11 Otto Mueller, Nudes, 1926

12 Heinrich Nauen, Bathers, 1913. Kaiser Wilhelm Museum, Krefeld

13 Wilhelm Morgner, The Entry into Jerusalem, 1912

14 Gabriele Münter, Flowers before a Moonlight Painting, 1939

15 Alexei von Jawlensky, Sicilian Woman, 1913

16 Marianne von Werefkin
The Boat, c. 1910

17 Wladimir von Bechtejeff,
Diana Hunting, c. 1910.
Bayerische Staatsgemälde-
sammlungen, Munich

18 Heinrich Campendonk, Cow Stable, 1917. Collection Fischer, Düsseldorf

19 Paul Klee, Around the Fish, 1926. The Museum of Modern Art, New York

20 Wassily Kandinsky, Reciprocal Conformity, 1942. Collection Nina Kandinsky, Paris

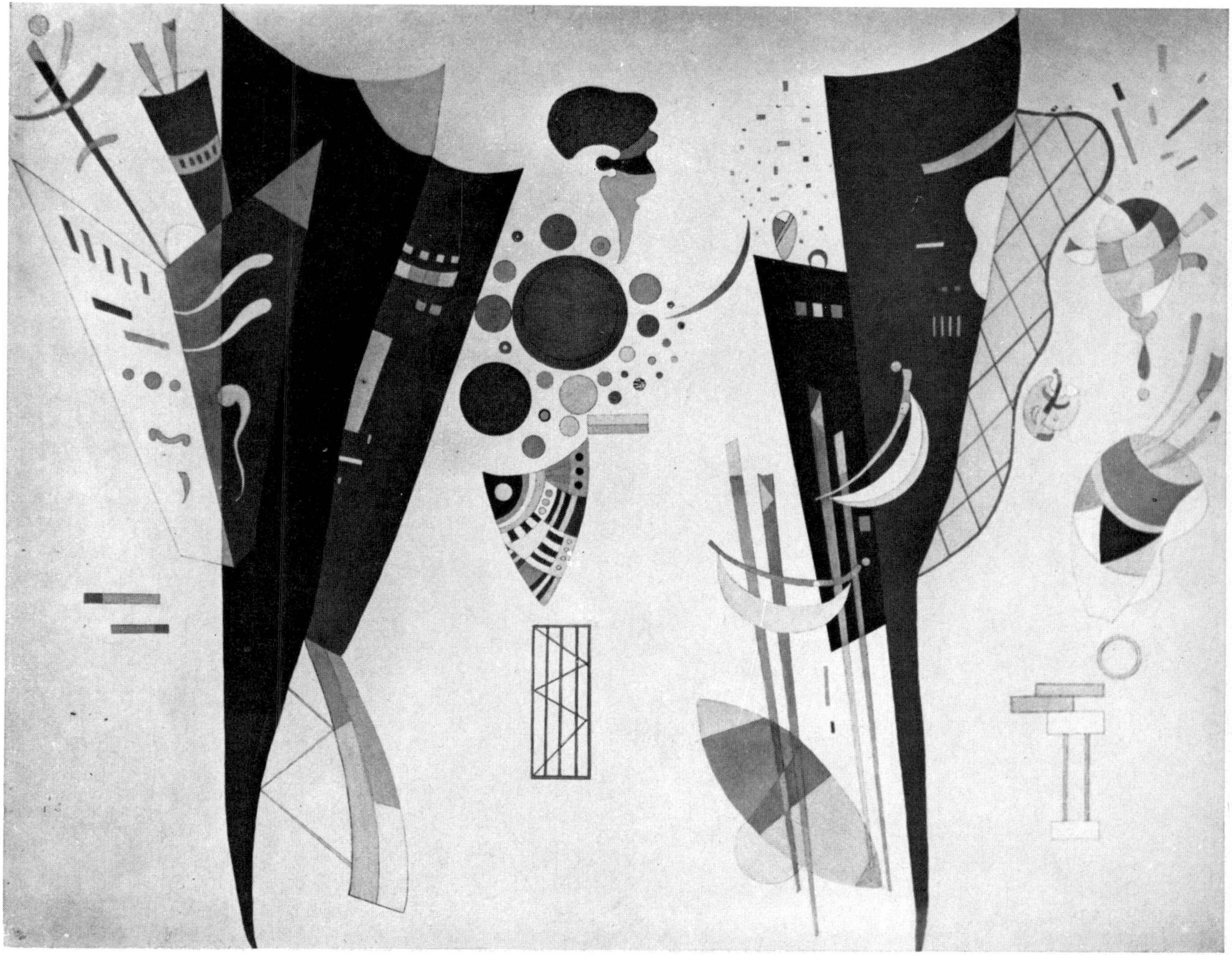

21 Oskar Schlemmer, Fifteen-group, 1929

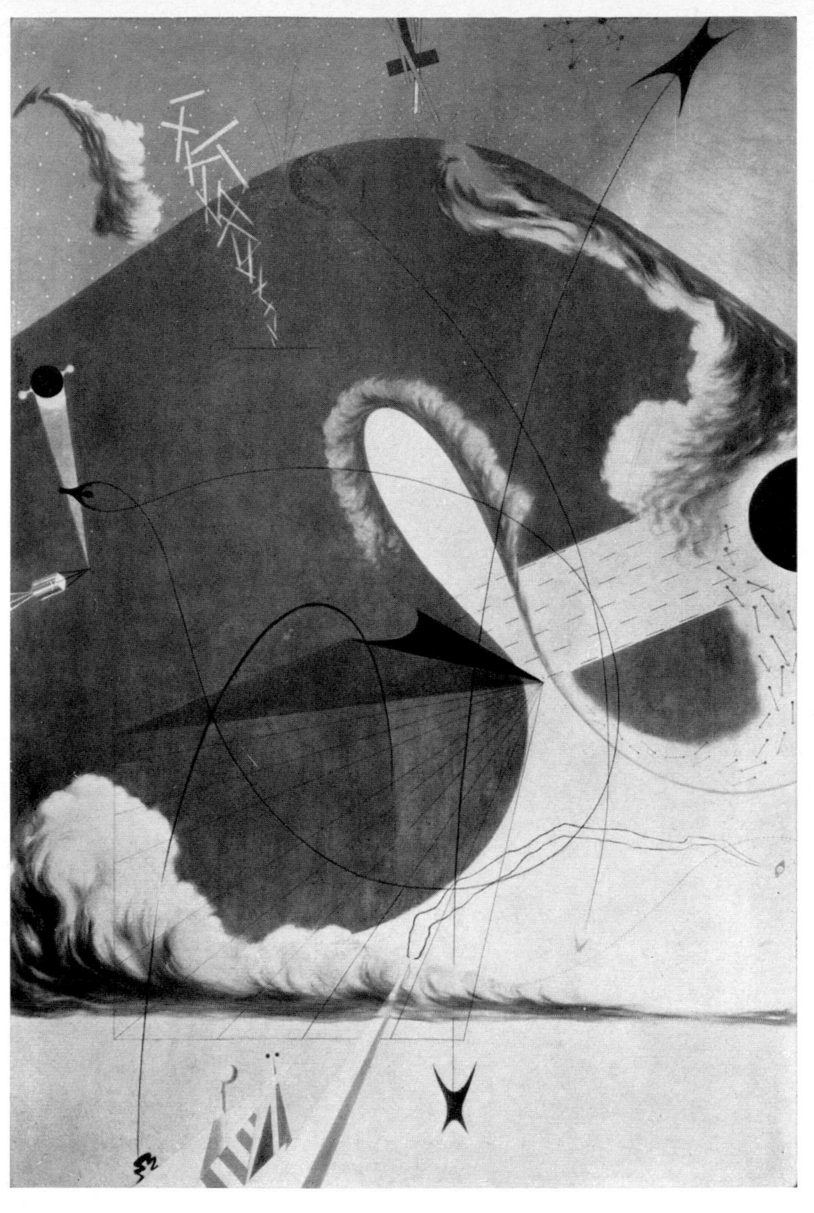

22 Herbert Bayer, Events in the Atmosphere, 1941. Collection Stendahl, Hollywood

23 Lyonel Feininger, Church, 1936. The Metropolitan Museum of Art, New York

24 Georg Muche, Flower Thirsting, 1954

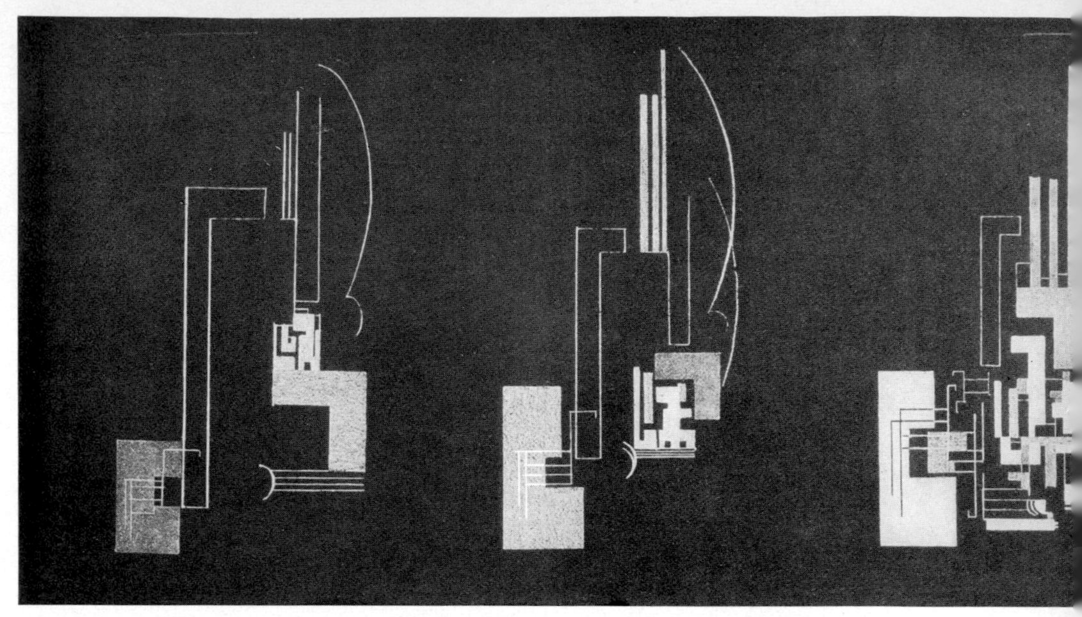

26 Josef Albers, City, 1928

25 Hans Richter, Detail of "Prelude," 1919

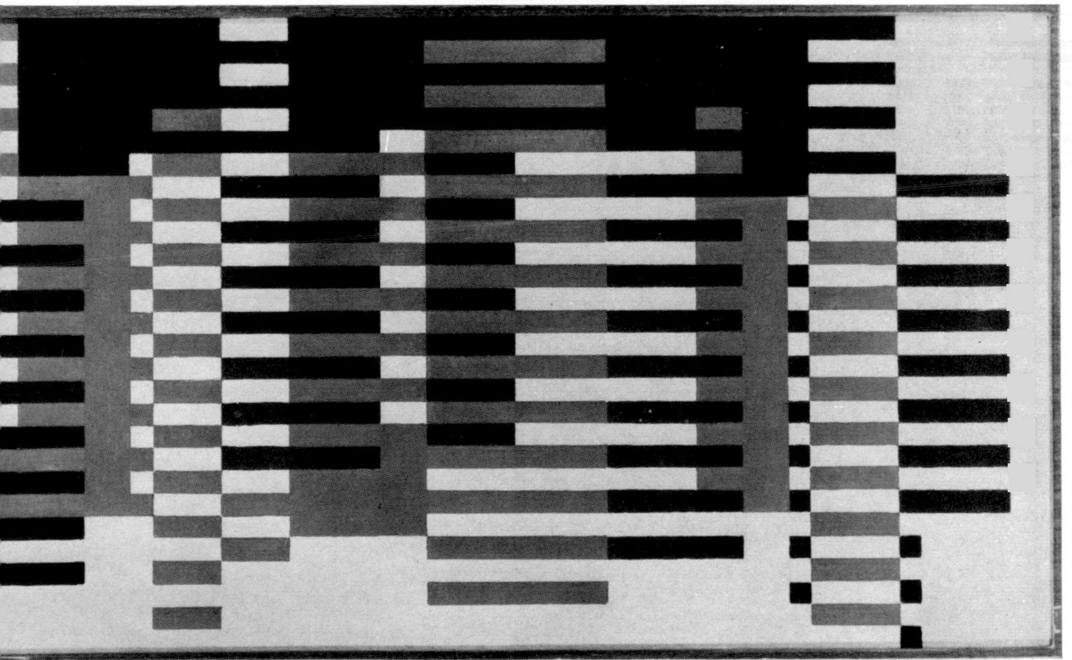

27 Ladislaus Moholy-Nagy, Z VIII, 1924

28 Max Bill, Undefined and Defined, 1947

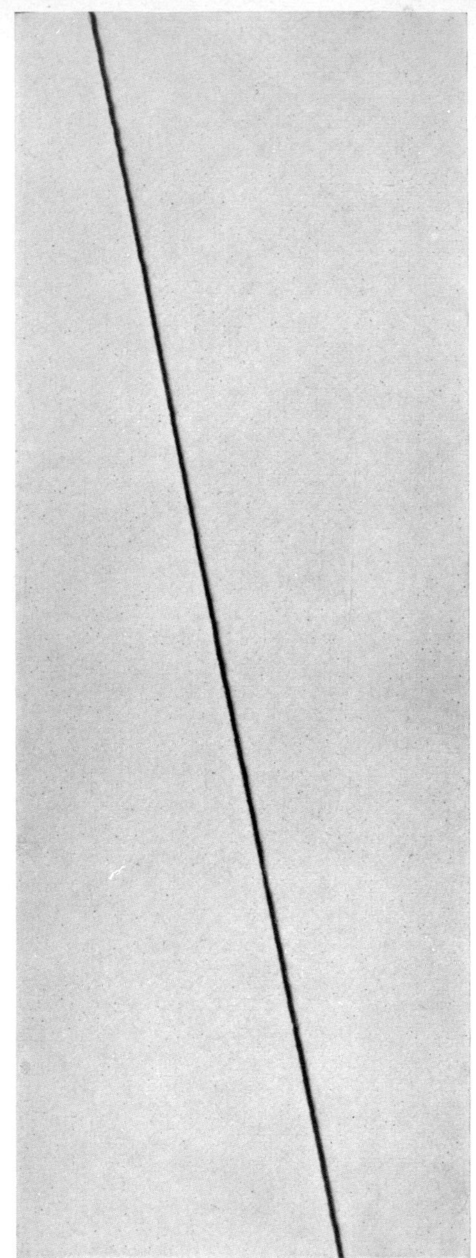

29 Friedrich Vordemberge-Gildewart, Compositions, 1948

30 Johannes Itten, Relief, 1919

31 Georg Schrimpf, Still Life, 1923

32 Alexander Kanoldt, Hoarfrost, 1921

33 George Grosz, Chamber of Horrors, 1920

34 Otto Dix, Match-seller, 1920. Staatsgalerie, Stuttgart

35 Walter Spiess, Farewell, 1921

36 Friedrich Schröder-Sonnenstern, from "Creatures," 1953

37 Raoul Hausmann, Photomontage, 1921–1924

38 Kurt Schwitters, Picture, 1921. Collection Tschichold, Basel

39 Max Ernst, Oedipus Rex, 1921

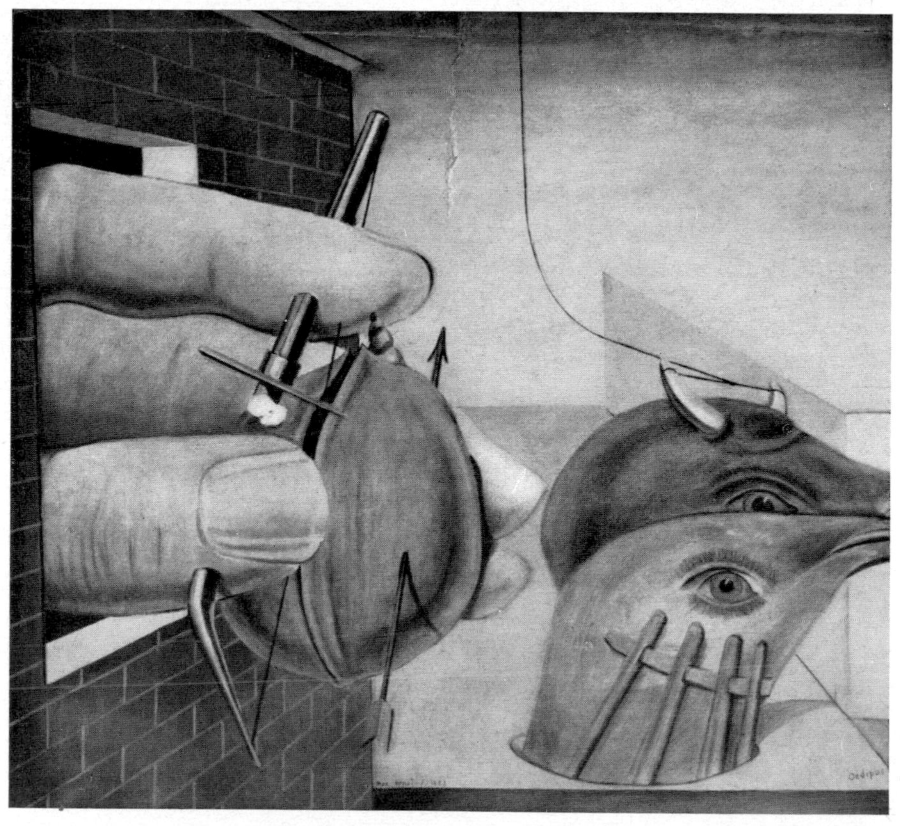

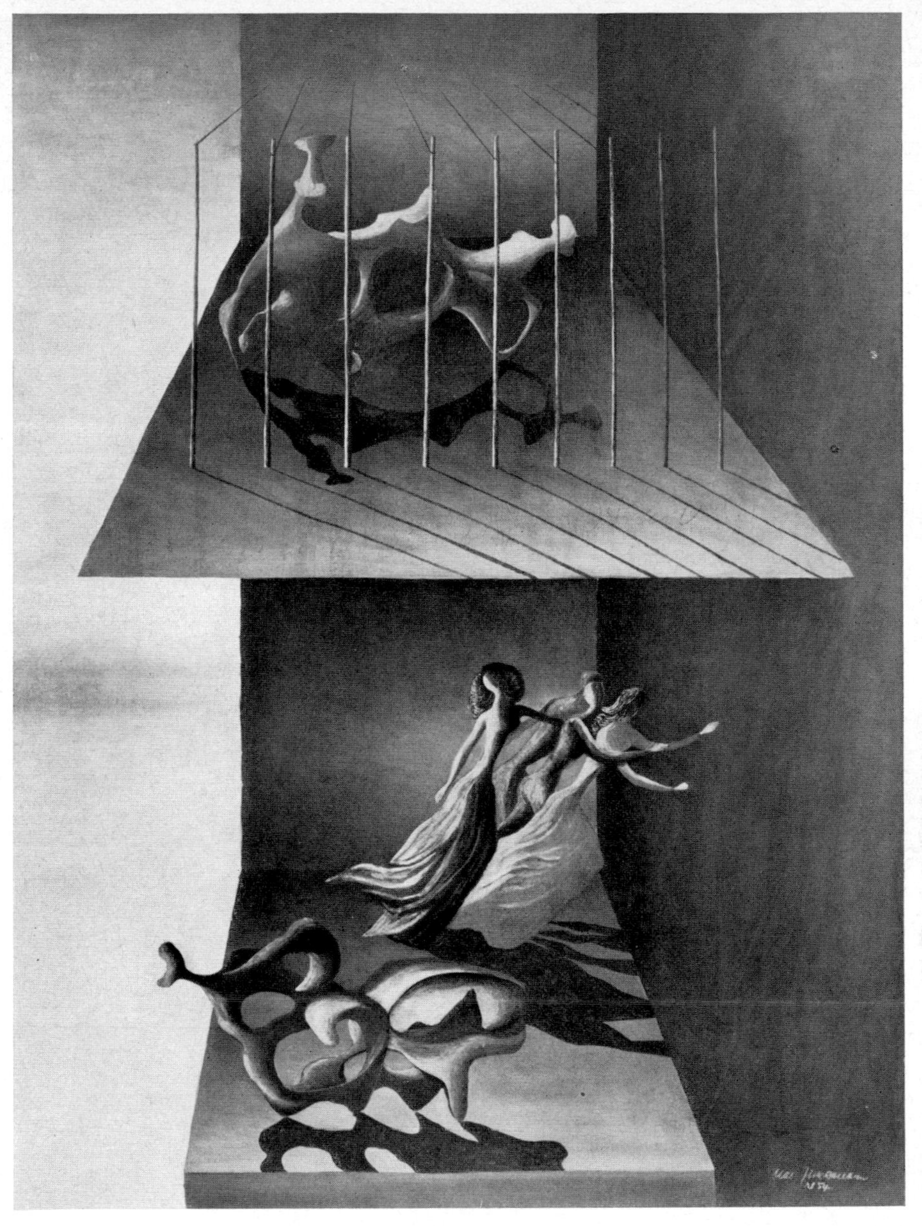

40 Mac Zimmermann, In Two Stages, 1954

41 Johannes Molzahn, New York, from Triptych III, 1946

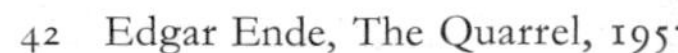

42 Edgar Ende, The Quarrel, 1957

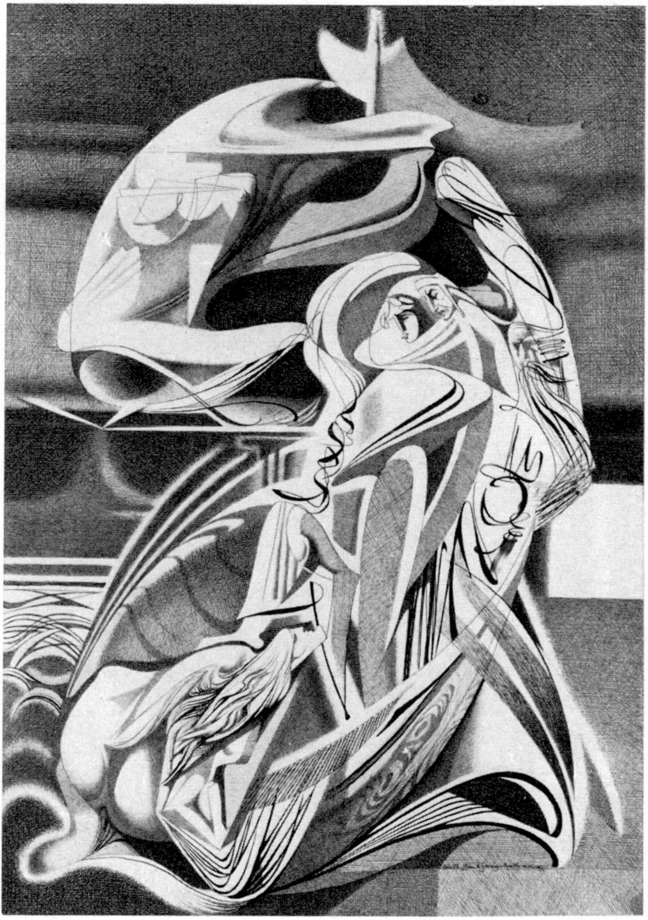

43 Karl Kunz, Dante's Inferno, Canto 8, 1955

44 Oskar Kokoschka, Portrait of L.B., 1959

45 Max Beckmann, Perseus Triptych, 1941 (detail)

46 Carl Hofer, Model with Fruitbasket, 1928

47 Jankel Adler, Old Man Reclining, 1925

48 Xaver Fuhr, Tree by the Harbor

49 Helmut Kolle, Large Still Life, c. 1920

50 Oskar Moll, Winter Window, 1935

51 Rolf Nesch, Trumpeter, 1934/35

52 Hans Purrmann, Italian Landscape

53 Karl Caspar, The Entry into Jerusalem, 1947

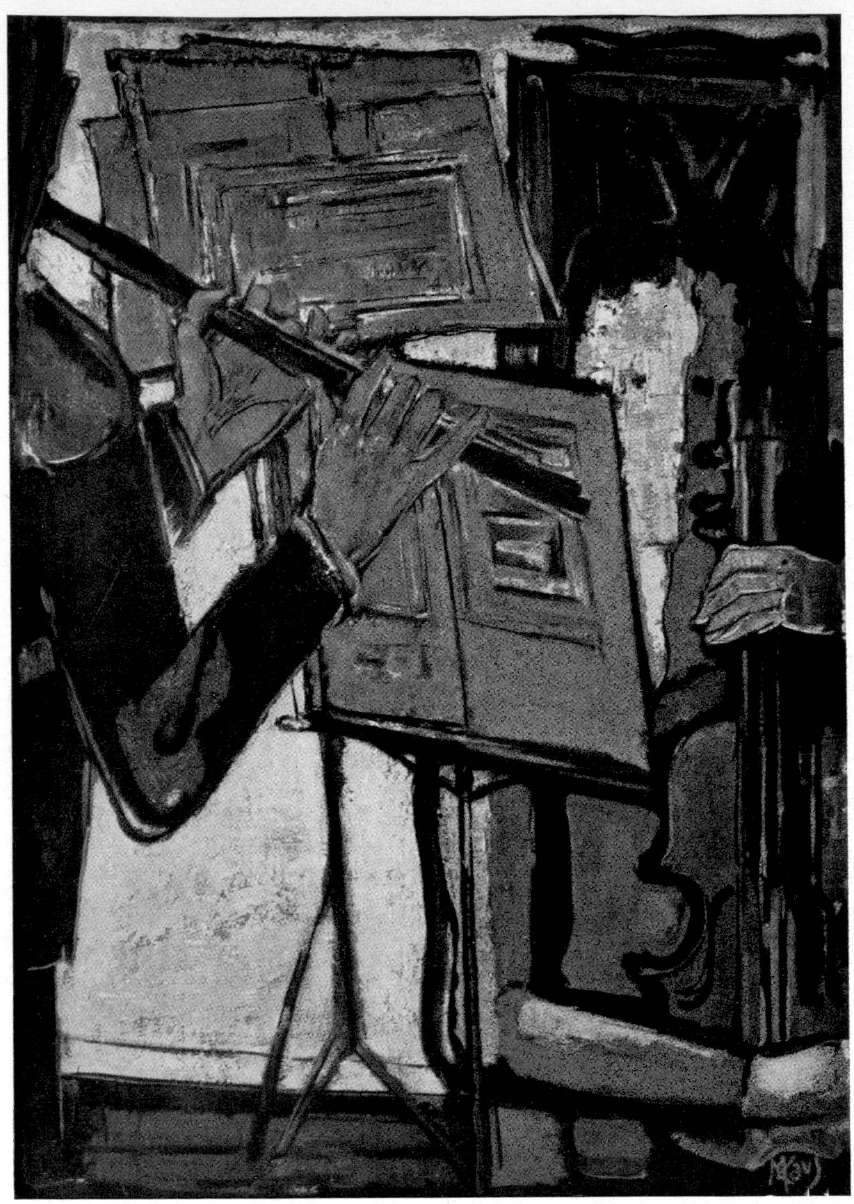

54 Max Kaus, Duet, 1955

55 Eberhard Schlotter, Still Life, 1958

56 Hans Reichel, Composition, 1953

57 Alexander Camaro, Autumn Angel, c. 1954

58 Theodor Werner, Mural, Musikhochschule, Berlin, 1954

59 Curt Lahs, Upper and Lower Field, 1951

60 Friedrich Karl Gotsch, Studio Interior, 1957

61 Fritz Kronenberg, Ana, 1955

62 Walter Becker, Street Picture, 1957

63 Peter Herkenrath, Space I, 1958

64 Willi Baumeister, Figure in Movement, 1936/37

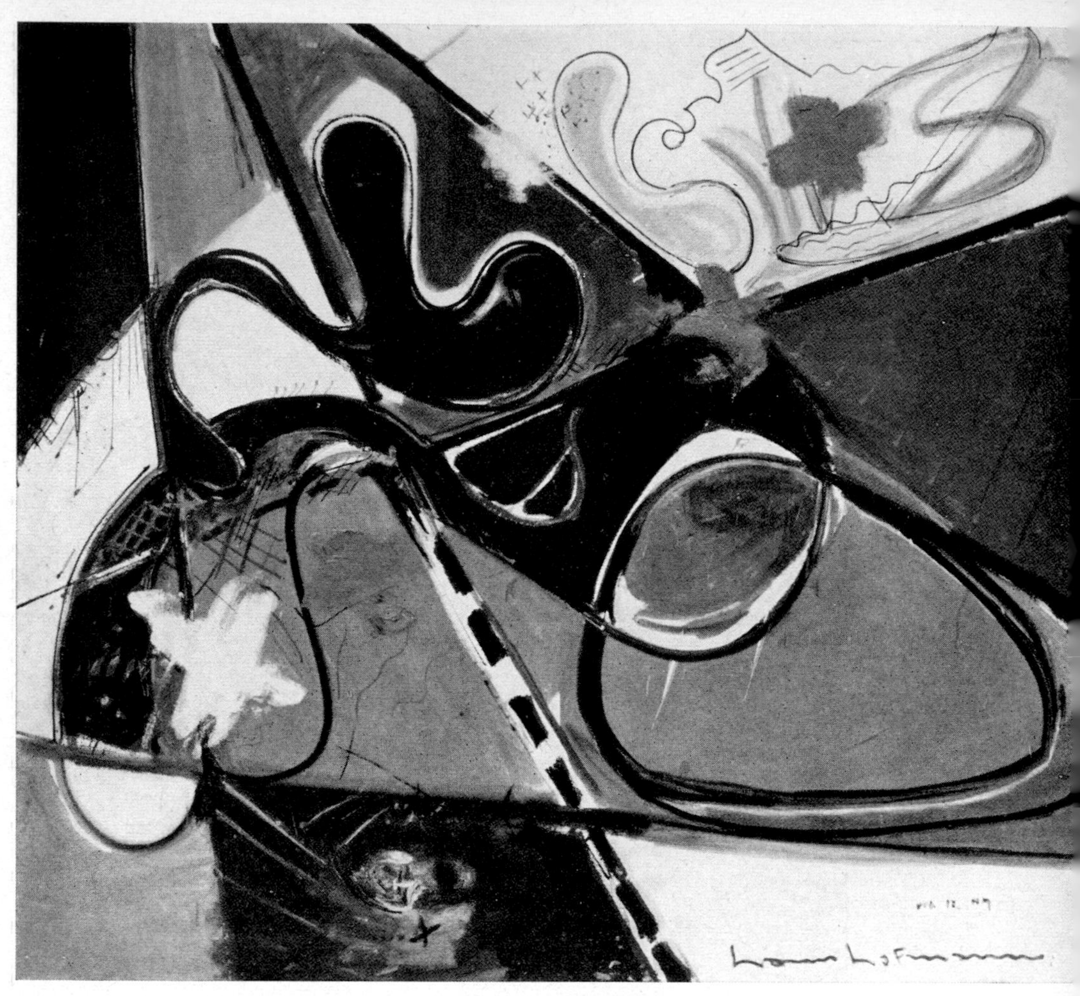

65 Hans Hofmann, Flooded, 1947

66 Otto Ritschl, Composition, 1959

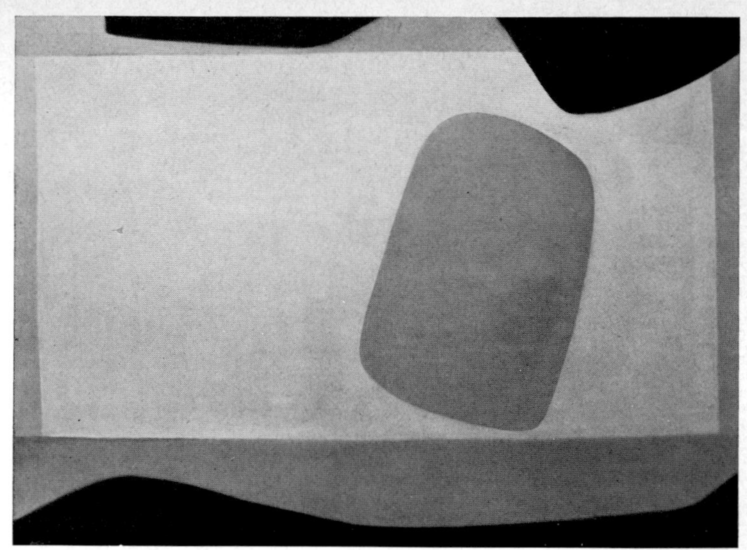

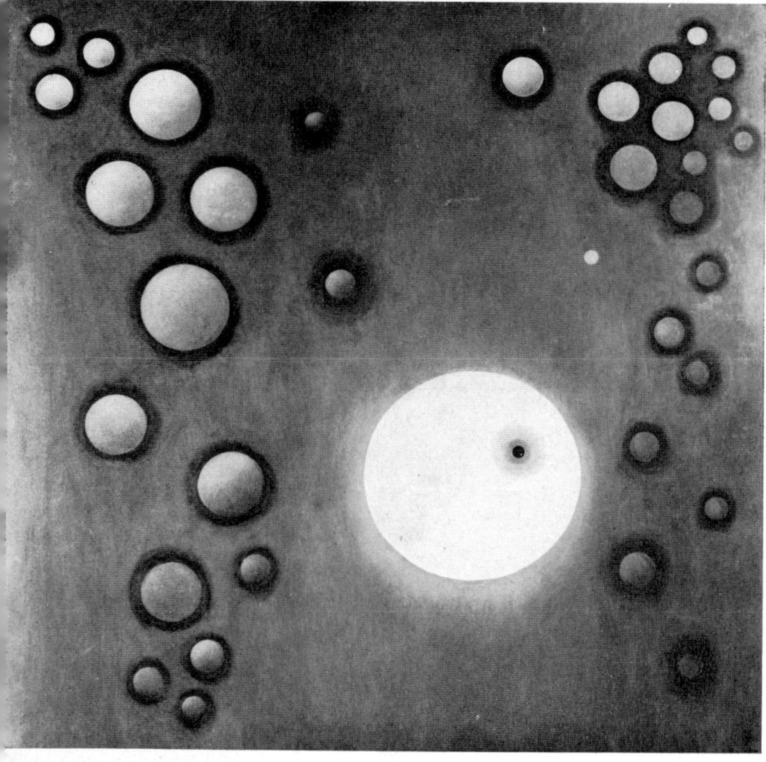

67 Rudolf Bauer, Blue Balls 1934

68 Hilla von Rebay, Leggiero, 1946

69 Joachim Albrecht, Composition, 1957

Günter Frühtrunk, Composition, 1955

71 Wols, Composition in Blue, 1951

72 Fritz Winter, Picture, 1960

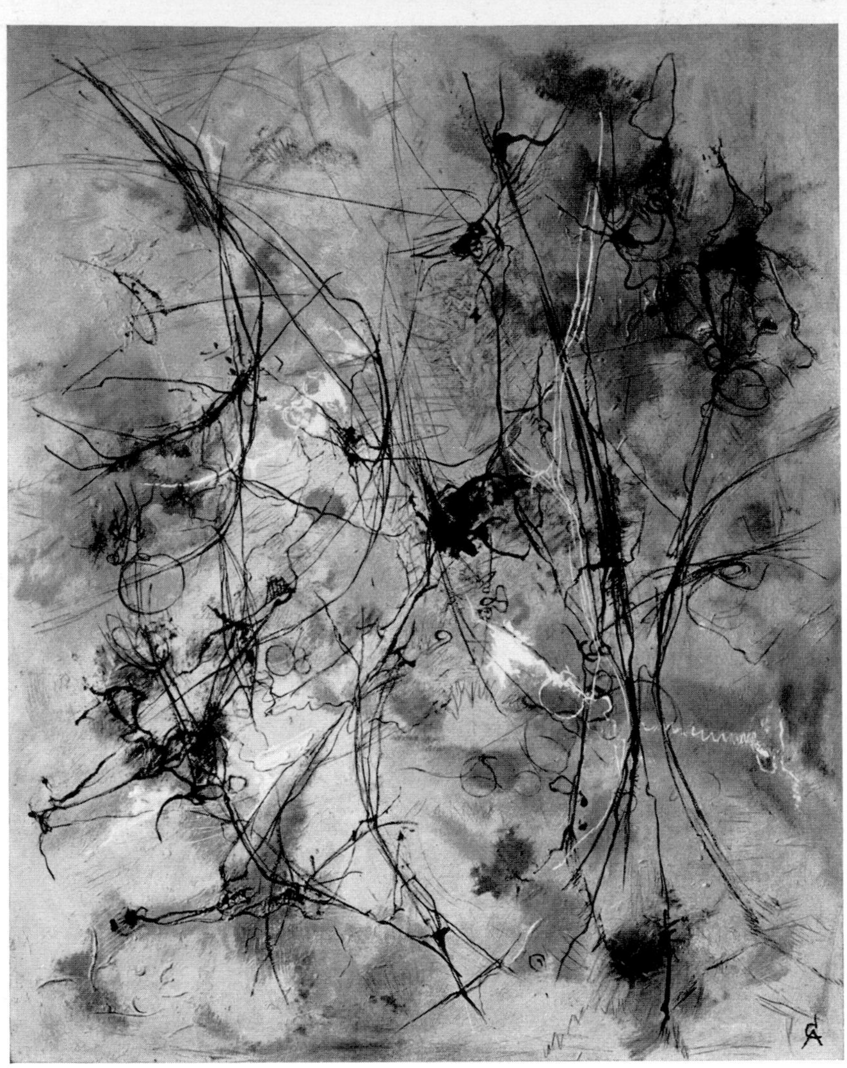

73 Rolf Cavael, F 9, 1958

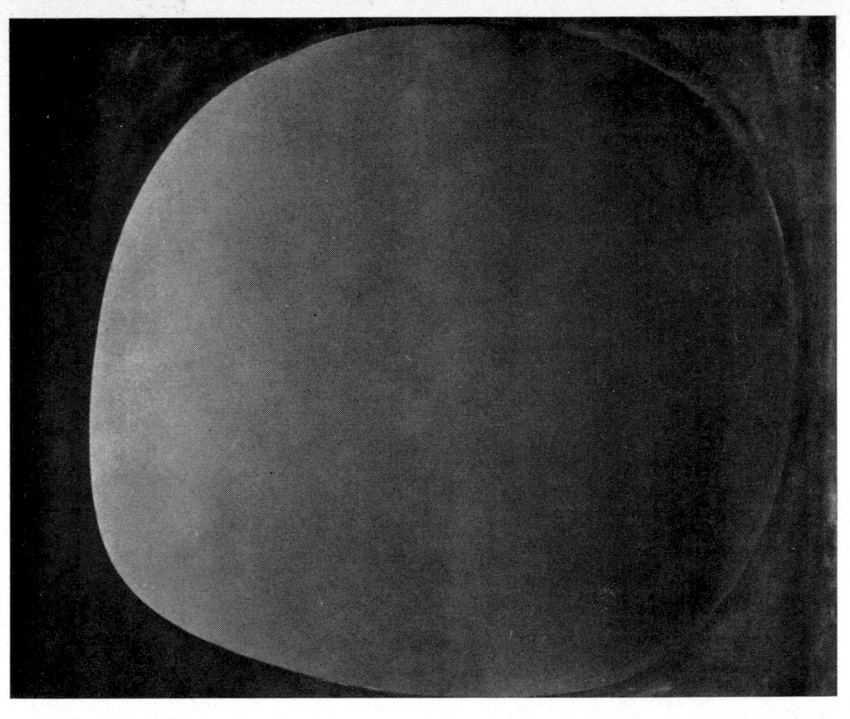

74 Rupprecht Geiger, 321/61, Blue Circle

75 Hans Platschek, Bardamu, 1961

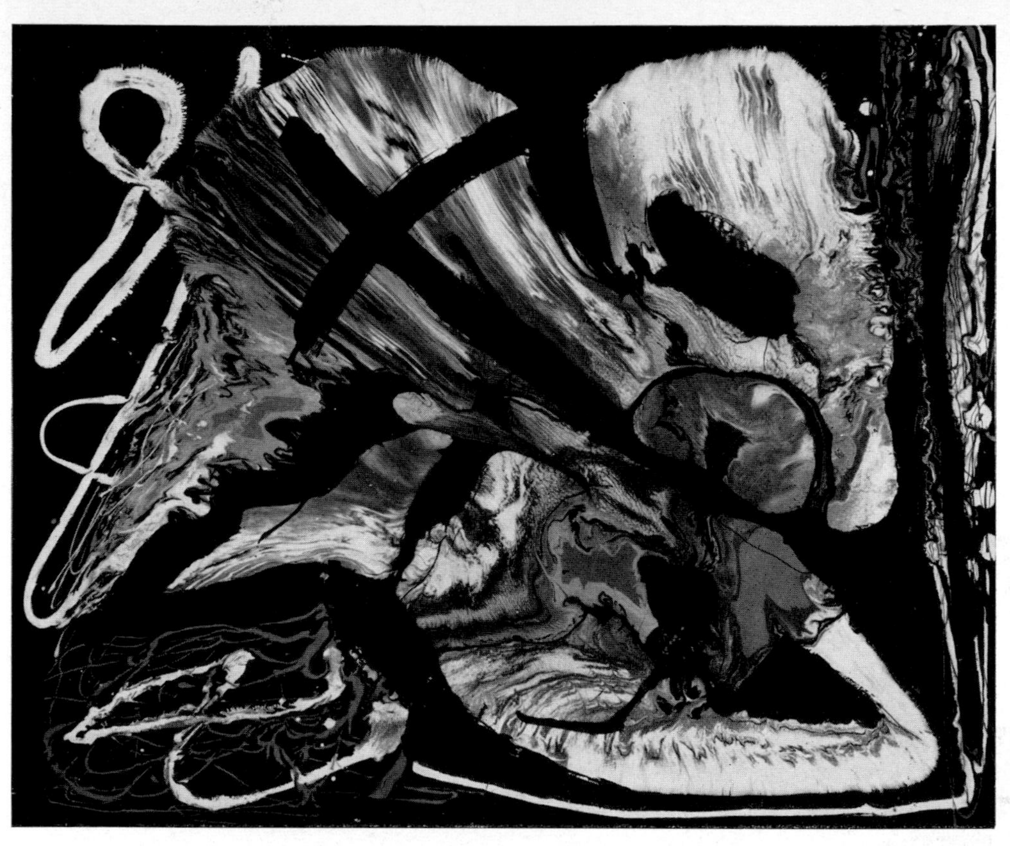

76 Hans Kuhn, Enamel Painting, 1957

77 K. R. H. Sonderborg, 3. XI. 1954

78 Ernst Wilhelm Nay, Picture, 1959

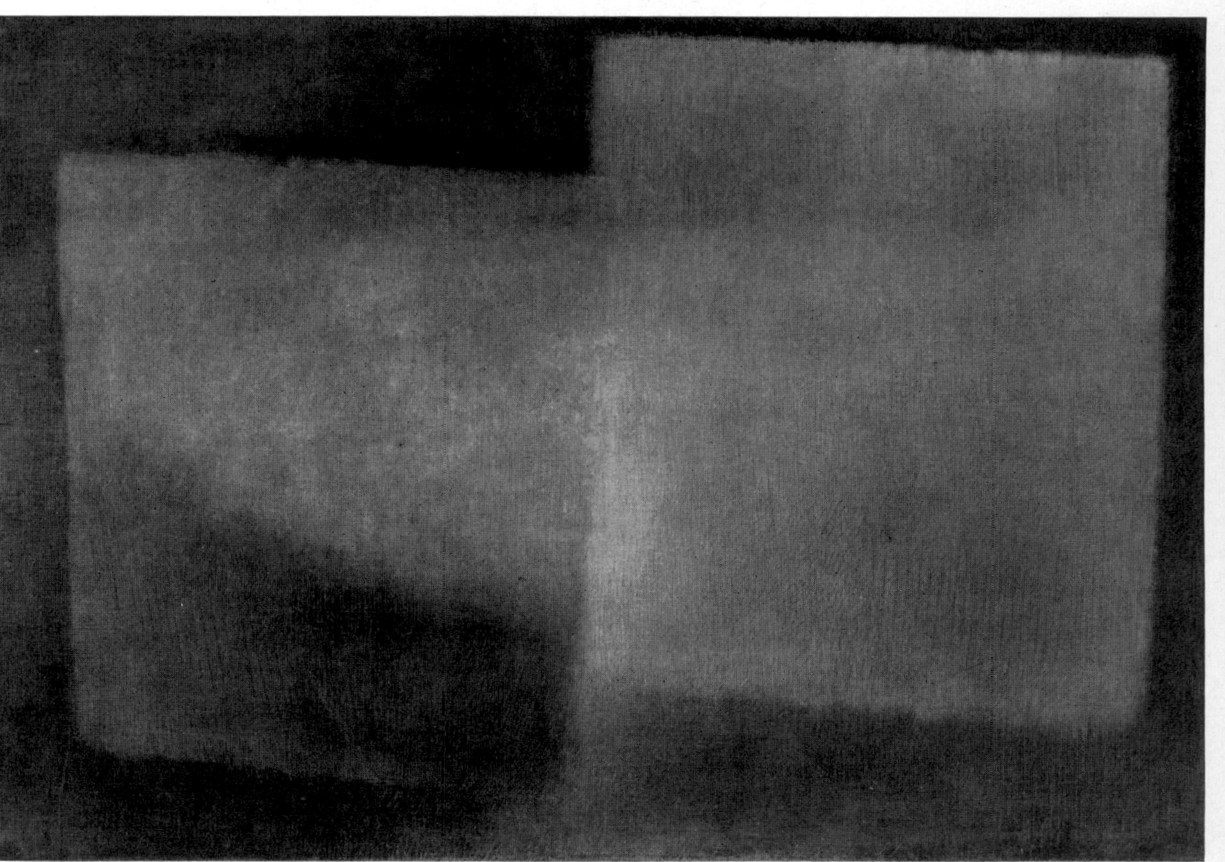

79 Georg Meistermann, Before Blue, 1959

80 Hann Trier, Gordian Knot, 1957

81 Josef Fassbender, Mural, Arndt Gymnasium, Bonn, 1954

82 Karl Buchheister, Composition Wu, 1956

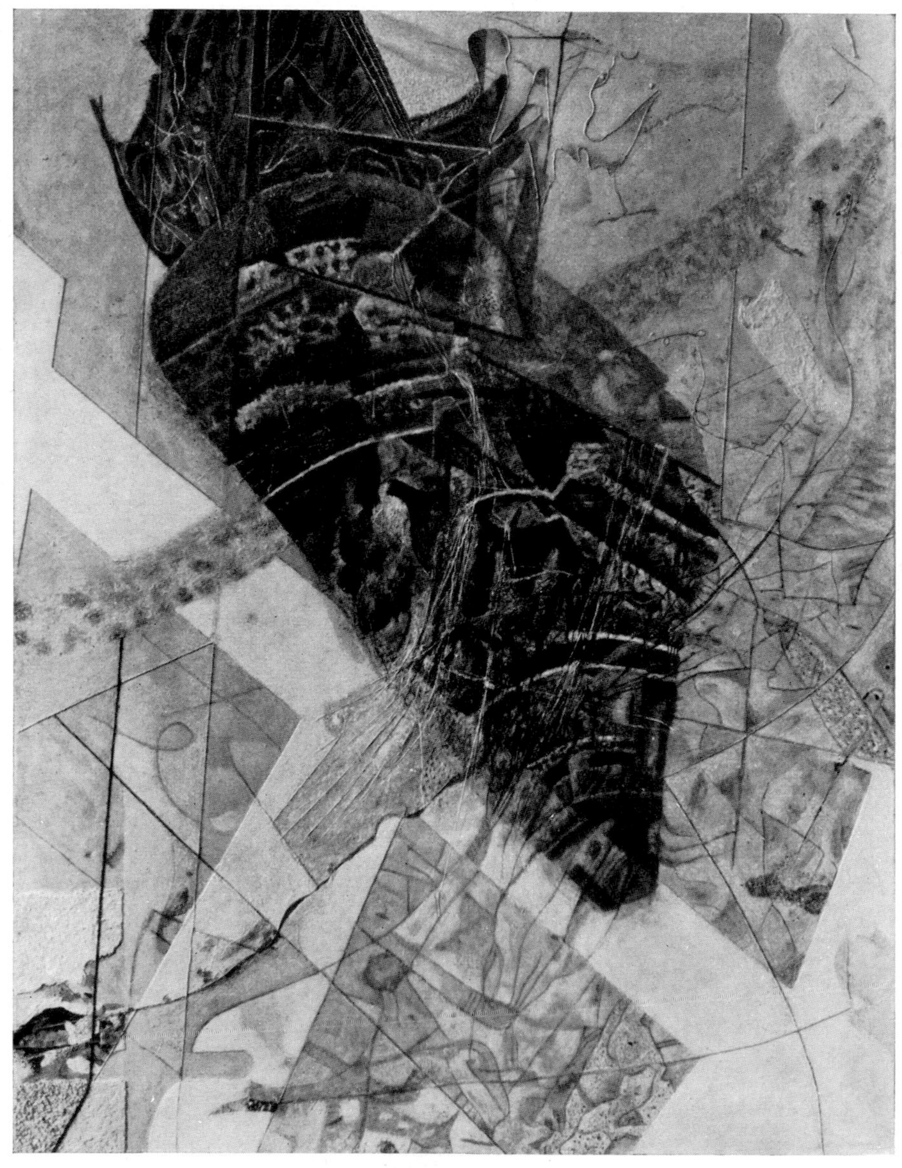

83 Gerhard Hoehme, Painting, 1957

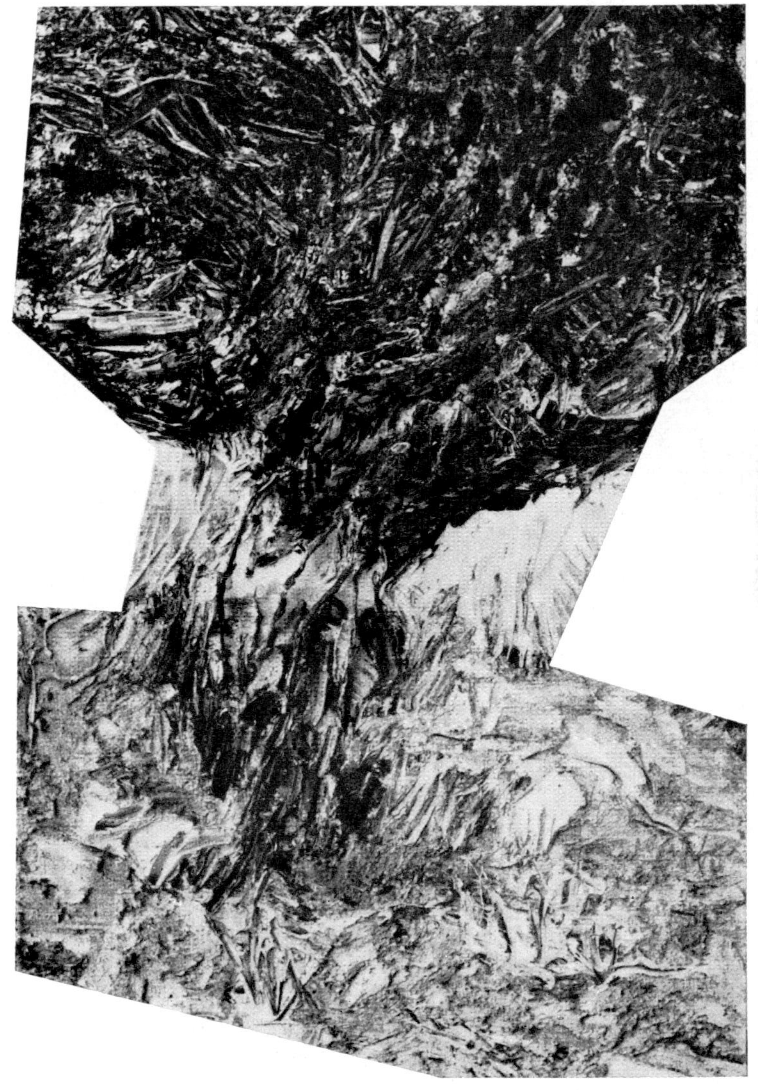

84 Emil Schumacher, Xerxes, 1960

85 Wilhelm Wessel, Relic in White, 1957

86 K. O. Götz, Gouache, 1956

87 Bernhard Schultze, Irradiated, 1957

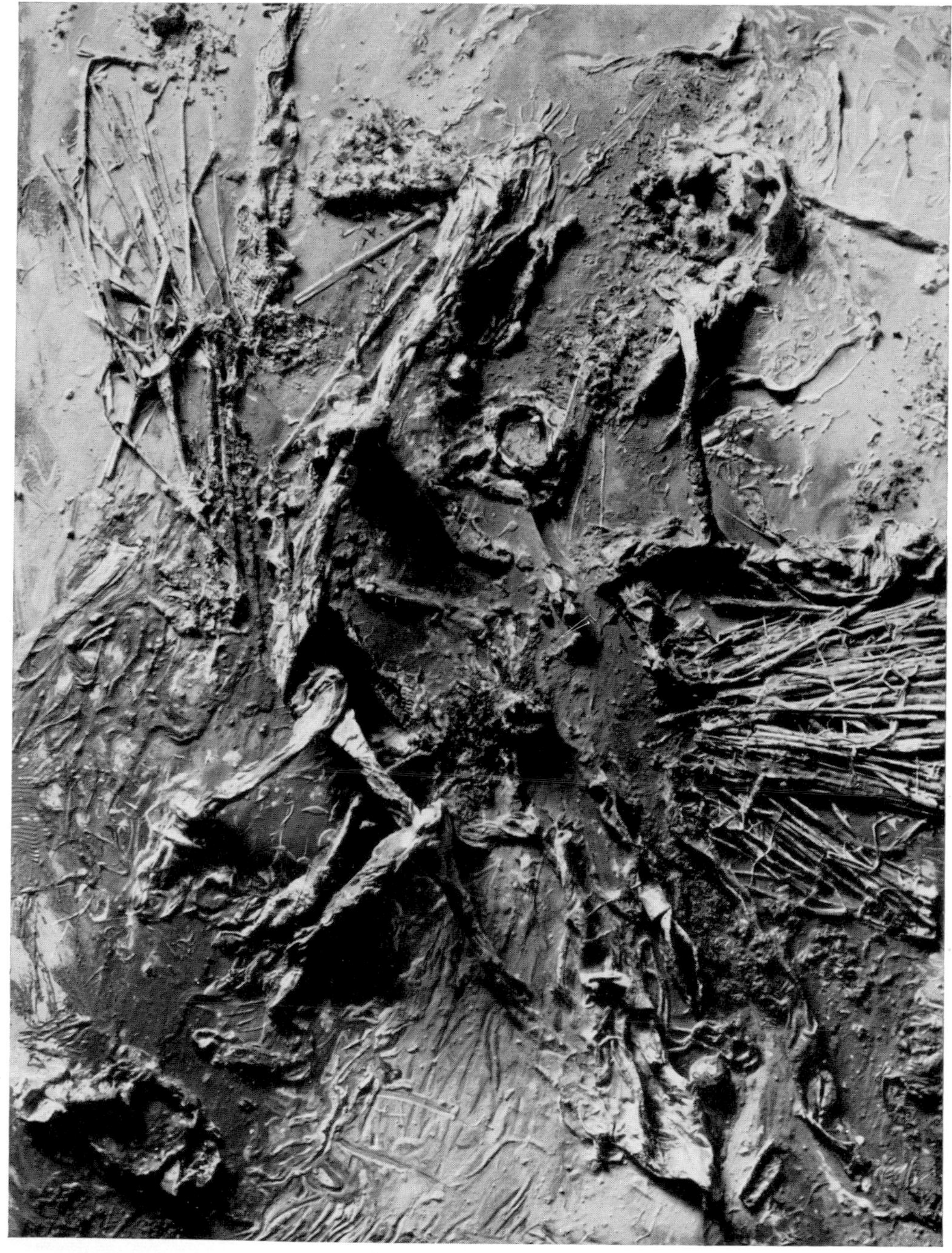

88 Max Ackermann, Original Cell, 1952

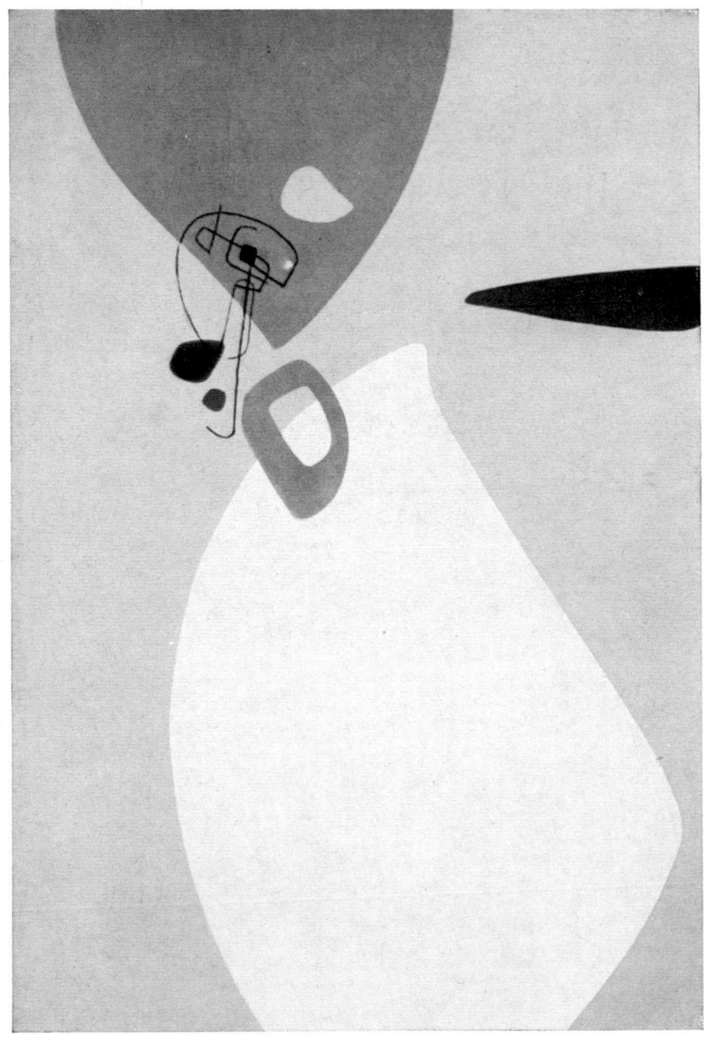

89 Julius Bissier, Arbogast, 1959

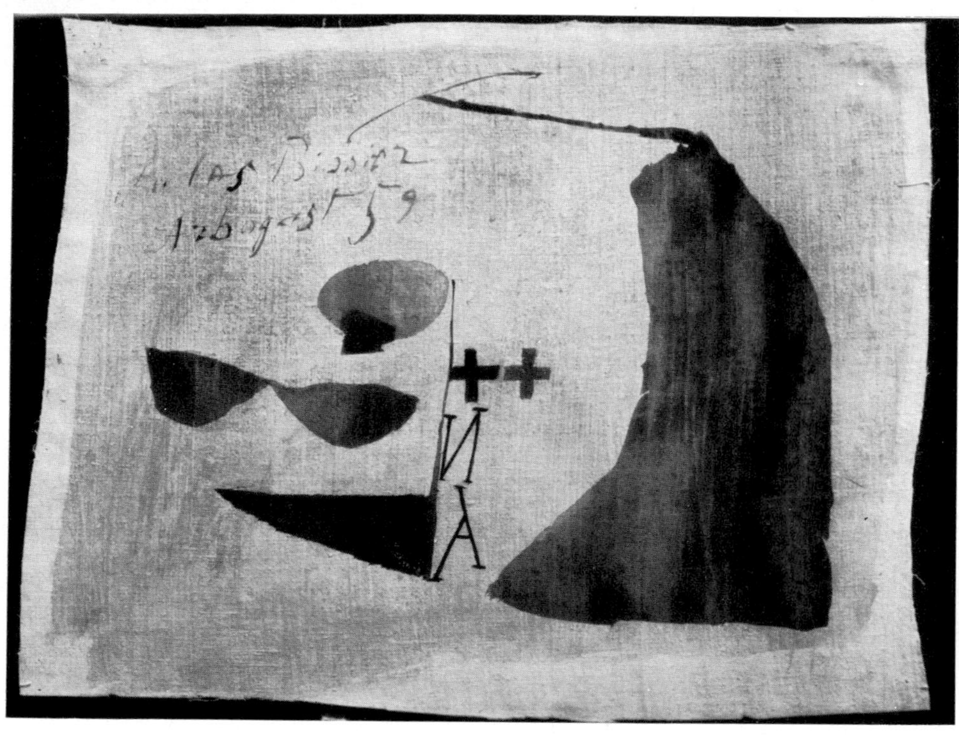

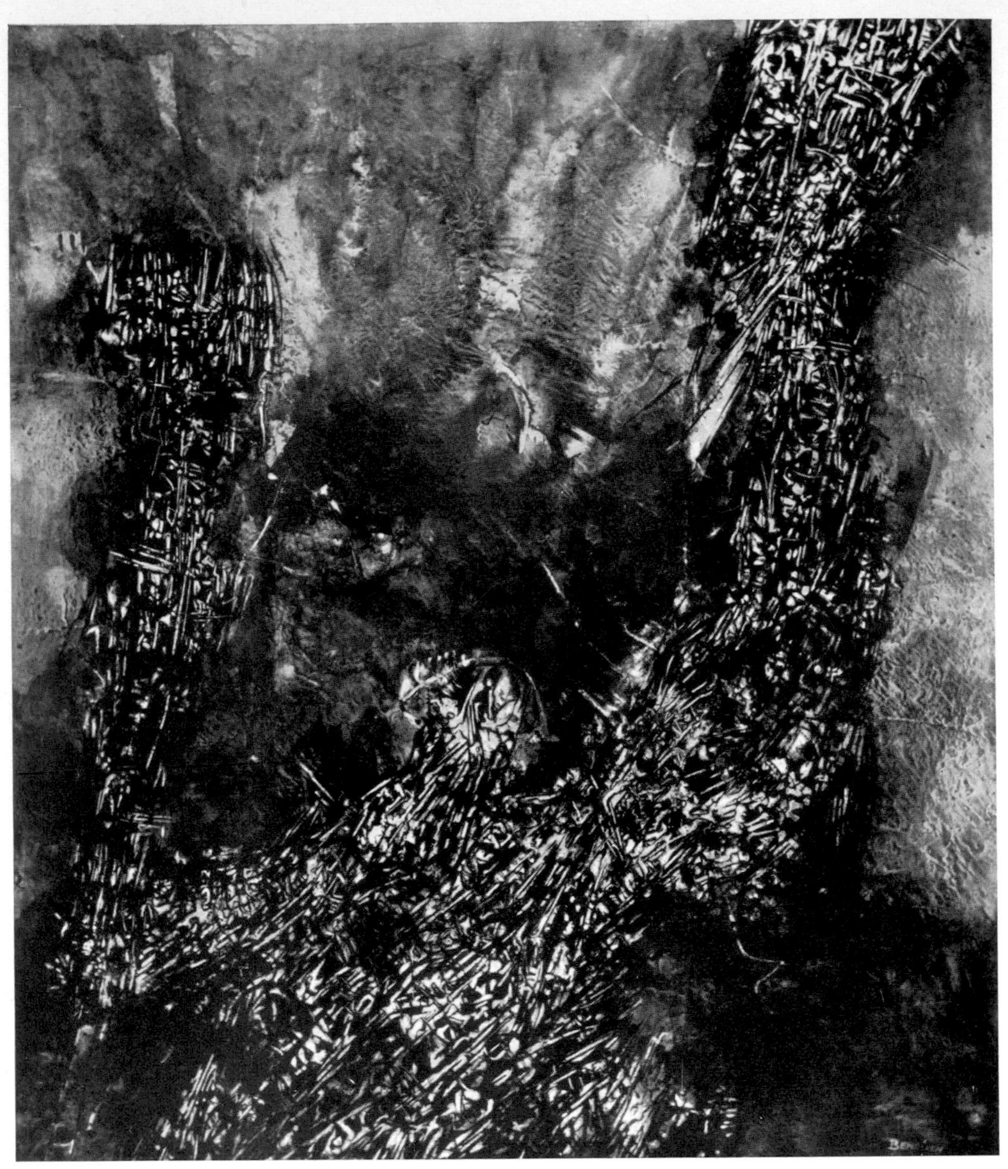

90 Klaus Bendixen, Transformation, 1960

91 K. F. Dahmen,
Object Picture, 1965

92 "Spur" Group, Spurbau, 1963

93 Gerhard Baumgartel, Picture 11/64

94 Hans Bellmer, La petite chaise Napoléon III, 1956

95 Horst Janssen, Self-portrait

96 Paul Wunderlich, Per aspera ad astra, 1964

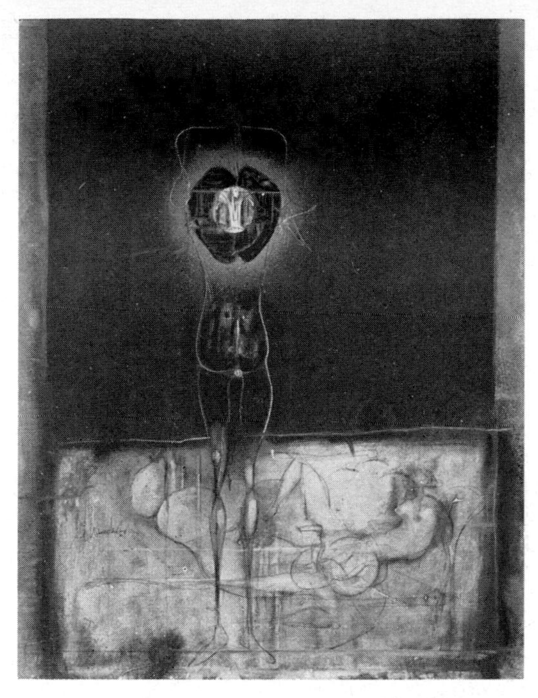

97 Konrad Klapheck,
The Capitulation, 1966

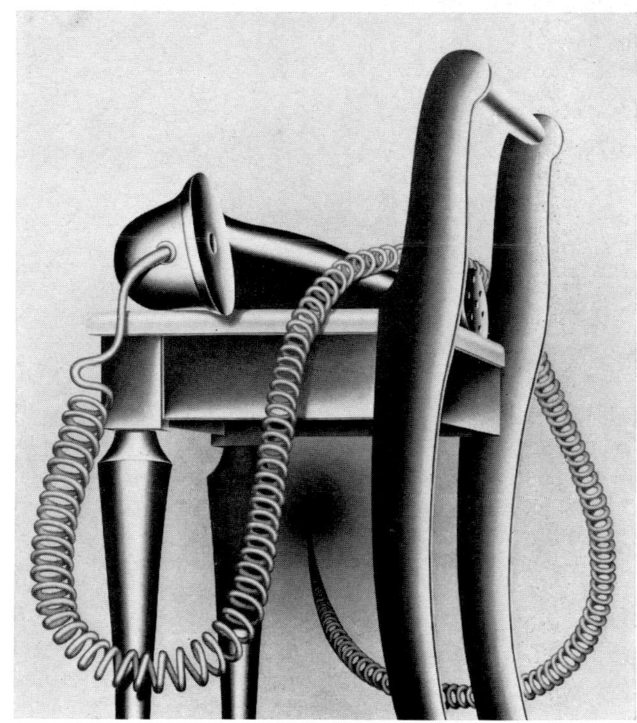

98 Rainer Küchenmeister, Body, 1964

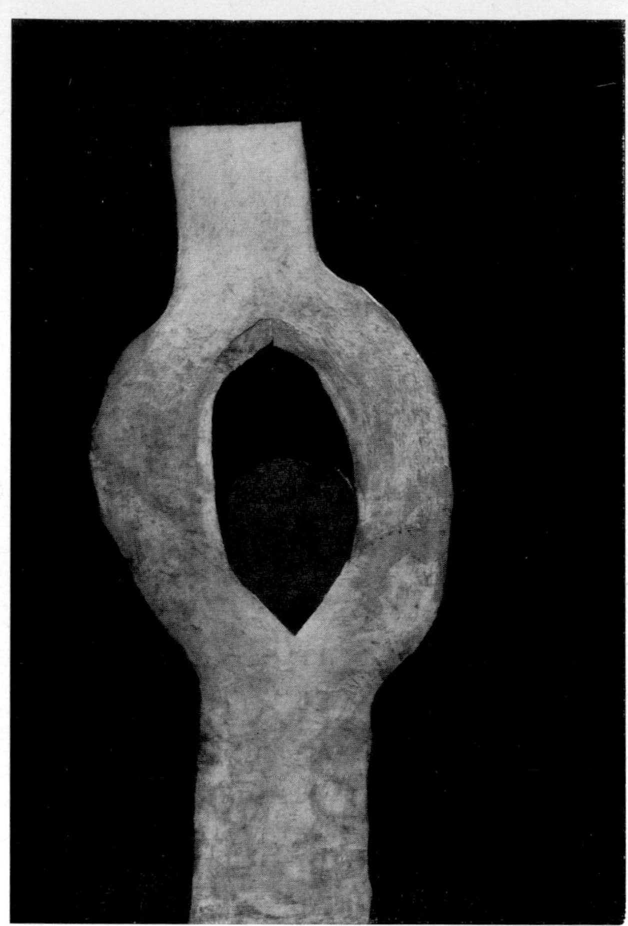

99 Lambert Wintersberger
Double Injury, 1968

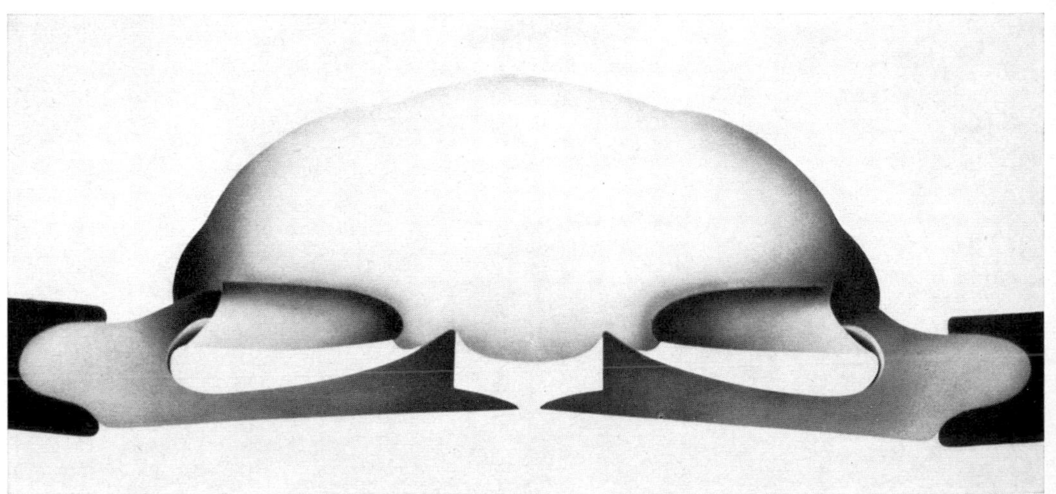

100 Uwe Lausen, Geometer 66

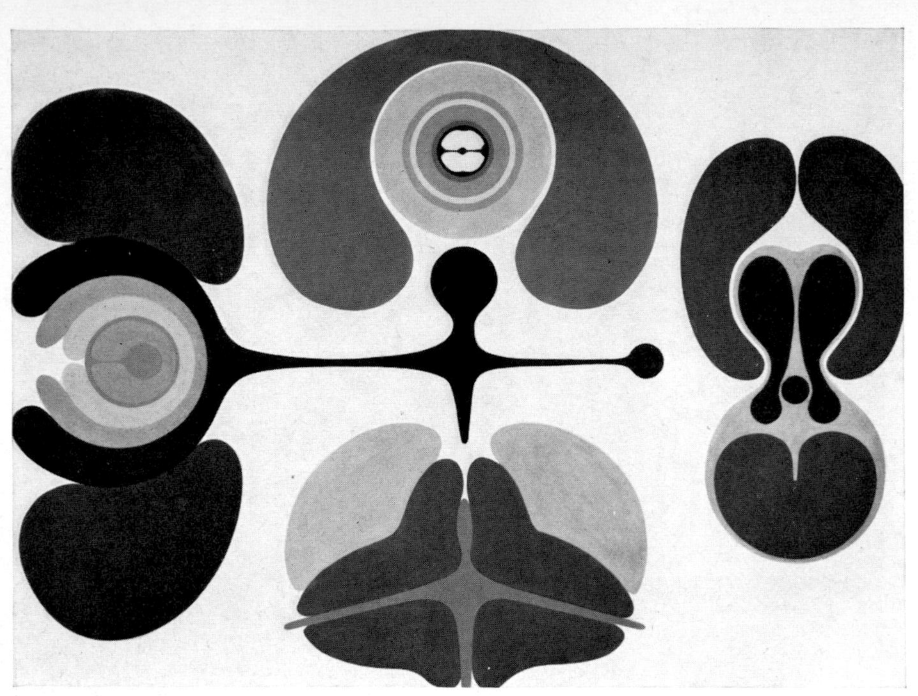

101 Geront Bubenik, Natural History-Realization II, 1966

102 Werner Schreib, Justine, Cachetage, 1965

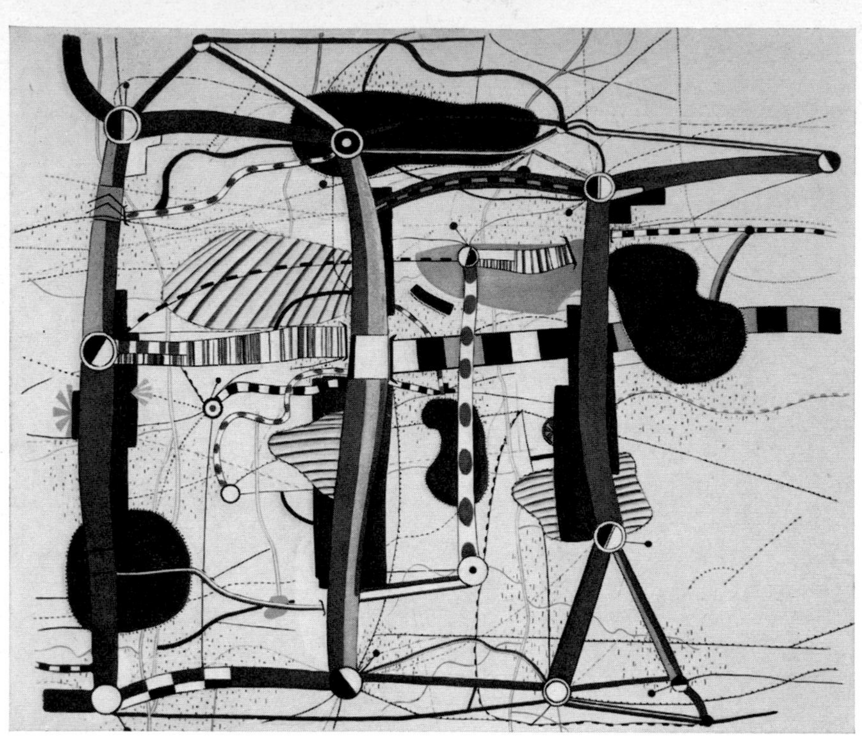

103 Peter Bruning, Légendes, 14/64

104 Otto Piene, Rouge et noir 1961

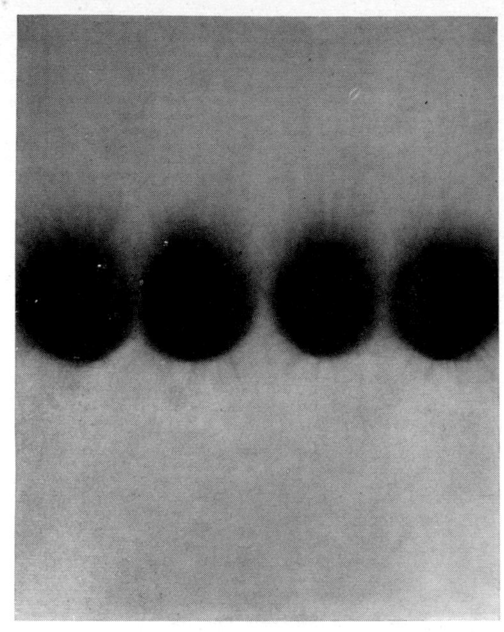

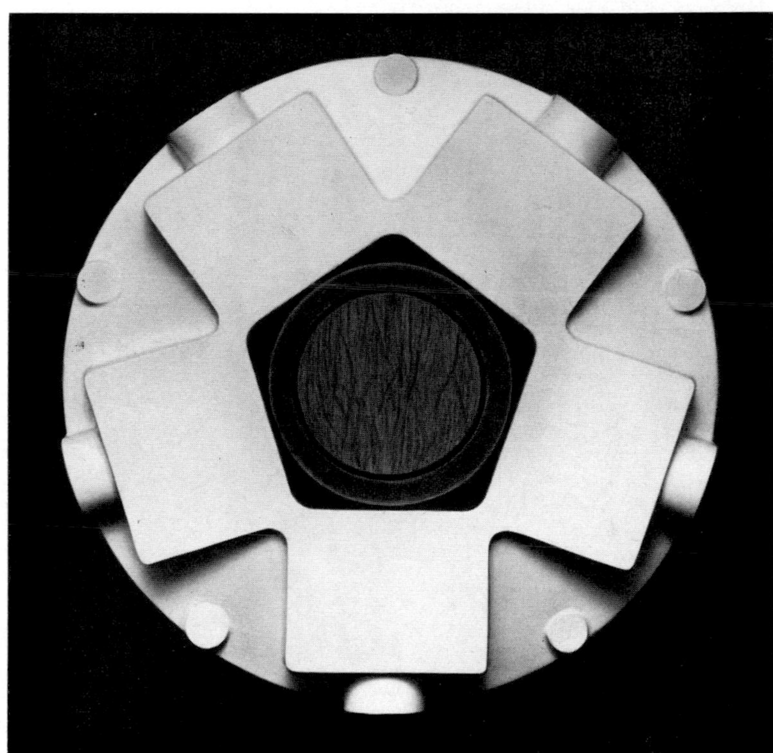

105 Claus Jürgen-Fischer, Double-picture, 1967 Mannheim, Galerie Lauter

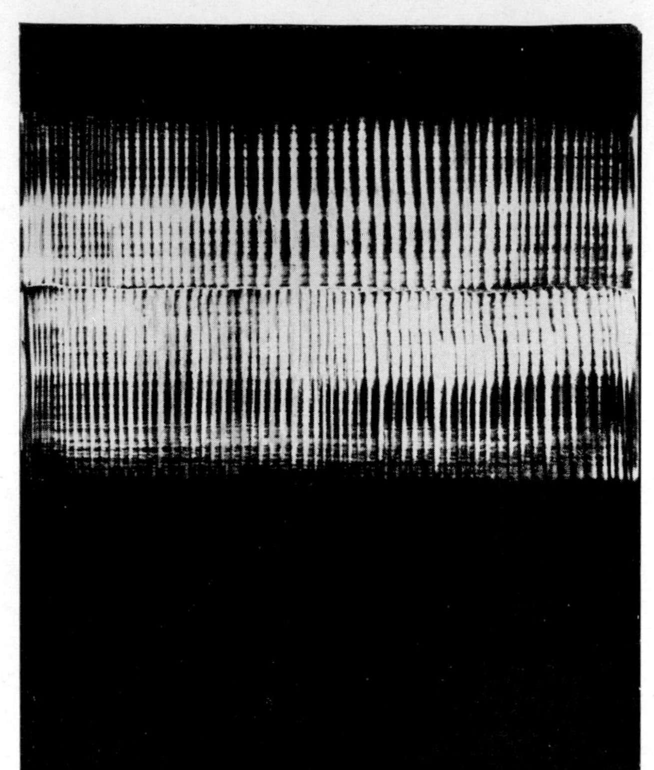

106 Heinz Mack, Dynamic Structure, White on Black, 1961

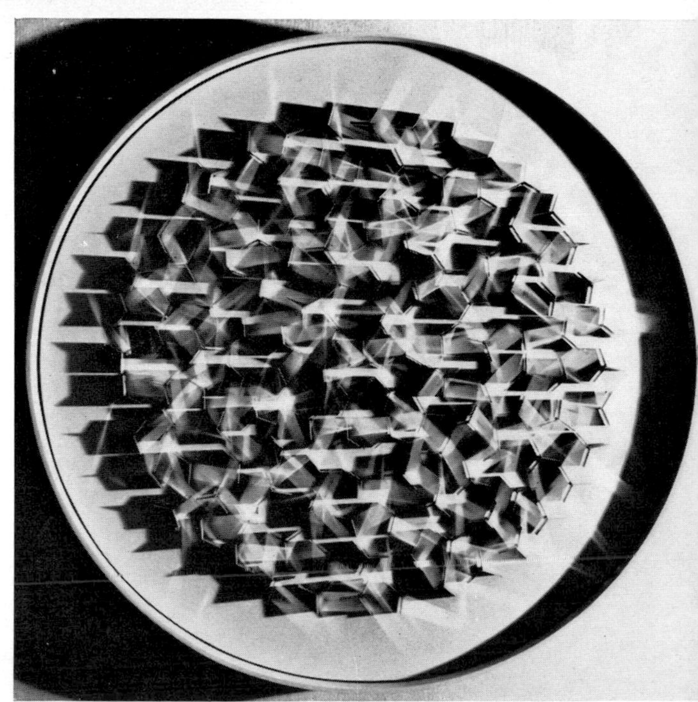

107 Gerhard von Graevenitz, Kinetic Object with Tri-winged Elements

INDEX

INDEX

Numbers in italics refer to black and white illustrations

ERRATA: On page 148, please read:

Werner Schreib (b. 1925)

Heinz Kreutz (b. 1923)